FAITHFUL MIND, THOUGHTFUL FAITH

FAITHFUL MIND
THOUGHTFUL FAITH
INTEGRATING FAITH AND LEARNING

Ph. D. in English

Robert A. Harris

Taught a pentecostal schools — Assembly of God

.:Virtual**Salt**
Publishing
Tustin

Faithful Mind, Thoughtful Faith
Integrating Faith and Learning

Copyright © 2014 Robert A. Harris

VirtualSalt Publishing
Tustin, California

ISBN 978-1-941233-13-9

Table of Contents

Introduction 1
1. Defining the Integration of Faith and Learning................3
   1.1 What Is Required for Integration to Succeed? 15
   1.2 Why is Integration Important?................................23
   1.3 Integration and the Five Elements of Learning 31
Chapter Summary 38
2. Overcoming Objections and Barriers to Integration......41
   2.1 Objections to Integration................................42
   2.3 Student Objections to Integration 55
   2.4 Barriers to Faith-Learning Integration 56
Chapter Summary 61
3. Foundations of Faith-Learning Integration....................63
   3.1. The Challenge 64
   3.2 What Knowledge and Skills Are Needed? 67
   3.3 Biblical Knowledge and Interpretation.....................67
   3.4 General Knowledge 86
   3.5 New Disciplinary Knowledge and Interpretation....93
   3.6 Critical Thinking..96
Chapter Summary 120
4. Integrative Frames: The Way Forward 123
   4.1 Alternative Views of Integration 124
   4.2 Steps Toward the Integration Process....................144
Chapter Summary 155
5. Strategic Integrative Practices 157
   5.1 The Christian Approach................................158
   5.2. Illuminate Course Content with Scripture 160
   5.3 Stress the Value of Learning 161
   5.4 Remember Black Swans and Unicorns 169

5.5 Determine the Integrative Outcome........................173

5.6 Remember: Fact and Interpretation Are Different.176

5.7 Integrative Challenges.................................177

Chapter Summary...185
6. Tactical Integrative Practices........................187

6.1 Model Integration for Your Students.................188

6.2 Teach Integrative Techniques........................188

6.3 Identify Disciplinary Issues..........................199

6.4 Syllabus Ideas..205

6.5 Discipline-Specific Integrative Practices...........210

Chapter Summary..226
Appendix 1: Using Scripture to Encourage Integration..229
A1.1 Scriptures Related to the Mind and Thinking......230

A1.2 Scriptures on the Importance of Truth.............233

A1.3 Scriptures Related to Reason.......................242

A1.4 The Bible and Knowledge and Wisdom.............243

A1.5 Wisdom..246

A1.6 Understanding...247

Appendix 2: Advancing Integration at the University....251
A2.1 Internal Faculty Development.......................252

A2.2 External Advancement................................254

A2.3 Student Development..................................258

Appendix 3: Resources......................................261
Appendix 4: The Fact/Value Dichotomy..................265
Appendix 5: A Quick Glossary............................301

INTRODUCTION

I would therefore inspire in others a desire to find truth, free from the distractions of emotion, and ready to follow the truth wherever it may be found.
— Blaise Pascal

My earlier book on this topic, *The Integration of Faith and Learning: A Worldview Approach*[1] was written with college and university students in mind. It is a book students can read on their own, in small groups, or—at Christian institutions—as part of a class. The book introduces students to the epistemological and ontological issues that surround the work of integrating Christian truth with disciplinary knowledge; it emphasizes the role of worldviews in shaping and assessing knowledge claims; and it provides students with theoretical and practical guidelines for doing integration.

The book you are reading now, aimed primarily at Christian faculty and scholars, adds much more *how* to the discussion of the *what* of integration. It is sometimes said that everyone talks about integrating faith and learning but not many are doing very much about it. Jay Rasmussen and Roberta Hernandez Rasmussen note that "most current literature available to college educators on faith-learning-living fails to address practical application."[2] What is needed, they continue, is material that answers the questions of, "What does integration of faith and learning

---

[1] Eugene, OR: Cascade Books, 2004.
[2] "Volume 1, Number 1: The Challenge of Integrating Faith-Learning-Living in Teacher Education," *ICCTE Journal*, n.d., page 2.

1

actually mean in operational terms? and How do teachers help students integrate faith and learning?"[3]

Answering these questions is the purpose of this book. In addition to theoretical discussions, here are many practical tools, resources, ideas, and example exercises that can be used right away. Think of this book as a toolkit and reference guide for Christian faculty who want to pursue integrative practices themselves and who want to teach their students how to integrate their own faith and learning. At the same time the book can be helpful to students also. Students majoring in education, religion, philosophy and many other subject areas will find the book a useful adjunct to their studies and preparation for their future careers.

This book is predicated on the conviction that Christian knowledge, Biblical truth, and the Christian worldview are not only relevant but central to a full and accurate understanding of reality. Integrating faith and learning is not an act of gratuitous obtrusion; rather it is an act of completing what otherwise will be a partial and shrunken view of the world and the understandings about it that the academy seeks. The Christian worldview offers an informing, structuring, and illuminating system for completing and comprehending every sort of knowledge. Far from being a stuck-on afterthought, a candle added at the last minute to the top of the mountain, Christian knowledge supplies the light from within, by which all can see the true nature and extent of the mountain, from jewels to mud.

The very term "Christian university" implies that Christian faith and academic knowledge will interact. This book offers ideas and methods for making that interaction a successful integration.

---

[3] Ibid., page 2.

1

1. DEFINING THE INTEGRATION OF FAITH AND LEARNING

I said, that, in order to have possession of truth at all, we must have the whole truth; and no one science, no two sciences, no one family of sciences, nay, not even all secular science, is the whole truth; that revealed truth enters to a very great extent into the province of science, philosophy, and literature, and that to put it on one side, in compliment to secular science, is simply under colour of a compliment, to do science a great damage.

—John Henry Newman[4]

Overview

This chapter answers these questions:

- What is the integration of faith and learning?
- What is the process of the integration of faith and learning?
- Why is the process of integration important?
- Who does this process?
- What are the results?
- What happens if integration doesn't take place?
- What is the relationship between integration and the other elements of knowledge?

---

[4] *The Idea of a University*, (1852). Rpt., ed. Martin J. Svaglic. San Francisco: Rinehart, 1960, Discourse 4, p. 54.

What is the integration of faith and learning? Let's start at the beginning with the integration of knowledge. Integration is not some odd religious ritual performed only by quaint Christian intellectuals. People of every faith and people of no faith perform integration every day—interconnecting new knowledge with existing knowledge to maintain a coherent set of beliefs, a unified picture of reality. As applied mathematician and network scientist Samuel Arbesman notes, "No one learns something new and then holds it entirely independent of what they already know. We incorporate it into the little edifice of personal knowledge that we have been creating in our minds our entire lives."[5] So integration is both natural and common to nearly every human being.

The integration of faith and learning is merely a special category of integrative activity. As Christians we believe that all truth is God's truth, that all knowledge must cohere in a rational way, and that ultimately, whatever the disparate sources of its parts, Truth must exist in the form of an interdynamic holism. That is, every aspect of truth must mesh with every other aspect and work together to present a unified picture of reality. Faith-learning integration is the process of connecting truth claims from the various arenas of knowledge, including the Christian (Biblical) arena, so that they all fit together this way. To draw on the root word, integration gives integrity to the set of truths a person believes.

When he was asked about the greatest commandment, Jesus replied, "Love the Lord your God with all your heart and with all your soul and with all your mind. This is the first and greatest commandment" (Matthew 22:37-38). In the same way that this is a call to an integration of the whole person—emotions, spirit, and mind—to love and

---

[5] *The Half-Life of Facts: Why Everything We Know has an Expiration Date.* New York: Current, 2012, p. 4.

serve God, so integrating faith with learning is a requisite activity for loving God with all our mind.

Now let's look at a couple of formal definitions.

> The integration of faith and learning is defined as any attempt of professors to discover, interpret, and/or articulate the various ways their faith impacts their learning or their learning impacts their faith.[6]

Note in this definition the operative term is "impacts" rather than "agrees with" or "disagrees with." There is a reason for that. But first, here is another definition:

> Faith-learning integration may be briefly described as a scholarly project whose goal is to ascertain and to develop integral relationships which exist between the Christian faith and human knowledge, particularly as expressed in the various academic disciplines.[7]

Here, the operative terms are "ascertain," that is, identify, and "develop," which means to elucidate, extend, and clarify.

> In the sense most commonly used, integrating faith and learning involves identifying and connecting compatible disciplinary knowledge with Christian knowledge, in a way that provides a two-way benefit. On the one hand, disciplinary knowledge extends and enriches the Christian worldview, while on the other hand, Biblical truth completes and adds further understanding to disciplinary knowledge.

---

[6] Laurie Matthias and Ruth-Anne Wideman, "Integrity and Integration: An Exploration of the Personal, Professional, and Pedagogical in the Professoriate. *Journal of the International Christian Community for Teacher Education* 4,1, no date.

[7] William Hasker, "Faith-Learning Integration: An Overview." *Christian Scholars Review* 21:3 (March 1992), p. 234.

Nicholas Wolterstorff connects Christian faith and scholarship by saying that the Christian scholar, "like everyone else ought to seek consistency, wholeness, and integrity in the body of his beliefs and commitments." Finding agreement between academic knowledge and Christian knowledge makes integrating and the maintenance of "consistency, wholeness, and integrity" easy.

Often, however, there will be conflict between academic content and Christian knowledge. In such cases, says Wolterstorff,

> the Christian scholar ought to reject certain theories on the ground that they conflict or do not comport well with the belief-content of his authentic commitment. And . . . he ought to devise theories which comport as well as possible with, or are at least consistent with, the belief-content of this authentic commitment.[8]

It is the role of the Christian professor, then, not to pass along disciplinary content as found, but to help students understand the relationship between the truths of their faith and the discipline's methodology, theoretical approaches, and knowledge claims. From this perspective, it is clear that Christian university faculty need to grow bold and confident in the truth content of their faith, and become willing to offer critiques of theories that conflict with it.

Having said that, though, it is crucial not to think that integration is merely a negative process, where the Christian scholar passes critical judgments on erroneous secular content and then tosses it away. Integration uses Christian knowledge to illuminate academic content so that the Christian student or faculty member will understand how

---

[8] *Reason within the Bounds of Religion*, 2nd Ed., Grand Rapids, MI: William B. Eerdmans, 1984, p. 76.

to process and hold that content. Whether supportive, neutral, or antagonistic to the Christian worldview, the ideas explored in the disciplines have a contribution to make to our knowledge—knowledge in general, and knowledge of the ideas shaping our lives and the lives of others.

Just to pull a random book example off the bookshelf, I think it is a good idea for every university student to read Karl Marx' *The Communist Manifesto*, not because Marx was right (100 million people have died under regimes trying to make communism work), but because of its historical importance and the profound effect it has had in the world of ideas even to this day. Marx' ideas are certainly not compatible with Christianity (remember that Marx was vehemently anti-Christian and anti-Semitic), so how are his ideas integrated into our Christian worldview? We learn to hold them in contrast with our worldview values and explore the differences. We ask questions such as,

- Why were his ideas so popular?
- What made them fade?
- Where are they still popular and why?
- What are some ways to answer those who still have this philosophy?

The fact is, there are many important bad ideas that we need to understand, and by learning about them and integrating them (yes, bear with me), those ideas not only are clarified by the light of the faith, but they help to clarify our faith, too. Contrast is an excellent tool for understanding. Ever hear of a non-example?[9]

All this to say that in addition to the usual definition of integration as weaving compatible truths into the fabric of our worldview, we must add that integration includes

---

[9] "Apples and bananas are examples of fruit. A tomato is a non-example."

learning and categorizing all kinds of knowledge claims. Wrong or incompatible ideas are not tossed away, because they are often profoundly important influences in our culture. (I didn't say *positive* influences.) Hence, the Integration Paradox: To practice integration effectively, you have to learn a lot of wrong ideas.

But before we continue, we need a definition. I've used the term *worldview* several times above, but I haven't defined it. Let me remedy that.

> A worldview is an individual's personal, comprehensive theory of everything. A worldview is a set of beliefs that allow a person to find meaning in life experience and to process new information in a way that maintains a coherent picture of reality. A coherent worldview makes the world make sense.

A worldview includes the values, beliefs, attitudes, assumptions—and biases—that are used in decision making and in evaluating new information and new experiences. What a person believes is real and unreal, possible and impossible, reasonable and unreasonable, true and untrue—all these are part of each person's worldview.

From this definition we can understand three things. First, some worldviews are more objective than others. The Christian worldview, for example, by including Biblical knowledge, provides an objective standard by which the Christian can evaluate new knowledge claims. It is objective because it has an external, fixed reference point in Scripture, which does not change.

Second, by including what is believed to be "true and untrue" we can understand that a worldview includes knowledge judged to be wrong or false. This information is used during integrative work: If, after discovering that a new knowledge claim is not in agreement with the other components of our worldview, we then check to see whether the new claim is similar to one determined earlier to be untrue.

And third, some worldviews are more comprehensive than others. The Christian worldview includes the realms of nature and of God, while the worldview of naturalism denies that supernatural knowledge has any reality or utility, making naturalism less complete and inadequately inclusive. Worldviews with self-imposed, circumscribed explanatory power may suit those who will do anything to escape from God, but the most complete worldview—the one that provides the most comprehensive explanation for all of reality—includes knowledge of the Creator of the universe.

Understanding the concept of a worldview and how it shapes beliefs of all kinds is essential for students studying integration and integrative issues. They might be surprised, for example, to learn that under the worldview of postmodernism, in place of the concept of *truth* we have *a circumstantially or politically derived narrative*.

Present the concept of worldviews early in the term and give examples during the term of various worldviews and how they approach one of the topics in your course.

Another way to clarify a worldview is to say that it is a mental model of reality. A mental model is an abstract or theoretical (and often simplified) way we understand how something works. Take a thermostat in a typical house, for example. The thermostat is an on-off switch in most houses. When the temperature drops below the desired warmth, the thermostat turns the heater on. When the desired temperature is reached, the thermostat turns the heat off. People sometimes assume that the thermostat works like a stove burner—turn it up farther and get more heat faster. But that's the wrong mental model. If the temperature in the room is 68 degrees, and you want 72 degrees, the room will not warm any faster by turning the thermostat to 80 than it will by setting it at 72.

You can see that possessing an accurate worldview is very important if you are to have a correct view of reality. Wrong worldview, wrong understanding of reality. Fortunately—I mean blessedly—we have the system's Owner's Manual. It's called the Bible.

From this digression I hope you can see that integration does not always mean committing to the truth of new knowledge found compatible with Biblical truth and adjusting one's worldview as a result. All of us know lots of things that we simply do not believe. That's how they ended up after our process of integration.

We don't want to reject and forget ideas that we have judged bad or false, because if we have forgotten them, the next time we encounter them we might mistakenly accept them. Instead, we "integrate" them by filing them in our memory as wrong or slanted or however we ultimately judged them. Thus, integration actually involves more than joining compatibilities; it includes *knowing how to hold new knowledge claims.*[10] Indeed, it is safe to say that most of the things we learn we do not take the time or make the effort to analyze and judge true or false. We simply add them to the part of our memory where we store knowledge claims whose factual status has not been determined.

Therefore, there are three ways of holding an idea in our memory (and in the broad way I'm using the term integrate, three ways to integrate an idea):

- **Believe it** and integrate it as a clarifier, extender, or even modifier of my worldview and knowledge set of true things.

---

[10] My definition of faith-learning integration is somewhat unusual in declaring suspended judgment and disbelief as integrated.

- **Disbelieve it** and hold it as a wrong idea, perhaps in conflict with my worldview or perhaps as simply false.
- **File it without Judging** and hold it as neither believed nor disbelieved, but merely as "this is claimed or believed by others" but its factual status is still not decided.

When enough time, thought, or new information can be brought to bear on a claim housed in the Uncertain or Filed without Judging bucket, a judgment can move the simply remembered claim either to the True and Believed bucket or the False and Rejected bucket. Similarly, an idea in the True and Believed bucket, if discovered not to be so, can be moved to the False and Rejected bucket; while a claim previously rejected can in some cases be rehabilitated and moved into truth.

What this means is that integration is not pouring concrete: instead, it is weaving a tapestry that sometimes needs to be adjusted. It is a dynamic process that goes on during every waking minute.

And just to be complete in drawing the map of integrated ideas, it must be pointed out that every idea in every bucket possesses a degree of strength with which that idea is held in that bucket. A given true or believed idea might be held weakly, moderately, or intensely, for example. Similarly, there might be a knowledge claim that you "sort of" disbelieve, while another you have judged "absolutely wrong."

For a working definition of the process and practice of integrating faith and learning, then, let us describe it like this:

The integration of faith and learning refers to the intellectual activity of evaluating and interconnecting the subject matter of the academic disciplines with Biblical truth by discovering the appropriate relationships between them.

The integrative process strengthens the Christian worldview and the faith (study the process of metamorphosis if you want to learn more about our creative, awesome God). Integrative activity by Christian faculty could also strengthen the disciplines, since so many disciplinary approaches currently operate under limited and distorted philosophical commitments.

Have students give examples of knowledge claims they hold in each of the three buckets: Believed, Disbelieved, and Filed without Judging. Discuss how some of these claims might move from one bucket to another.

Exercise

Below is one way to map the integration process.

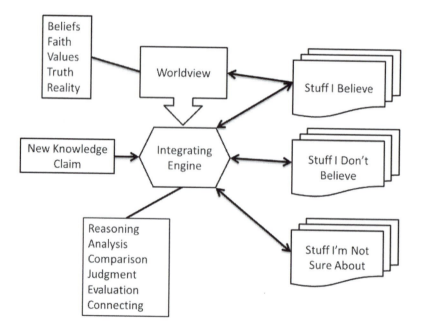

Biblical Truth?

Here, a new knowledge claim is brought into the mind, where the learner's integration engine compares it with current beliefs. This process involves using reasoning, analysis, comparison, judgment, evaluation, and connecting, and it draws on the individual's worldview map for the beliefs, faith, values, truth, and reality that are used as tests or measures of the knowledge claim. The results are placed in one of the three knowledge buckets: what is believed, what is disbelieved, and what is filed away as known but neither believed nor rejected as false. The knowledge claim that is accepted for belief also has an influence on the worldview of the learner, broadening it, weaving the tapestry of reality a little more complexly.

An additional definition, then, is that integration is the act of putting together new knowledge claims with current knowledge beliefs, using one's worldview map as a guide.

What is the faith that we are integrating? By faith is meant both the act of faith—trusting in God where we cannot see—but equally important, *the* Faith: that is, Christian knowledge as revealed in the Bible—revealed truth, God's words to us—together with the moral and esthetic values derived from the Christian worldview. For example, we are told that we are fallen creatures and that, without redemption, we are incapable of being good, much less heading for heaven. Integrating this faithful truth with learning causes us to reject secularist claims that human nature is perfectible and that utopia is possible on earth, just given the right type of government.

To be more exact, it should be clarified that the faith we are integrating refers to a correct understanding of Biblical truth. A wrong interpretation of what the Bible teaches, or a lack of knowledge of Scripture, will produce just as much confusion as a wrong understanding or ignorance of disciplinary knowledge.

What is learning? Learning refers primarily to the non-Biblical subject matter that students learn at the university: history, literature, biology, sociology, chemistry, music, psychology, and so forth. Learning includes facts, theories, methodologies, ideologies, and philosophies. Learning can also refer to any kind of knowledge from the world.

> Integration Key #1: The challenge of faith-learning integration involves the nature of the knowledge claims. Since, as we've said before, all truth is God's truth, integrating disciplinary truth or facts with Christian faith is or should be easy. However, knowledge claims frequently involve something besides statements of fact. They are often mixed with or are themselves opinions, judgments, interpretations, inferences, assumptions, presuppositions, extrapolations—all influenced by ideological slants, methodological biases, worldview skews and limitations, epistemological philosophy, and ontological commitments. Such knowledge claims may indeed be worthy and true, but then again, they might not. Discernment is the hard part.
> All truth is God's truth, but not all interpretations are God's interpretations.

What about "Faith-Learning-Living"? Some schools and universities add "living" to the goal announcements they set out for their students. They promise to transform students by incorporating into the curriculum "the integration of faith, learning, and living." The point of this otherwise redundant word is to make sure that the students understand that the Bible has behavioral claims on their lives. Some people do not realize that as Christians they are expected to act on their beliefs. That's what James means when he says,

> But someone might argue, "Some people have faith, and others have good works." My answer would be that you can't show me your faith if you don't do anything. But I will show you my faith by the good I do.
> —James 2:18 (ERV)

1.1 WHAT IS REQUIRED FOR INTEGRATION TO SUCCEED?

Successful integration of Christian faith with academic learning requires such theoretical underpinnings and commitments as

- A Christian understanding of human nature, together with the facts of creation in the image of God, rebellion, transgression, fall, and redemption
- The inclusion of the whole person—heart, soul, and mind—in all activities, worship, work, thinking, feeling, studying, deciding, interpreting
- Acknowledging the reasonableness and truth of Christianity
- Recognizing that Christianity is not a viewpoint imposed on world knowledge, but an epistemic foundation[11] (competing with lesser epistemes) that provides a clarifying platform for engaging all knowledge
- Applying the standards and worldview of Christianity to thought and behavior. "Ideas have consequences," as the proverb says
- A call to cultural evaluation by Christian standards: "Stop judging by mere appearances, and make a right judgment" (John 7:24)
- The understanding of human nature, human value, and human potential through the light of Biblical truth
- Valuing the mind, reason, and thinking: "I will pray with my spirit, but I will also pray with my mind; I will sing with my spirit, but I will also sing with my mind" (1 Corinthians. 14:15). And see Acts 17:2-3, 17:17, 18:4, 18:19 and 1 Corinthians 13:11)

---

[11] See the Quick Glossary in Appendix 5 for definitions of philosophical terms.

The methodology of integration requires a sharp mind with a positive mental outlook that includes

- A curiosity about and a love for learning all kinds of facts, ideas, viewpoints, and theories
- A cautious but not cynical approach to knowledge claims
- A robust critical thinking ability, including the capacity to engage in careful analysis and evaluation
- A profound respect for and use of reason
- A strong analytical approach to all knowledge
- A willingness to accept truth from any source, and the desire to follow truth wherever it leads

A well performed process of integration will have an impact on

- Values, choices, decision-making, and ethics by using Christian reference points
- The interpretation and meaning of history, events, books (both non-fiction and fiction)
- The purpose and goals of life
- Views of truth and a reasonable, well-grounded faith versus a blind faith
- A hierarchy of life: faith as a test of politics and ideology in the secular world

Scripture is filled with admonitions for believers to use our minds, to apply reason in every aspect of life. (See Appendix 1: Using Scripture to Encourage Integration.) Note, for example, Paul's prayer in Philippians 1:9-10:

> And this is my prayer: that your love may abound more and more in knowledge and depth of insight, so that you may be able to discern what is best and may be pure and blameless until the day of Christ. . . .

INERRANCY ?

"Knowledge," "depth of insight," "discern"—use your mind to serve God. In other words,

Get Serious About the Truth

It's often said that love is a verb—it's something you do rather than something you feel. I think the same way about truth. Truth is an activity of the mind, a seeking of the One who is Truth, knowing him by his truth.

To use the classical metaphor of Truth as a beautiful woman, we might say that especially in a culture where Truth is either out of fashion, locked in a closet so Falsehood can pretend to be Truth, or left standing in the rain by those who say they love her, it is all the more important to see her as someone to respect and fight for. So, as Peter says, "Therefore, prepare your minds for action" (1 Peter 1:13a).

1.1.1 IMPLICATIONS OF AN INTEGRATED MIND

As scholars, we recognize that many fact claims are actually interpretations imposed on filtered information, and that reigning paradigms are as much the products of philosophical commitments as they are of objective truth or purely empirical evidence. We also understand that many textbooks and journals contain claims which come from a perspective that includes various metaphysical assumptions and philosophical interpretations in conflict with Christian truth. For example, some of the claims of naturalist and postmodernist thought are clearly at odds with what we as Christians believe to be more complete and rational explanations.

With integration, the student can recognize that certain aspects of secular learning are processed through such knowledge filters and interpretive frames, and that new information must be ideologically acceptable by those with the cultural authority to define truth before it is declared to be true. A highly educated Christian can expose these practices and challenge such claims by identifying assumptions, and providing superior alternatives based on better evidence, more reasonable interpretations, and revealed truth.

With integration, the believer can more readily endure times of spiritual dryness that might threaten the emotion-only based Christian. The Christian supported by thought and knowledge will be less likely to have his or her faith damaged by those who would "deceive the hearts of the unsuspecting" (Romans 16:18, and compare Ephesians 5:6).

1.1.2 WHAT HAPPENS WITHOUT INTEGRATION?

If students do not learn to integrate faith and learning during their undergraduate years, then it may not occur. In graduate school and professional life, students may adopt the current paradigms of their field of study without realizing that those paradigms include a set of metaphysical assumptions, often naturalistic and humanistic, that conflict with Christian truth—not because there is a conflict between faith and fact but because there is a conflict of worldviews and assumptions, producing a conflict of interpretations. Not knowing this, the student may incur a split between faith and mind, with faith weakening as the mind grows more and more into the subject that has been infused with secular attitudes and values.

Without integration, Christians are in danger of turning their minds over to the secular framework while allowing their faith to become an emotional commitment and response, relying exclusively on feelings which can change—and be manipulated—more easily than an intellectually grounded and reinforced belief. Personal feelings are more subject to doubt than intellectual commitment.

Without integration, the students will risk compartmentalizing their faith, putting it in a box separate from their intellectual and working life. At the worst, the faith will become merely an emotional outlet, with God becoming a vending machine: put in a prayer and get out a blessing. Faith will become intellectually irrelevant and emotionally useful only as long as the blessings keep coming. Once God "lets them down," with an unanswered prayer or a negative life event, their faith will be at risk.

Without integration that includes the anchor of objective Biblical values, students will tend to exhibit a passive acceptance of current cultural values, lacking an active engagement and response to them, unable to separate entertainment values from moral and artistic values. Cultures with unfixed standards of reference move inevitably toward extremes, "pushing the envelope" without taste or decency.

In an era of constant cultural change, of a warfare over values, and even a subversion of the traditional meaning of the terms used to discuss values,[12] only a faithfully integrated heart and mind can see through the tinsel, the fog, and the dust and discern the difference between a cultural step forward and a mere click of the ratchet of excess. Such a one can recognize that many of the productions of modern culture are not contributing to a more humane, compassionate world where beauty and truth are celebrated, and that some entertainment products are harmful to such a vision. By realizing that, as Marcus Aurelius says, "The soul takes on the color of its ideas,"[13] the integrated Chris-

---

[12] For example, *tolerance* traditionally meant "willingness to endure something in spite of strong disapproval," whereas it now means "acceptance and approval."

[13] *Meditations*, 5.16.

tian can choose cultural inputs more wisely and therefore be influenced more positively.

1.1.3 Lifelong Integration

Integration is a process that must take place every day, because we are presented with new claims, new facts, new interpretations every day. This integration, this "faithful intellect," will guide and guard our students not just while at the university but throughout their journey through the postmodern sea, where they will face a lifelong barrage of demands for belief, indulgence, and consumption. Our role as faculty is to give them the tools they can hone and use both now and in the future.

It is often said that the major a student chooses as an undergraduate is less important than the primary goal of a university degree, which is to learn how to think, how to solve problems, and how to value everything appropriately. These are the activities of life, and how skillfully they are practiced will to a substantial degree determine the graduates' ultimate success and satisfaction in the practical areas of living. And each one of these activities is an inseparable part of the integration of faith and learning.

1.1.4 What Integration Is Not

1. Not the Bed of Procrustes. You remember the story of Procrustes from Greek mythology—the villain who forced travelers to fit into his bed exactly, by stretching the too short ones as if they were on a torture rack and by chopping off the "excess" length of the arms and legs of the too-tall ones. In other words, everyone was forced to fit exactly the same length, in spite of the resulting pain and gore.

Some non-Christian academic integrative work is that way. Whether the Bed of Procrustes is Marxist, feminist, postmodernist, naturalist, or some other theoretical approach, the interpreter forces the novel, historical event, action, or data into that bed of ideology and, to make it fit, lops off (ignores) whatever does not fit or stretches out the facts to match the theory.

Even in science there is pressure for researchers to apply a Procrustean bed. David Freedman points out that studies resulting in the wrong conclusion (as when a drug test shows the drug to be ineffective) are often not published.[14] Getting published, getting research grants, and increasing in personal status sometimes gets in the way of objectivity:

> It may seem strange to say it, but experts are rarely interested in getting at the truth, whatever it may be. What they want to do is prove that certain things are true. Which things? Well, whatever they happen to believe is true, for whatever reasons, or whatever will benefit their careers or status or funding the most.[15]

Christian scholarly integration is not that way. Christian academics working with theories informed by Scripture do not force every fact or theory to fit into the Christian worldview. For we all know that the foundations and conclusions of many disciplines are infused by ideologies that are not compatible with Christianity and cannot be harmonized or reconciled, no matter how much you chop off or stretch out.

Rather than the Bed of Procrustes, a better metaphor for Christian integration is that of a touchstone (a stone that goldsmiths used to determine the purity of a sample of gold). Christian integration involves testing secular knowledge claims and responding to the results. If the Christian scholar uses a bed to measure secular content, he

---

14 David Freedman, *Wrong: Why Experts Keep Failing Us — And How to Know When Not to Trust Them*. New York: Little, Brown, 2010, p. 55.
15 Ibid., p. 113.

or she does no stretching or lopping. The "too short" is declared inadequate and incomplete (an example might be claims arising from naturalist ideology which stubbornly refuses to consider supernatural truths). The "too long" idea is exposed for, say, its unjustifiable leaps or sweeping conclusions.

2. Not a form of Xeroxing. Duke University professor of literature Frank Lentricchia published an essay in a scholarly journal a number of years ago, saying that the interpretive frames regnant in the English departments of many universities produced a sameness in interpretation:

> What is now called literary criticism is a form of Xeroxing. Tell me your theory and I'll tell you in advance what you'll say about any work of literature, especially those you haven't read.[16]

Every work, he says, is exposed to exhibit a "cesspool" of racism, sexism, imperialism, or some other oppression, depending on the critic's particular theoretical school.[17]

But once again Christian integration is not that way. Instead, the Christian worldview provides a set of objective values, against which academic knowledge claims can be measured, categorized, and understood. Instead of declaring, "This is what this really means, in spite of what it seems to mean," the Christian scholar offers a clarifying insight, declaring, "This is how this compares (favorably and unfavorably) to Christian truth," or "These are the moral (or spiritual) implications of this idea, claim, or work." In a word, the Christian interpretive worldview is a ruler, not an axe.

---

[16] "Last Will and Testament of an Ex-Literary Critic," *Lingua Franca*, September/October 1996, p. 64.
[17] Lentricchia, p. 60.

1.2 WHY IS INTEGRATION IMPORTANT?

Characteristic of human nature is an impulse toward the pursuit of ever greater completeness of explanation, and ever greater systematic unity, in the body of our collective knowledge.[18]

There are two approaches to answering the why of integration. One is an approach based on learning theory and the second is an approach based on the importance of the faithful Christian mind. We turn to the latter approach first.

Sociologist William Graham Sumner entered college "outspokenly committed to orthodox Christian theological doctrines." When he became a professor at Yale, however, he put his religious beliefs "into a drawer," and proceeded to teach Herbert Spencer's theory of social evolutionism. Later on, when he opened up the drawer where he had put his faith, he discovered "there was nothing there at all."[19]

If Christianity is true, and if we want it to remain vibrant and impactful in our own and our students' lives, then we cannot treat its truth claims as irrelevant in practice during our academic engagements. Let's look at some specific reasons for the importance of doing the integration work.

1.2.1 IT IS IMPORTANT FOR FACULTY

1. Unify discipline and faith. Most Christian college and university faculty earned their higher degrees at secu-

---

[18] Wolterstorff, op. cit., p. 121.

[19] Christian Smith, "Secularizing American Higher Education: The Case of Early American Sociology," in Christian Smith, Ed., *The Secular Revolution: Power, Interests, and Conflicts in the Secularization of American Public Life*. Berkeley: University of California Press, 2003, p. 112.

lar institutions that paid little or no attention to the implications, challenges, or added richness that a Christian worldview could bring to disciplinary knowledge. However, faculty members, along with every other thoughtful person, want to have a coherent, overarching understanding of life, reality, human beings—and the content of their specific disciplines. Their Christian faith is fundamentally important to them, and their scholarly discipline is the arena in which they have chosen to invest their lives and intellectual energy.

Unless integrating these two areas becomes an ongoing, intentional activity, faculty will be at risk of developing two minds and two hearts. Such a dualism makes resolving unexpected conflicts between the two commitments quite problematic.

2. Model and teach. Needless to say that integration is critical for faculty at Christian colleges and universities so that they can (1) model it for their students, (2) demonstrate integrative practices and results in the classroom, and (3) teach their students how to integrate on their own. After all, most Christian institutions of higher learning are—often explicitly—committed to the integration project. Faculty are at the heart of this.

3. Impact the Great Conversation. Without a robust integration among Christian faculty, the faith will continue to be a doormat to secular worldviews. Surrendering to secular assumptions and knowledge claims is, in large part, what created the often enormous gap and need for current integration in the first place. According to Sociologist Christian Smith, many pastors and theologians in the nineteenth century, faced with the revolutionary and often anti-Christian ideologies of thinkers such as "Hume, Voltaire, Paine, Nietzsche, Swinburne, Carlyle, Owen, Holyoake, Darwin, Huxley, Wells, Spencer, Durkheim, Comte,

Brewster, and Freud," gave in to a "radical accommodation to secular modernism."[20] Smith continues:

> Rather than formulate and advance creative intellectual counters to the early secular movements from an historically orthodox Protestant perspective, they opted instead to embrace their challengers' suppositions and agendas and to redefine Christian faith in secular modernity's own terms.[21]

While these representatives of the faith might have thought they were simply accepting the inevitable flow of modern learning, the secularizers were engaged in a deliberate attempt to enthrone themselves as the sole source of knowledge. Smith notes, "What these secularizers were actually pursuing was not primarily a neutral public sphere, but a reconstructed moral order which would increase their own group status, autonomy, authority, and eventually income."[22] To do this, they seized "the power to construct reality through the production and control of knowledge."[23]

And just what is the secular world view that lack of Christian intellectual horsepower has permitted to reign? Bertrand Russell knows:

> Such, in outline, but even more purposeless, more void of meaning, is the world which Science presents for our belief. Amid such a world, if anywhere, our ideals henceforward must find a home. That man is the product of causes which had no prevision of the end they were achieving; that his origin, his growth, his

---

[20] Christian Smith, "Introduction: Rethinking the Secularization of American Public Life," in Smith, op. cit., p. 35.

[21] Ibid., p. 35.

[22] Ibid., p. 37.

[23] Ibid., p. 38.

hopes and fears, his loves and his beliefs, are but the outcome of accidental collocations of atoms; that no fire, no heroism, no intensity of thought and feeling, can preserve an individual life beyond the grave; that all the labours of the ages, all the devotion, all the inspiration, all the noonday brightness of human genius, are destined to extinction in the vast death of the solar system, and that the whole temple of Man's achievement must inevitably be buried beneath the debris of a universe in ruins—all these things, if not quite beyond dispute, are yet so nearly certain, that no philosophy which rejects them can hope to stand. Only within the scaffolding of these truths, only on the firm foundation of unyielding despair, can the soul's habitation henceforth be safely built.[24]

The scientists at the Christian universities know that it is wrong for anyone working in science to claim that science itself presents a purposeless world "void of meaning," and that we must live out our lives on a "firm foundation of unyielding despair." And yet, many scientists in the secular universities pound that drumbeat constantly and intensely, supported by the news and entertainment media. Unless Christian faculty can do the work of integration and show that the worldviews of naturalism and materialism not only provide inadequate explanations of reality but inhibit the progress of science and civilization, the Great Conversation will continue along the lines laid out by Bertrand Russell and our culture will continue to suffer as a result.

1.2.2 It is Important for Students

1. Gain intellectual courage. Students must drive out fear of their minds before they will allow full development

---

[24] "A Free Man's Worship," in *Mysticism and Logic and Other Essays*. London: George Allen & Unwin, 1917, pp. 47-48.

of them. Before they come to the university, many students have been warned by well-meaning friends, "Do not get so much education that you lose your faith." There is sometimes an assumed tension or even conflict between learning and faith. And it is not only some members of the Christian subculture who suffer from such a perceived split. Many academics on secular campuses appear to believe that faith and learning are incompatible also, to such a degree that they take it upon themselves to attempt to "liberate" entering students from their faith. Faith is often represented by these people as an obstacle to the modern world of "facts" (by which they often mean secularized interpretations of facts).

If we want our students to love truth and pursue it freely, we must liberate them from this fear of learning by showing them that learning can strengthen and extend their faith. They must come to understand that not only does truth belong to God, meaning that there is no need to fear it, but that the spiritual battle for the modern world is taking place in a sophisticated intellectual and philosophical marketplace that requires well-trained and well-informed minds to engage the combat.

We are told to do no less than to ready our minds: "Always be prepared to give an answer to everyone who asks you to give the reason for the hope that you have" (1 Peter 3:15b).

2. Improve intellectual performance. When students become aware that the mind (just as with heart and soul) can be an ally of faith—that they can strengthen their faith by strengthening their minds—they will see the importance and priority of mind training and take their academic work more seriously.

As evidence of this, about 50 or 60 Christian university students read J. P. Moreland's *Love Your God with All Your*

Mind[25] for a critical thinking class. This book promotes the use of reason and intellect in building Christian faith and as a tool in the philosophical battles of the modern world. In their written evaluations of the book, virtually all students reported being profoundly influenced by the realization that their minds were valuable instruments and that a well-developed intellect was necessary for the best service to God. Many students reported forming resolutions to work harder in their studies.

3. Strengthen faith. Faith finds a natural ally in learning because faith is built by understanding, by studying the world God has made:

> For since the creation of the world God's invisible qualities—his eternal power and divine nature—have been clearly seen, being understood from what has been made, so that men are without excuse. (Romans 1:20)

Giovanni Pico della Mirandola, one of the deeply influential figures of the Renaissance, argued that education was a necessary precursor to a deep spiritual life, and that, in fact, we should "prepare for ourselves, while we may, by means of philosophy, a road to future heavenly glory."[26]

A useful activity in any philosophy, literature, or history class is to assign students to read Pico's *Oration* and then comment, in a class discussion or in an essay about Pico's connection of the reason

Exercise   and intellect to the spiritual nature of mankind; the nexus of love, reason, and justice; how reason can lead to faith; how natural philosophy (science) points to theology;

---

[25] Colorado Springs: NavPress, 1997.
[26] *Oration on the Dignity of Man*, 1486. Tr. A. Robert Caponigri. Chicago: Regnery Gateway, 1956, p. 25.

and why Pico says that "God is a philosopher."[27] Such an activity is not only an example of integrating faith and learning, but also demonstrates the usefulness of the integrative task. And Pico has many ideas that are profitable for thought and analysis.

Indeed, knowledge itself — knowledge of God and his creation — is what allows us to love God as we should. As Brother Lawrence says, "We must know before we can love,"[28] so that the more we learn, the more we understand about the Creator:

> We must concentrate on knowing God: the more we know him, the more we want to know him. And, as knowledge is commonly the measure of love, the deeper and wider our knowledge, the greater will be our love.[29]

4. Extend Understanding. Christian faith and knowledge supply a more comprehensive picture of reality. Christian perspective must be understood not as just an "added bonus" or appended item to standard scholarship from a secular worldview, but instead as a more comprehensive and more rational epistemology than, say naturalism or materialism. Christianity, as a knowledge structure, is a standard of truth, providing an objectively critical approach for making corrective assessments in scholarship and intellectual work. In other words, Christianity should be an anchor and a touchstone for the analysis of culture and political structures rather than merely a point of view or another source of commentary on morals and manners.

---

[27] Ibid., p. 28.
[28] *The Practice of the Presence of God*, (1693) Letter 16. Tr. Donald Atwater. Springfield, IL: Templegate Publishers, 1974, p. 88.
[29] Ibid., p. 105.

James T. Burtchael argues that Christianity can provide "graced master insights" to approach the truth[30] and that "learning itself can be an act of piety."[31] Burtchael says that Christians should provide a "thoughtful critique of the world and its cultures"[32] from a faith that serves as a "critic and corrective in the very business of scholarship."[33]

Christianity is central to the shared enterprise of community learning at a Christian university. The university must emphasize that at the heart of Christianity are indeed relationship with Christ, guidance for life values, fulfillment of the heart's yearnings—and also truth: the faith is both a relationship, an experience of God, *and* an objective account of the world as it is, a roadmap or guidebook that tells us truths about ourselves, our origin, our purpose, and our ultimate future. What does Jesus say? "Sanctify them by the truth; your word is truth" (John 17:17). He doesn't say, "Your word offers some useful guidelines."

The more solidly rational and educated is the support for the faith, the stronger the faith will be and the more powerful the witness will be to an increasingly educated, skeptical, seeking, needy world. Christianity must therefore be seen not as a private emotion, not as a co-existing idea with little connection to reality, not as an "added plus" to an otherwise secular existence, not a balance in opposition to reason, but as an integrating truth that provides the world with meaning and coherence.

5. Empower Education. What is the purpose of education? Now, many students say, "To get a good job," but traditionally the answer—and still the real purpose—is, "To grow into a mature, circumspect, thoughtful person,"

---

[30] *The Dying of the Light.* Grand Rapids: Eerdmans, 1998, p. 844.
[31] Ibid., p. 842.
[32] Ibid., p. 836.
[33] Ibid., p. 774.

or for Christian education, "a mature, circumspect, thoughtful Christian." Without integrating faith into the curriculum and subject matter, this growth cannot happen. Dawn Morton writes, "Lacking of the foundation of faith, academics becomes merely an educational process instead of a life-changing process meant to impact and embrace the whole person."[34] Without integration, academics becomes transfer learning, where the professor merely offers — maybe even regurgitates — the lock, stock, and barrel of the secularly infused subject matter that he learned in graduate school.

1.3 INTEGRATION AND THE FIVE ELEMENTS OF LEARNING

We now turn to the approach based on learning theory, to see that, in the context of lasting learning, integration — of both Christian knowledge and secular knowledge is critical for the deepest learning to take place. The best learning engages five interacting elements, all of which are necessary for that interdynamic holism mentioned earlier to be constructed by the learner. Or, put another way, when learning engages all five elements, it will last. Knowledge must be applied, thought about, extended, and connected with other knowledge — in other words, worked with — in order to become a permanent part of an individual's learning. Learning that is not applied or practiced is likely to be forgotten quickly.

Briefly, here are the five elements of learning, presented all together so that the value of integration can be more clearly seen.

---

[34] "Embracing Faith-Learning Integration in Christian Higher Education," Ashland Theological Seminary, 2004, p. 63.

1.3.1. KNOWLEDGE

This element includes learning and understanding facts, ideas, philosophies, Biblical truth, concepts, and vocabulary. It also includes learning about knowledge claims (that might or might not be true), learning the steps in processes, and learning from experiment and reasoning. Knowledge is conveyed through presenting the facts, and through examples, definitions, non-examples, descriptions, drawings or other graphics.

Activities that add knowledge include

- Reading
- Lecture
- Experiment
- Discussion
- Question and answer
- Demonstration
- Watching educational film or video

- Example knowledge question: Explain Aristotle's concept that "virtue is a mean between extremes."
- Example knowledge question: List four facts from the case study that bear on the cause of the accident.

1.3.2. THINKING

Thinking is both a response to knowledge and a source of knowledge. A primary task of thinking is the analysis and evaluation of knowledge and knowledge claims—the analysis of arguments, reasons, and evidence for strengths, weaknesses, credibility, bias, and fallacies. Other forms of thinking are critical thinking, evaluation, judgment, creative thinking. Thinking includes the acquisition of new values or standards for judgment or evaluation, the use of quality criteria, and the categorization of knowledge elements. It also involves the ability to make comparisons and contrasts, to see similarities and differences.

Activities that produce thinking include

- Analyzing an argument, essay, poem, book to understand its structure, meaning, worldview, strengths and weaknesses
- Constructing a reasoned argument
- Discussing a reading assignment
- Brainstorming possible solutions to a problem
- Thinking through the implications of an idea or proposal to identify unintended consequences (asking "and then what?" to uncover unexpected downstream effects)

- Example: By placing courage at a midpoint between cowardice and recklessness, is Aristotle limiting heroism?
- Example: Based on the facts given in the case study, discuss what specifically could have prevented the accident.

1.3.3. APPLICATION

Application refers to what you can do with knowledge. According to the Hierarchy of Meaning, the application of knowledge results in wisdom.

To clarify the meaning of *applied* in the Hierarchy of Meaning below, think of *processed, organized,* and *used* as synonyms for *applied.*

Hierarchy of Meaning				
Applied Event Records	Applied Data	Applied Information	Applied Knowledge	Applied Wisdom
Data	Information	Knowledge	Wisdom	Good Judgment

Often, however, the application of knowledge has a direct purpose and outcome. Application can range from using the knowledge to dissect a frog, to applying knowledge of logical fallacies to rebut an argument, to a physical use involving learned skills (carpentry, dance, teaching). Any performance or problem solving activity requires the application of knowledge. Another important type of application is the transfer of knowledge from one realm to another. One last type of application is transforming knowledge itself into a new form or new knowledge.

The critical truth here is that knowledge must be worked with in order to be made lasting. Memorizing a bunch of facts for a multiple choice test will result in quickly lost knowledge. An assignment that requires students to work with—apply—their knowledge will make it stick.

Activities that involve applying learning include

- Using tools (of any kind, ranging from a wrench to a software app) to create or work on something
- Following a job aid or instruction sheet
- Giving a speech or presentation
- Writing a paper or posting a discussion topic or response

- Example: In his *Discourses on Art*, number 8, Joshua Reynolds says, "It is in art as in morals: no character would inspire us with an enthusiastic admiration of his virtue, if that virtue consisted only in an absence of vice; something more is required; a man must do more than merely his duty to be a hero." Use your knowledge of Book 4 of Aristotle's *Nicomachean Ethics* to explain how Aristotle would react to Reynolds' comment. Quote appropriately.
- Write a persuasive essay arguing for or against a federal mileage-based driving tax.

1.3.4. INTEGRATION

As we have discussed, integrating learning means making connections between what is newly learned and what is previously known, connecting ideas with each other, seeing similarities, differences, harmonies, and conflicts. Integration includes making connections across disciplines. New learning influences your worldview and your worldview influences new learning as you work toward an ongoing epistemological coherence. The world gains richer meaning as you interconnect everything you understand about everything.

Activities that involve the integration of learning include

- Explaining the relevance of new learning to what the learner already knows
- Creating analogies or comparisons (contrasts, too) between new learning and previous learning
- Explaining a chain of causation or historical chain of events
- Cross-disciplinary connections, such as learning from a history class applied to a literature class

- Example: Connect, compare, or contrast Aristotle's remarks on self-indulgence in III.12 of the *Nicomachean Ethics* with the psychological theory of cognitive dissonance.
- Example: Construct an analogy that compares the skills of carpentry with the skills of writing an essay.

1.3.5. METACOGNITION

Metacognition involves thinking about thinking, or better, thinking about learning (metalearning). For learning to be most lasting, the learner must be intentional about whether the learning is taking place and how well. Learners need to ask questions such as,

- Do I understand this material?
- What questions do I have about this?
- How could I learn this more thoroughly?
- What is the connection or relationship between this new knowledge and what I already know?

Monitoring your learning produces a self-awareness of learning progress and enables you to prioritize studying, revisit what needs to be covered again, and practice applying the learning.

Examples of metacognitive activities include:

- Paraphrasing
- Summarizing
- Creating questions and answering them

- Example: Write three sentences summarizing the content of the assigned chapter.

The Five Elements of Learning can be represented by a pentagonal spider (or radar) chart that allows you to analyze how significantly each element is addressed in a curriculum design project.

Use the blank chart on the following page to analyze a syllabus, classroom experience, or a plan for a future class. Follow the instructions to complete a diagram that shows visually which elements are stronger and which possibly need some additional emphasis.

The chart can also be used by students to sketch out how well rounded they believe their learning is for a particular course. Have each student complete a chart about a quarter of the way through the course. Collect the charts and examine them for commonly perceived deficiencies.

Exercise

The Five Elements of Learning Spider Chart

Name _____ Project _____ Date _____

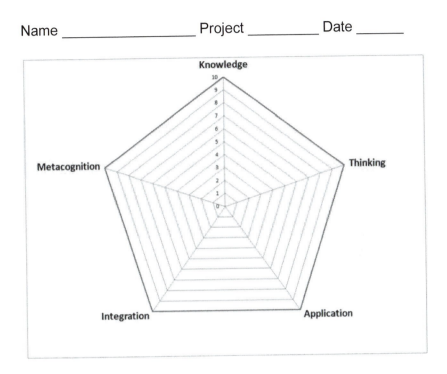

On each element scale, draw a dot on the number from zero to 10 that you believe best represents the emphasis, time, or attention paid to that element. Next, draw lines connecting the dots. The resulting shape will reveal how balanced the design is and where you might need to add emphasis.

Analysis:

Action Plan:

CHAPTER SUMMARY

The integration of faith and learning refers to the intellectual activity of interconnecting Biblical truth with the subject matter of the academic disciplines—and with knowledge claims from everywhere.

Integrating learning means making connections between what is newly learned and what is previously known, connecting ideas with each other, seeing similarities, differences, harmonies, and conflicts. Integration includes making connections across disciplines.

For integration to occur effectively, the scholar or student must adopt an appropriate attitude toward learning, the Christian worldview, and the vital role of the intellect—he or she must "get serious about the truth." Without practicing effective integration, the scholar or student is in danger of a weakened faith, shut up in a box away from the vital controversies of the day.

A worldview is a personal theory of everything, including a person's basic beliefs, values, and attitudes. The world and experience and new knowledge are all filtered through the worldview, so it is important to have a worldview that most accurately reflects reality—things as they are. Christianity is that worldview.

Developing the skills for integrating faith and learning can strengthen faith as well as strengthening knowledge and understanding of the world.

Good integration is closely tied to good thinking. Developing the ability to reason and to analyze are critical thinking skills (pun intended).

Integration is an inseparable part of the Five Elements of Learning: Knowledge, Thinking, Application, Integration, and Metacognition.

Questions for Thought and Discussion

1. Explain the similarities and differences between the ordinary process of integrating knowledge and the Christian process of integrating faith and learning.
2. How does Christian integration differ from the secular process of imposing an ideological framework on, say, a historical event?
3. In what sense is the Christian worldview objective?
4. Why is it important to learn how to integrate faith and learning?

Activities

1. Define the integration of faith and learning in your own words, and then give an example of an integrative work that you might pursue in your own discipline.
2. Redraw the integration model on page 12, making it align with your understanding of how integration works or should work.
3. Fill out the Five Elements of Learning pentagon on page 37. Where are you strongest? Where do you need to improve? What action plan can you create to bring you to your goal?

Notes

2

2. OVERCOMING OBJECTIONS AND BARRIERS TO INTEGRATION

Thinking means connecting things, and stops if they cannot be connected.
— G. K. Chesterton[35]

Overview
This chapter answers these questions:
- What are some of the objections to the idea of faith and learning integration raised by secularists and by Christian university faculty?
- What anti-integration arguments are raised and what are the responses?
- What objections might students raise against learning and doing integrative work? How can they be answered?
- What are some of the barriers that hinder or prevent faculty and students from doing integration successfully? How can these barriers be overcome?

Integrating faith and learning presents inherent challenges because of the deeply secular orientation of academic subject areas, the minimal integrative training and experience of many Christian faculty, and the lack of

---

[35] *Orthodoxy* (1908). Rpt., San Francisco: Ignatius Press, 1995, p. 40.

preparation of incoming students. As if this were not problematic enough, the entire enterprise is often met with strident objections.

Not only do secularists object to the integration of Christian knowledge with disciplinary content, but many Christian professors—even at Christian colleges and universities—do, too, preferring to follow a "two realms" or "two spheres" view of reality, where religious truth is kept separate and distinct from disciplinary knowledge. As we will see, this viewpoint is supported by a number of arguments.

In addition to the theoretical objections, there are several practical barriers that keep robust integration from occurring to the extent it should among Christian academics and their students. Let's look at these two categories each in turn.

2.1 Objections to Integration

This section responds to common objections that secular and some Christian professors have raised against practicing faith-learning integration in scholarly work.

2.1.1 Objection 1

Religious perspectives toward academic knowledge do not exist.

First Response: Religious perspectives do exist.

The objection is an argument from ignorance and it is false. Religious perspectives, or better, items of relevant Christian knowledge, exist for most if not all academic areas. The usual flippant rhetorical question is, "How does Christianity apply to mathematics or chemistry?" The answer is, quite extensively. Whether the mathematics and chemistry are used to explore the nature of God's creative ability, the rational world, or whether Christian principles are brought to bear at the interpretive level ("What is the real meaning of chaos theory or complexity theory?" for example), there is much for Christian truth to contribute. Generating data and working with facts are only part of doing academic work; interpreting those data and facts makes up the often more substantial part. And wherever there is interpretation, there are worldview assumptions, pre-theoretical commitments, philosophical preferences, and methodological habits. All of these need to be tested and can be enhanced and clarified by Christian knowledge.

Second Response: Additional religious perspectives can be developed.

If we are generous and grant that in some area there is no Christian perspective, the point then is that *nonexistent* does not mean *impossible to develop*. Many problems currently have "nonexistent" solutions but we don't claim that they therefore will never have solutions. If therefore Objection 1 is true in your area of specialization, don't sit back and say, "Therefore I can't teach a Christian perspective." Develop one.

2.1.2 OBJECTION 2

Religious perspectives are irrelevant to disciplinary knowledge.

Response: The meaning of knowledge involves religious assumptions.

When Objection 1 is overcome, this appeal to irrelevance is often a fallback position. But it is also false, for reasons hinted at above. Objectors are fond of saying, for example, "There is no Christian physics or sociology." But this claim is only half true. The foundational assumptions of the disciplines and their interpretive frameworks are both connected to a metaphysical structure (their ontology—theory of what exists—and epistemology—theory of knowledge) that control both the identification of new knowledge and the meaning of that knowledge. When physics and sociology touch on the meaning of their findings, such as the origin of creation or the characteristics of human nature, then the Christian worldview has enormous, even decisive relevance to the subject. And even at the methodological level, the Christian perspective encourages us to challenge the philosophical naturalism behind the disciplinary processes and the limits naturalism places on the identification of knowledge.

The claim that "religious perspectives are irrelevant" is really the claim that "the religious perspective of Christianity should be kept out of the discipline so that only the religious perspective of naturalism will influence the discipline's findings and interpretations."

For an extensive discussion about the interconnectedness of facts and values, including values embodied in various "religious" perspectives, see Appendix 4: The Fact/Value Dichotomy.

2.1.3 Objection 3

There is no uniquely or exclusively Christian theory or approach to this subject, no "Christian economics" or "Christian biology."
Response: Most theories involve elements in common with other approaches.

Few theories, approaches, models, assumption sets, or even worldviews are unique in the sense of being completely unlike all others. The goal is to find truth and to gain understanding, not to elaborate an arbitrary or pet theory. In the process of developing a theory that covers the data the best, the Christian theory will likely overlap and include elements of other theories, insofar as they reflect accurate knowledge and provide a coherent understanding. Therefore, Christian theory may reflect (1) affirmation of parts of other models, (2) refinement or revision of parts of other models, and (3) unique parts, aspects, and components. New theories often reconstruct material from older theories rather than replacing them completely. The goal of Christian approaches is not uniqueness, but truth.

2.1.4 OBJECTION 4

Attempts to define a Christian theory for a discipline would not produce a very good theory.

Response: All theoretical work must start somewhere.

Initial attempts to build an airplane in your backyard probably wouldn't produce an excellent aircraft, either. What's true in the garage workshop is also true in the mental workshop. David Claerbaut notes that even if we agree that "initial attempts at a 'Christian sociology' or 'Christian economics' may not be particularly 'good' sociology or economics, . . ."[36] the same is true for most initial attempts to develop a discipline. After all, he continues, first attempts "are what academics call 'first approximations' — models to be improved upon. Consider that the first mainstream formulations in medicine, sociology, and psychology were incredibly crude attempts."[37] Most first attempts may be rough, tentative and in need of development and refinement, but that is no reason for avoiding the attempts in the first place. And, with the advantage of a clarifying worldview that can take what is worthy from established content, there is every hope that even first attempts may be substantial and of high quality.

No discipline will be advanced if the argument holds that we shouldn't attempt to develop a new pathway because the attempt will be hard, fraught with peril, or less than perfectly successful on first attempt. That's self-defeating.

2.1.5 OBJECTION 5

Because there is no single, agreed-upon "Christian perspective," a Christian perspective cannot be taught. It doesn't exist.

---

[36] Claerbaut, David. *Faith and Learning on the Edge: A Bold New Look at Religion in Higher Education.* Grand Rapids: Zondervan, 2004, p. 16.
[37] Ibid., p. 16.

Response: It is natural to expect variation within Christian approaches.

This "single-perspective" objection is a case of special pleading that singles out Christian theory for criticism while ignoring the simple facts about the status of other theories. For example, in evolutionary theory, there is no single evolutionist perspective (for there is Darwinian, Neo-Darwinian, Goldschmidt's hopeful monster, Eldredge and Gould's punctuated equilibria, Hoyle and Wickramasinghe's panspermia, etc.). And while Neo-Darwinism might be the most common, there are disagreements within it. For example, some or even most Darwinists believe that birds evolved from dinosaurs, while others do not.

Similarly there is no single Marxist, feminist, or Freudian perspective, but no one claims that because a single, agreed-upon perspective does not exist, none of these therefore can be taught or further developed. Of course, each perspective within each of these theoretical areas contains features that are found in common, which is why they share the same general name, and yet there are many variations of thought within each. It might even be said that there are as many perspectives as there are writers, because every scholar has some unique outlook to contribute. A Christian perspective or approach is likely to exist in several variations, also, each sharing a set of core features that make it Christian.

Further, each perspective is constantly under development and subject to change, combination, revision and so forth. This is the nature of theory and of academic work itself. Christian scholars working to develop Christian perspectives or Christian theories within their subject matter will likely continue to develop a variety approaches and interpretations within the general Christian framework. That is to be expected.

2.1.6 OBJECTION 6

It would be wrong to teach a Christian perspective because that would present "a biased view that is unfair to other religious perspectives."[38]

Response: This falsely assumes that Christianity provides not knowledge but subjective belief.

The objection is a cultural relativist argument that assumes that no "religious perspective" is true, but that all religious perspectives are equally false (or to be postmodern, equally "true"). Part of the problem is the use of the term *perspective*, which is sometimes taken to mean a subjective viewpoint or even an opinion rather than a knowledge claim. Those of us arguing for the integration of Christian faith (that is, Christian knowledge) and learning believe that Christianity brings not just a viewpoint but objective knowledge to the table that must be incorporated into the world of learning in order for that world to be complete, accurate, and fully true. Christianity proposes unique truth claims. Christian faculty should have the courage of their convictions.

Note that those who object to the introduction of Christian assumptions and knowledge never also object that "it would be wrong to teach from a naturalist perspective because that would present a biased view that is unfair to other religious perspectives." Once again we find a case of special pleading. My (naturalist) religion is okay in scholarship, but your (Christian) religion is not.

2.1.7 OBJECTION 7

Christian scholarship would be biased and subjective.

---

[38] Larry Lyon and Michael Beaty. "Integration, Secularization, and the Two-Spheres View at Religious Colleges: Comparing Baylor University with the University of Notre Dame and Georgetown College." *Christian Scholar's Review* 29:1 (Fall, 1999) , 73-112.

First Response: Christianity provides an objective foundation for knowledge.

All knowledge is discovered and developed through the reliance on an interpretive paradigm to bring intelligibility and meaning to individual and collected facts. Kerry Magruder and Mike Keas note that "no one can theorize without worldview precommitments."[39] To call Christian scholarship biased and subjective would be to open up the same charge toward all scholarship. It might be more profitable instead to say that scholars typically seek truth based on their understanding of the world and of the nature of truth itself. They apply interpretive models or paradigms to assess data. The Christian worldview might be seen as an alternative paradigm or interpretive framework, interested in objective truth wherever it may lead.

Second Response: Christian scholarship should be the least biased and least subjective of all.

Because it is based on objective knowledge (Biblical truth) and it holds up truth as the highest value, the operative framework of Christian scholarship facilitates objectivity (unlike some of the ideologies in academia where political correctness and the suppression of dissent are more important than facing the truth).

At the bottom of this objection lies a large set of assumptions and preferences relating to epistemology (the theory of knowledge—how and what we can know) and ontology (which things are to be considered real and which not). Commitments to theory and methodology may or may not be labeled bias (after all, you're biased but I'm just focused). A better discussion would result from the examination and assessment of the assumptions and

---

[39] Kerry Magruder and Mike Keas, "Reflections on Science and Faith: Four Theses by Kerry Magruder and Mike Keas." Oklahoma Baptist University. January 28, 2003. <http://www.okbu.edu/academics/natsci/us/general/sci_faith.htm>.

commitments connected to all the competing paradigms, using tests such as coherence, correspondence, explanatory power and so forth.

2.1.8 OBJECTION 8

A Christian perspective would cause instruction to lack integrity because it is not based on religiously neutral presuppositions.[40]

Response: To the contrary, including Christian truth in the educational process supports rather than inhibits integrity.

First Support of Integrity. There is no such thing as religious (or metaphysical) neutrality. The process of all research and interpretation is based on "pre-scientific belief commitments."[41] Scholarship proceeds either on the assumption that God exists or that he does not exist. Either God has created the universe and humankind or he has not. Neither position is religiously neutral.

The advantage and first guarantee of integrity of a Christian approach is that not only does it identify its own religious perspective and puts it admittedly on the table (thus avoiding hidden bias), but it also identifies the religious perspective (the metaphysical commitment) of all other worldviews and exposes them to awareness and evaluation. Integrity is guaranteed by removing the veil of neutrality from, say, naturalism, and enabling the learner to see its religious biases. Only in an academic arena where religious perspectives are clear and on the table for discussion can this situation occur. As John Henry Newman wrote, [Without theology in its proper place in the academy,] "sciences will assume certain principles as true,

---

[40] Michael Beaty, Todd Buras, Larry Lyon. "Christian Higher Education: An Historical and Philosophical Perspective." *Perspectives in Religious Studies* 24:2, (Summer, 1997), pp. 151, 152.
[41] Ibid., p. 156.

and act upon them, which they neither have authority to lay down themselves, nor appeal to any other higher science to lay down for them."[42] Without the watchdog of a Christian perspective, the disciplines will make claims that are metaphysical (or even theological) rather than scientific or factual and will not be called to account.

Second Support of Integrity. A Christian perspective guarantees integrity by supplying a check on the self-aggrandizement of other disciplinary areas.

In secular universities, taking Christianity or any religion seriously is virtually banned. Yet students and faculty alike still have both spiritual and factual questions about their own lives. In the absence of answers from an accepted revealed truth and with the failure of purely empirical demonstration, the hard and social sciences move into these religious realms and make philosophical or theological pronouncements—about the meaning of life, man's origin, man's destiny, human nature, even the meaning of worship. Such pronouncements are neither scientific (in the strictly empirical sense) nor within the scope or competency of the disciplines from which they come. But without a Christian knowledge source to supply the missing answers, the disciplines strive to answer such questions themselves. Once again quoting Newman: "I observe, then, that, if you drop any science [and by *science*, Newman means *arena of knowledge*, including theology] out of the circle of knowledge, you cannot keep its place vacant for it; that science is forgotten; the other sciences close up, or, in other words, they exceed their proper bounds, and intrude where they have no right."[43]

Third Support of Integrity. A third guarantee is the Christian exaltation of truth as the primary goal and value

[42] Newman, John Henry. *The Idea of a University: Defined and Illustrated.* 1873; rpt., San Francisco: Rinehart Press, 1960, p. 73.
[43] Newman, p. 55.

in education. Truth is the objective measure. Unfortunately, the secular academy has been overtaken by ideology and power politics where truth is often no longer viewed as paramount (or sometimes even as objective). This sad state of affairs raises the daunting question, "Can you have academic excellence or integrity *without* a Christian perspective?" The Christian touchstone exposes, challenges, and corrects all kinds of knowledge claims, and it provides standards and tests of truth against sloppy, ideological, agenda laden, tendentious scholarship that is the real inhibitor of academic excellence and integrity.

Fourth Support of Integrity. The word *integrity* includes the sense of wholeness or completeness, and from that sense, *the Christian perspective provides the integrity of a holistic view of knowledge* by including those spiritual dimensions that are usually ignored or even rejected with hostility in secular teaching. The secular academy has suffered severe damage to its integratedness (to its integrity?) by the narrow view of knowledge arising out of positivism and still evident in scientism and by the relativism and dogmatism arising out of postmodernist attitudes. Christian scholars have the singular opportunity to repair the realm of learning and to restore genuine integrity to it.

2.1.9 OBJECTION 9
Trying "to work within a Christian context in one's teaching . . . [would be] to lower the academic quality of the pedagogy."[44]
Response: Working out God's truth should raise rather than lower the bar.

First, from a religious motivation, seeking truth to honor God, seeking truth to learn more about God, and seeking truth to understand ourselves and the creation more fully should provide a powerful motivation to strive for excellence.

---

[44] Claerbaut, p. 21.

Second, the fact that Christianity seeks truth rather than political correctness or rhetorical power should increase the desire for knowledge and even information quality because accuracy does indeed matter. The very fact that we can use the word *truth* unashamedly, without feeling the need to dress it in sneer quotes demonstrates that we believe in real standards of objective knowledge.

Third, Christianity's holistic view of truth seeks to delineate a grand theory of the knowable universe, wider and more inclusive of all we can experience, wider than the truncated view offered by naturalism (limiting itself to material reality).

Seeking unity and transcendent meaning and the interconnections — that is, the integration — of all knowledge is a high and motivating calling. Careful thinking and analysis are more important than ever when the perceived consequences — right or wrong knowledge of God's creation — are more serious than under competing perspectives.

This "lower Christian quality" objection appears to arise from the fear that working from a Christian perspective will make Christian scholarship look different from secular scholarship, and secular scholars will denigrate it for that reason. Christian scholarship will indeed have differences, but those differences do not imply "lower academic quality." Christian scholars should work to meet the highest standards and stop worrying about the respect of the secular scholarly establishment (which grants or removes respect often on the basis of politics and power and conformance with currently accepted ideas). Christian scholars should reject the inferiority complex that the secular academy wants to foist on them.

2.1.10 OBJECTION 10

Wait a minute. Some disciplines have more than one theoretical approach, each with its own worldview and truth claims. And these truth claims can change from time to time. So integration is shooting at a moving target.

Response: Integration must begin with what is currently thought.

Whether it is people or their ideas, they must be reached at first where they are. Changes are addressed as they come. This isn't magic; it's life. Disciplinary approaches often change or require adjustment as new knowledge forces a correction, and sometimes a major theoretical frame is shown to be so involved with error that it must be either abandoned or largely redacted. At the same time, however, the overarching worldview or methodology is retained, and that is the point of impact with the Christian worldview.

For example, Margaret Mead's conclusions that promiscuous sex among the Samoans in the late 1920s kept them happy and free of anxiety were exposed as the consequence of a hoax played on her by her two Samoan interviewees. However, her ideas so permeated American and European culture that even today they remain as a subtext in many movies and books.

There is also a saying that applies to the information age, where every idea, good and bad, can circulate all over the world in seconds.

A lie can travel halfway around the world while the truth is putting on its shoes.

And just to rub in that very fact, there is a lie associated with this quotation about lies. The quotation is almost always attributed to atheist Mark Twain, when in fact it originated, slightly reworded, with Christian minister Charles Haddon Spurgeon, who attributed it to an old proverb:

It is a great deal easier to set a story afloat than to stop
it. If you want truth to go round the world you must
hire an express train to pull it; but if you want a lie to
go round the world, it will fly: it is as light as a feather,
and a breath will carry it. It is well said in the old proverb, "A lie will go round the world while truth is pull-
ing its boots on."[45]

To the point also is the fact that the attribution to Mark
Twain will continue on into the future. The proverb for
this phenomenon is, "Undead information walks ever on."
Many ideas and fact claims have been proved wrong or
false, and yet they are still circulated.

Because disciplinary knowledge can change, it is also
risky for Christian scholars to leap onto the latest finding
that appears to support our worldview. Citing it cautious-
ly is the better practice.

2.1.11 OBJECTION 11

But the Bible is not a science book.

**Response: The Bible contains knowledge relevant to the
scientific understanding of reality.**

It's quite the case that most of the content of the Bible
concerns non-scientific matters. In addition to behavioral
laws and theology and moral teaching, we find figurative
language like metaphors: "How precious is Your lovingkindness, O God! And the children of men take refuge in
the shadow of Your wings" (Psalm 36:7). We find phe-
nomenological and experiential viewpoints rather than lit-
eral (or "scientific") descriptions: "It was very early after
sunrise" (Mark 16:2b). We find rhetorical devices such as
personification: "Let the rivers clap their hands, Let the
mountains sing together for joy" (Psalm 98:8).

---

[45] "Joseph Attacked by the Archers," Sermon 17, delivered April 1,
1855. The Spurgeon Archive. <http:// www.spurgeon.org
/sermons/0017.htm>.

But the Bible also contains truths that directly impact the disciplines: God created the heavens and the earth; we are created in the image of God; we are sinners; we have a redeemer. From these truths and other Biblical teachings, we can know that our lives have purpose and meaning.

Criticizing the Bible because it is a religious book that makes pronouncements about "scientific" matters seems hypocritical coming from some scientists whose science books aren't supposed to be books of theology, but the books make theological pronouncements, such as that God does not exist.

Anti-Christian wags who have attempted to co-opt the respect of science in order to advance their philosophical agenda like to mock Christians who argue for Biblical relevance and authority in the natural world. "The Bible says nothing about the chemistry of nylon manufacture," they say. "I don't see any instructions on how to solve complex equations." But these are just irrelevancies, or worse, red herrings designed to shift the argument away from the actual issue, which almost always boils down to the view of what it means to be human.

2.3 STUDENT OBJECTIONS TO INTEGRATION

Some students might object to the practice of integrating faith and learning, mostly because it requires active rather than passive engagement with the course content, therefore involving more thinking and more work. The objections, however, might be phrased differently.

2.3.1 STUDENT OBJECTION 1
Why can't we just learn the same material they do over at State University?
Response: We are learning the same material that students at State University learn.

And more. We're going to learn the material in the context of the worldviews and theoretical strengths and weaknesses surrounding the content. We will learn the importance of knowing where an author is "coming from" — the worldview that shapes discourse — and we will use Christian knowledge to improve our understanding of the difference between fact and interpretation.

Even more than that, we will discover that the learning students get at State U can be enriched by the additional knowledge our worldview brings. And with the touchstone of faith, we can gain additional insights into our own worldview through the subject matter we are learning.

2.3.2 Student Objection 2

You say that some of the ideas behind the course content are wrong, misguided, or limited. Why should we study stuff that's wrong?

Response: To be wise, we must have more knowledge than just what is perfectly true.

The use of contrast and the exploration of why an idea is weak or wrong make a powerful learning technique. Analyzing errors is an excellent way to find and understand truth. Second, it's important to study ideas that many millions of people believe so that we can understand why they believe what they do and so we can understand how to reach them with the truth. And third, and perhaps most importantly, there is much worthy knowledge to be gleaned, even though it is presented through a worldview we believe is limited or distorted. That's what critical thinking is all about — separating the wheat from the tares.

2.4 Barriers to Faith-Learning Integration

Now, let's look at some practical barriers to the integration process, and how they can be overcome.

2.4.1 BARRIER 1: LACK OF TRAINING

Few faculty have training or experience with integrative practices. Graduate schools do not train faculty to integrate their disciplines with their faith. Most graduate programs, especially at the PhD level, are operated by secular institutions, which are unsympathetic or openly hostile to helping their students along the integration path.

Overcoming the barrier. Christian universities and colleges should provide the necessary resources and offer programs to address this barrier. Every college and university should create the following:

- New faculty training in the how-to of integration should be offered.
- New faculty should be paired with a mentor experienced in integrative work.
- All-faculty colloquia that share integrative techniques, successes, and problems should be offered regularly. A multi-day retreat each fall and an all-day colloquium in the spring will keep faculty fresh with new ideas and focused on the intentionality of integration.
- The library should create a special collection area and fund the acquisition of books about integration, the Christian mind, thinking Christianly, issues of faith and reason, and so on.
- Each year the administration should identify a book for all faculty to read and include a discussion of it during the fall colloquium.
- Faculty should be required to write an essay each year outlining their understanding, performance, and growth of their faith-learning work.
- A student essay contest should held, awarding a prize each spring to the essay that best demonstrates the integration of faith and learning within a disciplinary area.

2.4.2 Barrier 2: Deeply Embedded Secularism

Many academic disciplines include secularist assumptions and methodologies that are in tension with a Christian worldview. Postmodernism, Marxism, Darwinism, Naturalism, Materialism, Mind-Body monism, and various other ideologies are intertwined within the framework of the discipline, making it difficult for the Christian faculty member to comprehend and teach knowledge that opposes those assumptions.

Overcoming the barrier. Individual departments should meet to discuss the schools of interpretation and the assumptions underlying their discipline. Discussion of Christian alternatives and the Christian worldview should be included in department meetings.

Exercise

Faculty (and with the help of faculty, students too) can grow in their understanding of their discipline by completing a session answering questions about the philosophical commitments, values, and methodologies that influence or control that discipline's interpretive process. A worksheet that specifies and organizes the task could include questions like these:

1. **Epistemological assumptions**
- What can be true?
- How does your discipline's view of truth compare to a Biblical view?

2. **Ontological assumptions**
- What are the dimensions of reality—is reality circumscribed to include only material things?
- What is the discipline's view of human nature? Is it changeable by changing political structures or by changing human hearts?

3. **Axiological commitments**
- What is considered "good" or "bad" in the discipline?
- What set of values is used to judge facts, behaviors, actions, and circumstances?
- Are values fixed, or relative to circumstance, applied selectively?
- How do the discipline's values compare to Biblical values?

4. **Methodological rules**
- Are facts restricted to what can be demonstrated empirically?
- What is the logic of reasoning in your discipline?
- Does the methodology constrain the search for truth?

2.4.3 BARRIER 3: FEAR OF CONSEQUENCES

In an environment where publication and presentation at scholarly meetings is important for promotion and tenure, many Christian faculty are afraid to rock the boat of their discipline and write something that would appear threatening to the status quo. In addition to fear of ridicule and lack of respect from their secular colleagues, faculty are concerned about repercussions (denial of grants, jobs, presentations at conferences, etc.) for stepping away from established orthodoxy.

Peer review for publications in most fields (with the power of rejection) means that Christian faculty must toe the line of "correct" theoretical approaches if they want to get published. Therefore, they shy away from bringing conflicting but Biblical ideas into the great conversation.

Overcoming the barrier. Christian faculty should adopt a two-pronged approach: (1) increase efforts to get published in their discipline's flagship journals and (2) start up new peer-reviewed journals that will be friendly to high quality articles that offer investigation, analysis, and interpretation from a Christian standpoint.

Another possibility is for faculty to write books and articles that run parallel to instead of directly against disciplinary views. See the examples discussed in Chapter 4.

2.4.4 BARRIER 4: TOO MUCH WORK

Integration has been so long neglected that there will be a tremendous amount of work involved in generating alternative theoretical models and then demonstrating that those models provide a superior account of the data.

Christian faculty have much on their to-do lists, and without intentionality and support from administrators, it is likely that integration will be nominal.

Overcoming the barrier. The saying is, What gets rewarded gets done. Department chairs, provosts, deans, and university presidents should adopt policies that encourage and reward integrative work. Demonstrated integrative work and student assignments should be considered as part of promotion and tenure decisions. At the same time, administrators should help faculty prioritize (and simplify by reducing work where possible). If integration is presented or viewed as "just one more thing," it will not succeed. It must become an essential, foundational part of the school's academic culture.

CHAPTER SUMMARY

This chapter answered a number of objections to the process of faith-learning integration and argued that both the academic disciplines and Christendom will benefit greatly from it. Students need to understand the benefits of a Christian higher educational experience that helps them develop and maintain a coherent, holistic worldview. Practical barriers to integrative work were also addressed, with some suggested ways to overcome them.

Questions for Thought and Discussion

1. Do any of the objections to integrative work seem especially cogent to you? Was the response convincing? Why or why not?
2. Are there other objections to integration that you have heard (or raised yourself)? What answers have you thought of?
3. Did this chapter encourage you to engage more actively and deeply in the practice of integrating faith and learning? Why or why not?
4. Of the barriers to integration discussed in this chapter, do any apply with particular force to your own discipline? If so, what ideas do you have to overcome them?

Activities

1. Convene a department meeting to discuss the objections to integration detailed in this chapter. Develop discipline-specific answers to those objections that seem most relevant.
2. In a department meeting, discuss the barriers you think apply especially to your discipline. What strategies can you think of now that will help overcome those barriers?
3. Meet with colleagues from other disciplinary areas to discuss the "lack of training" barrier. Develop a plan

for faculty development in integrative work. (Possibilities include colloquia, retreats, reading and discussion sessions, assigned book, focused faculty or department meetings, presentations by experienced faculty, outside speakers.)

4. Develop syllabus language or a short discussion note that responds to possible student objections to learning about and doing integrative tasks themselves.

3

3. FOUNDATIONS OF FAITH-LEARNING INTEGRATION

There is no wholly neutral epistemology that can settle disputes over what areas of human knowledge are neutral and objective. Rather, a Christian epistemology must frankly begin . . .not only with common sense but also with data derived from revelation.

—George Marsden[46]

Overview
This chapter answers the following questions:
- What Biblical knowledge and interpretive skills do faculty and students need to have in order to perform integrative tasks successfully?
- How does general knowledge help in the integrative process?
- Why is critical thinking important to good faith-learning integration?
- How are facts dependent on values?
- Why is decompartmentalizing faith and learning important to a holistic view of reality?

---

[46] George Marsden, "The Collapse of American Evangelical Academia," in Alvin Plantinga and Nicholas Wolterstorff, eds., *Faith and Rationality: Reason and Belief in God.* Notre Dame, IN: University of Notre Dame Press, 1983, p. 247.

3.1. The Challenge

A principal reason for the existence of the Christian college or university is to provide an educational environment that includes both academic subject matter and Christian knowledge. For many Christian institutions of higher education, academic knowledge and Christian knowledge are viewed not merely as co-existent, but as compatible—so much so that many of these institutions emphasize the integration of faith (or Christian knowledge) and academic disciplinary learning. What we know as Christians is viewed as relevant to and even a part of the great, holistic knowledge environment. As John Henry Cardinal Newman noted, "In a word, Religious Truth is not only a portion but a condition of general knowledge."[47]

Many Christian colleges and universities identify the integration of faith and learning as an important—or even core—goal in the educational experience of their students. However, entering freshmen often arrive unprepared to develop the process of integration because they lack the necessary foundational skills and knowledge. This chapter identifies the areas that require careful attention for preparing students for integrative activities and provides a set of strategies and questions for developing these areas.[48]

New faculty at Christian colleges and universities often face the daunting prospect of helping students integrate academic knowledge claims with Christian truth. The process is daunting in part because it is frequently foreign to the faculty members who have spent many years in secu-

---

[47] John Henry Cardinal Newman, *The Idea of a University*, 1852, 1873. III.10. Rpt. San Francisco: Rinehart Press, 1960, pp. 52-53.

[48] This chapter is a revision of a poster session presented at the National Faculty Leadership Conference in Washington, DC on June 25, 2004.

lar graduate schools without hearing the slightest hint about integrating their faith with learning. In fact, in many graduate programs, faith is seen as a liability—a guilty bias to be ashamedly suppressed, lest it interfere with the discipline's claims and methodologies.

Learning to integrate faith and learning in their personal scholarly lives is therefore a definite challenge for many new faculty. Compounding this challenge is the fact that new faculty are often assigned the introductory and other lower division courses that are the first experiences of postsecondary education for incoming students. Today's incoming college freshmen present their own challenge. Many of them arrive ill equipped to begin the process of faith-learning integration.

This chapter looks at the four areas in need of attention to help students prepare and begin the lifelong great work of integration. Employing these strategies either at the course level or at the curriculum design level will produce the foundations needed for integrative thinking and learning. The most powerful implementation is to include numerous questions that will stimulate Socratic dialog.

Let me begin by offering three anecdotes about contemporary Christian college students.

- A church youth leader needed a roommate, and in the course of advertising the opening at his church met a youth group member, a college student, who had been living with his girlfriend for quite some time, only recently to be told that such behavior was wrong for Christians. Surprised, he immediately decided to move out and into another apartment. Hence, his interest in the roommate spot.

- A faculty member at a Christian university remarked offhand one morning in class, in connection with a comment made by a student, that the Bible has claims on one's personal behavior. Several students in the class appeared to be shocked.

- A Christian graduate student was asked how his spiritual life was going. The student replied that he had been so busy that he hadn't had time to pray or read the Bible, so his spiritual life was nonexistent. When asked if his laboratory work was going well, he said yes. When asked if he thought God helped him in his laboratory work, he said yes, also. But he had not connected his lab work, God's guidance, and God's help to his spiritual life.

While these stories may appear to represent a surprising naïveté, they are not so untypical as to be anomalous. These students have clearly failed to integrate faith and living, to perceive that their faith is a life-and-behavior encompassing commitment, not a hobby to be indulged on carefully marked off days. The failure to connect life and faith (as evidenced by many surveys that reveal little difference between the behavior of Christians and non-Christians) is important for our purposes because the inability to integrate faith and learning is a subproblem of the failure to integrate faith and living. Those who do not practice integration well are those unwilling to allow faith to shape their understanding of the world.

Therefore, the four foundational areas discussed here are not only important for preparing students to integrate faith and learning, but are necessary for them to integrate faith and living overall. Effective integration requires a foundation of knowledge, skills, habits, attitudes, and values. Without a proper foundation, integration of some sort will still take place, but on an improper foundation, making the resulting beliefs confused, conflicting, and error filled. The four foundational areas at issue are Biblical knowledge and interpretation (a Christian knowledge environment), a robust supply of thoughtfully assimilated knowledge, both intellectual and spiritual, a decompartmentalized faith capable of working with new knowledge claims, and critical thinking skills.

3.2 WHAT KNOWLEDGE AND SKILLS ARE NEEDED?

In order for students to integrate their faith and their learning successfully, they must develop four areas, as shown by the graphic here, for use by the student's integration engine:

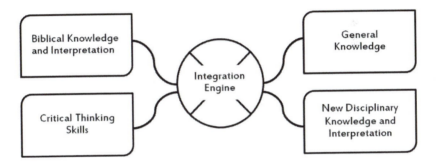

Each of these four areas has several components, all important to the integration process. Here is an explanation of each area and what needs to be included for successful integrative practices.

3.3 BIBLICAL KNOWLEDGE AND INTERPRETATION

The first of the four areas consists of what might be called a Christian knowledge environment, which includes a deep knowledge of the Bible, combined with first-quality interpretive skills (hermeneutics). No one can integrate the faith with any learning if he or she lacks an accurate knowledge of the source of the faith. Trying to integrate an erroneous interpretation of the Bible is equally fruitless—or misleading.

Christians are "people of the Book," and our identity, our Christian knowledge, even our epistemology, are all dependent on the Bible. Such a declaration, to a long-time believer, may appear to verge on "a firm grasp of the obvious," but to the Christian student who enters a Christian college after having been saved only three months prior, or for the Christian student whose background has de-emphasized Scripture (the nominal Christian family, for example), such a concept may not be obvious or may be given only lip service. The result is a Biblical knowledge that is scant and a Biblical facility (the ability to use and apply relevant Scriptures to life and learning problems) that is nonexistent.

Exercise To determine your students' level of Biblical knowledge, give a short quiz at the beginning of the term. It can be as simple as a matching test (match the father or mother to the son or daughter, match the person with the item, such as Moses-Ten Commandments, etc.). You might also coordinate with other faculty in your department to assign a New Testament book to be read carefully during the term of the course.

The first foundational requirement to prepare to integrate faith and learning, then, is a knowledge of what the faith involves, not only as a personal relationship with Christ, but as propositional content knowledge, especially as derived from the Bible itself. The integration process will involve connecting academic learning with Christian knowledge coming either directly from the Bible or though interpretation of Biblical texts.

The three components of the Christian knowledge environment are a Biblical worldview, Biblical literacy, and hermeneutical skills.

3.3.1 A BIBLICAL WORLDVIEW

A worldview is a set of beliefs, values, and attitudes that enable us to process new information and maintain a coherent view of reality. Through our worldview we apply the standards that allow us to make connections between what we know, what we experience, and what new knowledge claims we encounter. In other words, our worldview supplies the interpretive framework for understanding our experiences and the events of the world, and it provides the values that form the basis for decision making. In terms of a process flow, we might think of the role of worldview as the foundation for the production of knowledge, or "properly justified true belief." In the diagram below, the arrows might be translated as "influences" or even "helps determine."

Knowledge depends on judgment, what we conclude to be true after thoughtful investigation. The quality of our judgment depends on the quality of our evaluation or analysis of claims and counterclaims, our sorting out of the evidence. The type of evaluation we perform relies on our standards for evaluation, our standards for truth and evidence, and our standards for proof. And the standards we bring to bear on our analysis are directly dependent on our worldview. Is truth one of our values? Is reason effective? Does the Bible provide us with a source of ultimate values and therefore standards of evaluation and judgment — or is there another source?

Because faith-learning integration is closely linked with judgments about what is or is not knowledge, our worldview is therefore clearly crucial to the proper functioning of faith and learning integration. Indeed, our worldview is the philosophical engine that drives the integrative process. An integrative diagram might look like this:

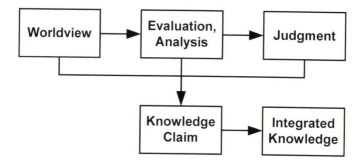

A challenge facing Christian educators is that a Biblical worldview foundation has been taken for granted. The assumption seems to be, "Our students are Christians, raised in the church, so of course they have a Biblical worldview." Such is, unfortunately, not necessarily the case. Most young people could not explain their worldview, where it came from, or what causes it to change. According to a survey by the Barna Research Group,[49] only 9% of born-again Christians[50] have a Biblical worldview.[51] Worse still, among teenagers who are born

---

[49] "A Biblical Worldview Has a Radical Effect on a Person's Life." Barna Research Online. December 1, 2003. Retrieved from http://www.barna.org.

[50] Barna defines born-again Christians as "people who have made a personal commitment to Jesus Christ that is important in their life and believe that they will go up to Heaven because they have confessed their sins and accepted Jesus Christ as their Savior. . . ." See George Barna, *Think Like Jesus.* Nashville, TN: Integrity, 2003, p. 28.

[51] Barna defines a Biblical worldview as including eight criteria: the Bible is the moral standard for behavior, absolute moral truths exist, God is the all-knowing, all-powerful creator of the universe, Jesus led a sinless life, Satan is a real person, a person cannot earn salvation by being good or doing good, Christians have a responsibility to share

again (which is to say, Christian high school and college students), only 2% have a Biblical worldview.[52]

Of course, that doesn't mean they have no worldview. The worldview they do have tends to be a mix of ideas, sometimes contradictory, drawn perhaps by osmosis from the surrounding culture. Teenagers' daily lives are filled with TV, films, MTV, advertisements, magazines, and peers who provide a constant and seemingly plausible stream of worldview alternatives to Biblical values, often sold as the latest or what's hip. Again quoting Barna, "Christians have increasingly been adopting spiritual views that come from Islam, Wicca, secular humanism, the Eastern religions and other sources. Because we remain a largely Bible-illiterate society, few are alarmed or even aware of the slide toward syncretism. . . ."[53] The "trend away from adopting biblical theology in favor of syncretic, culture-based theology" is especially prominent among teenagers and adolescents, he says.[54] Strong postmodernist influences have dominated the marketplace of ideas long enough so that many students have adopted cultural and even philosophical relativism.

Clearly, successful faith-learning integration is impossible for students who lack a clear and well defined Biblical worldview. To begin the process of worldview improvement, and to set the first foundation stone for later faith-learning integration, the following questions are offered for exploration.

---

their faith, and the Bible is completely accurate. See George Barna, *Think Like Jesus*. Nashville, TN: Integrity, 2003, pp. 22-23.

[52] Barna, George. *Think Like Jesus*. Nashville, TN: Integrity, 2003, p. 23.

[53] "Americans Draw Theological Beliefs From Diverse Points of View." Barna Research Online. October 8, 2002. Retrieved from http://www.barna.org.

[54] Ibid.

General worldview questions. These questions will serve to open the subject of worldview thinking and to help students understand that everyone has a worldview, whether or not he or she is aware of it. Exposing hidden assumptions is one of the key principles to clear thinking, and the identification of worldview components and sources is essentially an exercise in assumption identification. (Recall that assumptions include propositions, methodologies, and values.)

- *What is my worldview?* This question is a thought-starter, and many students will find difficulty answering it. You may need to define a worldview not only as a "theory of everything that makes the world make sense," but in more concrete terms, such as "those beliefs and values that we truly use when we make decisions or interpret our own experiences."

- *Is my worldview Biblical?* Students who acknowledge that their worldview is Biblical might be asked further, "How do you know?" or "What specific values from the Bible do you use to make decisions or interpret events?" A related and even more important question is, "Are there parts of my worldview that conflict with Biblical teaching?" Most students will likely have a mixed worldview, containing elements drawn from various sources. This question will allow them to begin the process of eliminating elements that conflict with reality.

- *Where did the components of my worldview come from?* Most of us develop our values, attitudes, and thinking habits almost by osmosis, from things we read, hear, or see. We often do not recognize when we are being influenced. Answering this question about the source of a particular value, then, may be impossible. However, the question does expose the

fact that we do adopt worldview components sometimes unthinkingly and that we should question
and test both those components and their sources.
During the discussion of this question, it may be
useful to identify either a specific value (such as attitudes toward dress or the basis for deciding on
which films to see) or a specific source of some values (such as MTV or other media, peers, or parents)
and ask whether any specific influences can be re-
called.

- *Is my theology (belief about the spiritual realm, belief
  about the origin, purpose, and destiny of human beings)
  Biblical or extrabiblical?* Most Americans, students
  and adults alike, appear to be highly syncretic in
  their theology today. A confused or mixed-together
  theology cannot serve as a proper foundation for integration. The study of world religions and the
  identification of sources for many common ideas
  (such as reincarnation, karma, divination) will help
  to clarify the difference between Scriptural and un-
  scriptural ideas. *No Buckd hists hm !*

- *How does my worldview affect my beliefs, actions, and
  understanding of the world?* This is something of a
  trick question because our genuine worldview
  forms the basis for our actions and understanding
  of the world. It may be that we claim to have a Biblical worldview but then act contrary to it. In that
  case, our genuine worldview may not be fully Biblical. Our actions are usually a better key to what we
  really believe than our protestations about what we
  believe. Of course, sometimes we act against our belief (Romans 7:14-23) but usually our beliefs are revealed by our actions.

Because our worldview encompasses a "theory of everything" for making sense of all our experience and knowledge, there may be some components to it that are not directly relevant to academic integration issues. However, the aspects of our worldview that touch on ontological sets (what is real, what exists) and epistemological requisites (how we can have knowledge) are central to faith and learning integration.

Worldview questions relating to truth.[55] The following questions will provide a basis for contrasting Biblical epistemology with relativistic and postmodern views about truth. In each case here, a Yes answer conforms with a Biblical worldview and a No answer does not.

- *Does absolute truth exist?* Truth exists whether we know it or not, since God is the source and knower of truth. Some truths are absolute and eternal. The truth, "God is," might serve as an example.
- *Does absolute moral truth exist?* This question should stimulate discussion about cultural and moral relativism. Both modernist and postmodernist ideology have pressed for relativism in moral and cultural behaviors, and many students have absorbed this idea to a greater or lesser extent.
- *Can truth be known?* Logically, this question cannot be answered without affirming that truth can be known. Even a No answer embodies a truth claim, that it is true that truth cannot be known. In spite of this self-refuting problem, a few people adopt a skeptical pose toward truth. The Biblical view is that truth can be known (for example, John 8:32) or at least approached (for example, 1 Corinthians 13:12).

---

[55] These questions do not cover all of Biblical epistemology (such as the capacity to reason *a priori* (Proverbs 1:7) and *a posteriori* (Romans 1:18-21).

- *Is truth unified?* This question touches on the problem of compartmentalization (see below), where some Christians are tempted to divide truth into nearly independent realms. If faith-learning integration is to be successful, we must take the position that "all truth is God's truth," and that all truth coheres. The "two realms" view, where we see our lives as having somewhat separate religious and secular commitments, produces a fragmented reality.
- *What are the sources of truth?* Experiment, experience, observation, and reason are the answers most epistemologies share. However, we must add revelation to the list for a Biblical epistemology because the Bible provides knowledge that cannot be gained through other means.

The unity of truth—including academic and Biblical or theological truth—is at the heart of integration. The phrase "integration of faith and learning" might be expanded to say "the integration of faith-truth or Christian truth and learning truth or academic discipline truth." Much of Christian truth (such as God as creator or the nature of humanity) directly impacts the content of academic disciplines. It is not a question of spiritual truth versus scientific truth. Without a commitment to a unified truth, students will feel an increasing dissonance between heartfelt belief (faith) and what they feel compelled to accept intellectually; so their faith will be in danger of becoming increasingly personal and emotional and thus self-marginalizing. Faith will no longer make any claim to influence the arena of "real" or objective truth. Some aspects of the contemporary culture, especially multiculturalism, already encourage this division, as does postmodernism, which posits many "truths," either all equally valid or none true in an objective sense.

Exercise

A useful exercise for examining Biblical epistemology and the Biblical teaching about truth is to ask students to search the Bible for occurrences of *truth, knowledge, know, reason, understand, think,* and related words, and to discuss the implications of some of the uses. (For example, in the NASB-U, *truth, truthful, or true* occurs 149 times in just the New Testament; *reason, reasoned, or reasoning* occurs 95 times in the NT alone.) Such a task can be accomplished rapidly with Bible software or by using one of the online Bibles available on the Web (see Bible Gateway at bible.gospelcom.net or my Bible study page at www.virtualsalt.com/bibstudy.htm).

Worldview questions relating to human nature. The question of what it means to be a human being is central to both the culture war and to our worldview. Moral values, personal behavior, law, and social policy are all deeply influenced by the view of human nature we adopt. Very different social and political problems are identified and very different solutions and behaviors are justified depending on whether humans are viewed as merely material machines, devoid of creator or soul, or whether we are seen as the creatures of a God who has made us in his image. Below are three questions related to human nature in a larger context:

- *Did God create the world and mankind?* Man's destiny is intertwined with his origin. If we arose by chance, then we have no purpose (other than "differential reproduction") and life has only humanly constructed meaning. If God created us, we have not only a rich meaning and purpose to our lives, but also a responsibility to know and serve God.

- *Is God sovereign over history?* Does God care about his creatures and does he guide world events? Or is there merely random action by blind matter stumbling around in the dark?

- *Is the Bible accurate in all its teaching?* Scripture tells us many things about our nature. Do we accept all of those teachings or do we pick and choose?

Integration Key #2: What does it mean to be human? The answer to this question influences or determines the worldviews, interpretations, and conclusions of much scholarly research. Man: Image of God or accidental product of undirected chance?

Questions relating to human nature more specifically include these:

- *What is human nature?* That is, Is human nature fixed or changeable? Are we basically good or are we fallen in sin?
- *What is the value of human life?* A common saying is that you cannot know the value of something unless you know its purpose. If you find a mechanical device while you are lost in the forest, it may have no value to you at all. If you are told that its purpose is to guide you back to safety, then it suddenly has great value to you. Thus, answering the purpose question answers the value question.
- *Why are we here on earth?* This is the purpose question. See above.
- *Why should we do one thing rather than another?* This is the axiology question, the question of ethics and morality. What is our basis for choice and decision making? How should we live? What should be our life goals?

The construction of a Biblical worldview must be an ongoing process. It must be built and added to in every course. However, it should begin early. In college, a University 101 or Freshman Orientation class is a good start. However, to cover the ground best, freshmen should be required to take individual courses in critical thinking and Christian worldview. The critical thinking course would include hermeneutics, and the Christian worldview course would include a study of competing worldviews, such as naturalism and postmodernism.

In addition to such a formal addressing of worldview issues, however, every faculty member teaching freshmen should include these ideas and help students develop their worldviews.

A useful, clarifying activity is to discuss a work of literature, a historical event, as a philosophical concept, or a disciplinary theory from both a secular (or popular theoretical) worldview and from a

Exercise   Christian worldview. What difference does each viewpoint make when considering the meaning and implications of the idea or theory or event?

3.3.2 Biblical Literacy

A significant cause of this lack of a Biblical worldview is Biblical ignorance. One of the false assumptions that some faculty at Christian colleges and universities make is that their incoming students have an accurate knowledge of the Bible. The fact is, many incoming students have little familiarity with the Biblical text. It has become almost a cliché to call the Bible "the most unread book of all time," but the assertion appears to have increasing strength. Busy lifestyles, with so many choices for consuming time, prevent many young people from doing regular Bible reading.[56] Barna's research indicates that "comparatively few early teens say that they learned enough Bible content to enable them to make important life decisions on the basis

---

[56] See for example, "Why Johnny Can't Read . . . the Bible." Retrieved from http://home.snu.edu/~hculbert.fs/flesch.htm.

of biblical principles."[57] Without a solid grounding in Scriptural knowledge and a commitment to a Biblical worldview, students will be unable to integrate their academic learning with a clear and accurate Christian knowledge.

Questions about Biblical knowledge. The following are general questions about Biblical literacy. If general questions like these are used, in each case, the first answer of Yes or No should not be accepted as the final word, but additional probing questions such as, "How do you know?" or "Explain your answer" should be added. However, a better method is to "translate" each question into one of specific content. For example, the first question might be translated into one that asks, "Tell me about the fall of mankind," or "What happened at the wedding in Cana?"

- *Am I thoroughly familiar with the Biblical text, including content, concepts, and themes?* Students must be encouraged to read the Bible not only regularly but completely. A few verses here and there are not enough.
- *Do I understand the different genres (such as law, history, prophecy, poetry) and the purposes and audiences of the various books?* Included here should be awareness of imagery (metaphor, simile, synecdoche) and rhetoric (hyperbole, understatement, irony). No, God does not actually have the body of a bird (Psalm 17:8).
- *Am I familiar with the major doctrines of the Bible, and can I locate the supporting verses for those doctrines?* An introduction to theology course is probably the best way to help students answer this question. A

---

[57] "Spiritual Progress Hard to Find in 2003." Barna Research Online. December 22, 2003. Retrieved from http://www.barna.org.

book on the major doctrines of the Bible would be good also.

- *Can I find the Biblical view of a given question?* Familiarity with the Bible is the most effective way to answer this question with a Yes. Concordances or Bible software are a less effective substitute.

Questions about the application of Biblical knowledge. Biblical knowledge is best tested in context, where students are asked to supply appropriate passages, doctrines, or values from Scripture during the course of ordinary classroom discussion.

- *What does the Bible say about this idea?* This question asks for a specific teaching, in the case where the Bible has a specific passage about the idea under discussion. For example, "You shall not steal" prohibits embezzlement.

- *Can you think of a Biblical passage that's relevant to this problem [or theme or idea or claim]?* This question asks for a passage that is thematically or morally connected to the issue under discussion, even though the passage may not address the case specifically. For example, "You shall not give false testimony" speaks to the issue of fraudulent inducement in contracts.

- *Is there a value we can take from our knowledge of Biblical truth that applies here?* This question asks for a value belonging to the Biblical worldview rather than a specific Scriptural passage. For example, the values of human life and humanity in the image of God speak to the issue of human cloning or stem cell research.

Most students have a Bible, or even several. The challenge is getting the students to read the book they already have. Required courses in Bible survey or Introduction to the Bible can be helpful, as can the use of a substantial amount of Scripture in other courses. One or more Biblical literacy tests might also encourage students to be Bible readers and give the institution insight into general Biblical knowledge. Reading techniques used for understanding academic material, such as SQ3R (survey, question, read, recite, review) might prove helpful.

Ask students to locate Biblical texts that relate to the subject of your course or your current topic. Those students who have little Bible knowledge can perform keyword searches at one of the online Bible sites or with PC software on their own or school computers. Be sure to teach students about (1) the importance of context and capturing surrounding verses when needed and (2) how to develop synonyms for the concepts they want to find, and (3) the use of multiple translations to increase the possibility of locating a particular search word. You might also introduce them to a resource like the *Treasury of Scripture Knowledge*, that giant collection of cross references.

Among the many online resources and free downloads are some audio versions of the Bible. The King James Version, read by Alexander Scourby can be listened to at Audio Bible (www.audio-bible.com/bible/bible.html), and the World English Bible (a modernized American Standard Version) can be listened to or downloaded and copied freely in mp3 format at the Audio Treasure Web site (www.audiotreasure.com/webindex.htm). Students can listen to the Bible on their portable mp3 players or convert the files to audio CD's for use in their stereos or automobiles. The "read, hear, discuss" format can then be applied.

3.3.3 HERMENEUTIC SKILLS

Do not assume that incoming freshmen are trained and experienced interpreters of the Bible or of any literature.

We are still suffering from the widespread practice of "reader response" interpretation, where students are allowed to adduce nearly any interpretation of a passage they want. The postmodernist idea that every text has an infinite number of interpretations (all of which are actually "misinterpretations") is still popular. Students therefore may need encouragement in developing good analytic skills and evidence-based interpretations and inferences.

At the simplest level, students might be encouraged to adopt the three-step process suggested by Roy Zuck: [58]

- *What does it say?* This is an issue of understanding the vocabulary and syntax of the passage. For especially important passages, consult several translations, and study the original language words to get a better feel for the meaning. (Use an interlinear Greek-English New Testament, for example.)

  As a case in point, the King James translation of the Bible (1611) sometimes presents problems of interpretation simply because of language changes between the early seventeenth century and today. A simple example comes from Luke 5:37: "And no man putteth new wine into old bottles: else the new wine will burst the bottles, and be spilled, and the bottles perish." At first glance, there seems to be something wrong. Why not put new wine into old bottles? Glass is pretty strong. But did they even have glass bottles in Israel in Jesus' day? So we consult an etymological dictionary and discover that *bottle* is from the Latin *bota*, skin.[59] In 1611, a bottle referred to a wineskin. So the King James, in its

---

[58] Roy B. Zuck, *Basic Bible Interpretation: A Practical Guide to Discovering Biblical Truth.* Colorado Springs, CO: Victor, 1991, p. 10.
[59] Joseph T. Shipley, *Dictionary of Word Origins.* 2nd Ed., New York: Philosophical Library, 1945, p. 53, *bottle.*

time, accurately translated the original Greek *askos*, wineskin.

- *What does it mean?* Is the passage intended to be understood literally, or are there literary figures (metaphors, similes), irony, or a recounting of an event or behavior without endorsing it? And do Christians differ about the meaning? For example, does the word *day* in the first chapter of Genesis refer to a 24-hour solar day or to a longer period? Consult several commentaries to see how various Bible scholars interpret the passage.

- *How does it apply to me?* Answering this question emphasizes the relevance and application of Scripture to our lives as well as the *how* of application. Ask yourself, What behavior is required (or prohibited) by this passage? How should I alter my current lifestyle in order to conform with this teaching?

The question about how the passage applies can be further elaborated by differentiating between principle and the specific behavioral example given in the passage. Henry Virkler notes three possibilities:

- *Retain both the principle and its behavioral expression.* For example, in the commandment, "You shall not covet your neighbor's house" (Exodus 20:17a) we should retain both the principle (the prohibition against coveting) and the behavioral expression (coveting a house).

- *Retain the principle but suggest a change in the way that principle is behaviorally expressed in our culture.* For example, in Paul's comment that "if anyone says to you, 'This is meat sacrificed to idols,' do not eat it" (1 Cor. 10:28), we understand that the principle of avoiding behavior which may cause other believers to stumble is still relevant, we no longer have the specific case of meat being sacrificed to idols in our culture.

- *Change both the principle and its behavioral expression, assuming that both were culture-bound and are therefore no longer applicable.* An example might be the Old Testament prohibition against eating pork (Deut. 14:8), which may have been related to the danger of trichinosis.[60]

The last choice, of course, where we decide to give up both principle and specific practice, should be handled with great fear and trepidation, lest we open the swinging door to relativism and to a counterscriptural pick-and-choose theology. It's one thing to pick an example, as I have, from old covenant law, but another to discard a New Testament teaching without especially good reason, based on the interpretation of other Scriptures.

Questions about interpretation. These questions are designed to get students to think deliberately about their interpretive practices.

- *What method of interpretation do I use to understand Biblical teaching?* Articulating an answer to this question may be a struggle for some students, but the effort should help students clarify how they gain Biblical understanding. During discussion, the instructor can also supply some new possibilities (use Scripture to interpret Scripture, use a Bible dictionary, a word study, or systematic theology).
- *How do I discern and interpret figurative language or parables?* Only a few students may still be confused over the claim that the Bible is "literally true" as opposed to "accurate in all its claims" or "without

---

[60] Henry A. Virkler, *Hermeneutics: Principles and Processes of Biblical Interpretation.* Grand Rapids: Baker Books, 1981, p. 225.

error in its original manuscripts." Should we really hate our father and mother (Luke 14:26), or is that a figure of speech? Students who still need help with figurative language might consult Bullinger's *Figures of Speech Used in the Bible*.[61]

- *How do I find the meaning of a passage?* Here students can come to the understanding that meaning is derived, gained, or discovered rather than "developed" or "constructed" as the postmodernists would have us believe. We may not always understand the full meaning of a passage, but that does not mean that we can overlay our own meaning on it. This question is also a good one for bringing up the unity of Scripture, the fact that Scripture interprets Scripture (one passage clarifies or supports another passage), and that issues of context (historical and textual) are important.

- *How do I discover underlying principles beneath specific examples?* Help students to see the generalizations underlying arguments. Teach syllogisms and enthymemes.

- *What method do I use to apply Biblical teaching to my own life?* There seems to be a dearth of personal application among some students. Yes, the Bible makes claims on our behavior and lifestyles. This question allows for that discussion to take place.

- *What interpretive resources do I use?* This question will discover what familiarity students have with commentaries, Bible dictionaries, concordances, word studies, and so forth.

---

[61] E. W. Bullinger, *Figures of Speech Used in the Bible*. 1898. Rpt., Grand Rapids: Baker Books, 1968.

If a course in hermeneutics is not required of all students, then some aids and discussion in several classes might have to suffice. Books such as *How to Read the Bible for All Its Worth* are valuable, too.[62]

3.4 General Knowledge

A good mental warehouse stocked with learning is important for the purposes of comparison, contrast, analogy, context, circumspection—and that's just for the purposes of running a well-oiled integration engine. General knowledge is good for the soul, too, and rightly processed, can help make a person wise. Therefore, students should be strongly encouraged to read, read, read—worthy books, of course. (I once saw an interview on TV with a woman who had read several thousand romance novels, and she was none the wiser for it.)

Students should be reassured that learning gets easier as they apply themselves. The more you learn, the easier learning is. There is a sound basis for this in learning theory, where the mind reaches into long-term memory to retrieve a schema that can function as an analogical learning bridge: comparing the new idea with an old idea makes the new idea easier to learn.

A good stock of general knowledge also helps students (or anyone) identify the degree of plausibility of new claims, because they have encountered the false and fake as well as the genuine and good. Getting a sense of what is possible and what is impossible, what kinds of ideas (true or false) the purveyors of information frequently offer, and having an ever-increasing collection of knowledge will

---

[62] Gordon D. Fee and Douglas Stuart, *How to Read the Bible for All It's Worth*. 4th Ed. Grand Rapids: Zondervan, 2014.

help in the easier and faster understanding and evaluating of new claims.

For faculty, a good stock of general knowledge, including knowledge from popular culture, is valuable for teaching students through the use of analogy. Seventeenth century pastor and poet George Herbert noted the power of analogy for teaching:

> The Country Parson is full of all knowledge. They say, it is an ill mason that refuseth any stone: and there is no knowledge, but, in a skillful hand, serves either positively as it is, or else to illustrate some other knowledge. He condescends even to the knowledge of tillage and pastorage, and makes great use of them in teaching, because people by what they understand are best led to what they understand not.[63]

Those familiar with learning theory know that analogy is one of the principal and most effective ways of learning.

As a way of beginning the unification process, students should be made aware of interdependencies. These three pairs of ideas are often split and held to be independent or nearly independent of each other. To help students unify their thinking, these pairs must be recognized as ultimately inseparable.

3.4.1 BEHAVIOR AND BELIEF

As mentioned above, ideas have consequences for action. At the same time, our actions reveal our real beliefs. If we say we love coffee ice cream more than any other flavor, but we always order pistachio, our true belief about ice cream will be rightly questioned. Much of the time we do follow our beliefs, so that it is true that our beliefs in-

---

[63] George Herbert, *A Priest to the Temple* (1652); rpt. in *The Works of George Herbert*, ed. F. E. Hutchinson, Oxford: Clarendon Press, 1941, Chapter 4, p. 228 (spelling modernized).

fluence how we behave. But it is also true that our behavior influences what we believe.

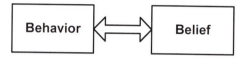

Aristotle says that virtue is "formed by habit": Our moral "characteristics develop from corresponding activities."[64] If we behave consistently in a certain way, such as being honest or dishonest, our beliefs will eventually conform to our actions. (Cognitive dissonance theory is one explanation of this phenomenon, and simple habituation may be another.)

The Bible also teaches us that faith is an activity, not just a state of belief: Jesus tells us, "If you love me, you will keep my commandments" (John 14:15). Love and discipleship are not mere states of assent or feeling, but the commitment is revealed by action. The sense of Colossians 2:6 is, "Now that you have received Christ, live like it. Don't just follow his ideas; follow him."

There is a comic scene in Henry Fielding's novel *Joseph Andrews* where Parson Adams quotes an imaginary villain seeking entrance into heaven: "Lord, it is true, I never obeyed one of thy commandments, yet punish me not, for I believe them all."[65] Such an argument lacks the power of conviction. And, of course, Scripture tells us, "But prove yourselves doers of the word, and not merely hearers who delude themselves" (James 1:22). We are to develop values that influence our behavior.

---

[64] *Nicomachean Ethics* II.1, 1103a, 1103b.
[65] Henry Fielding, *Joseph Andrews*. 1742, rpt. Boston: Houghton Mifflin, 1969, p. 67 (Book I, Chapter 17).

- *Do I know the Scriptures that call me to live out my faith, that show that faith is an activity?*[66] If Christian faith is something more than a feeling indulged on Sunday mornings, if it has implications for life and personal behavior (as well as for intellectual interaction with the world of knowledge), then faith must be an activity, something we do as well as something we assent to or believe.

- *Do I realize that my behavior over time both reveals what I really believe and shapes that belief?* We cannot do one thing and believe another on a consistent, ongoing basis. Usually, cognitive dissonance will eventually cause us to reconcile behavior and belief. If we believe that stealing is wrong but continue to steal office supplies, then eventually we will probably conclude that either stealing is not always wrong or that taking office supplies is not really stealing. On the positive side, if we make ourselves perform unselfish and charitable actions even though we don't feel unselfish or charitable, we should eventually come to be and feel giving and generous.

3.4.2 INTELLECTUAL AND SPIRITUAL

Ultimately, what we believe intellectually influences what we believe spiritually. And more than just spiritual belief, what we believe intellectually influences the quality of our spiritual life. These influences are clear evidence that the compartmentalization of faith—keeping it away from learning or the attempt to put faith into a separate realm from scholarly knowledge—is not only unwise, but

---

[66] Suggestions include Matthew 19:17, John 14:15, John 14:23-24, John 15:10 and of course that "right thorny epistle," James, especially verses 2:14-16. For faith and obedience, see John 3:36, Romans 2:5-8, 2 Thessalonians 1:6-8, and Hebrews 5:8-10.

it is also ultimately impossible. When it comes to faith and intellect, compartmentalization is marginalization—for faith.

In the same way that our intellectual commitments influence what we believe about spiritual matters, so, too, our spiritual life influences our intellectual life. This is what Saint Anselm meant by his dictum, *Credo Ut Intelligam,* "I believe in order that I may know." Or as Proverbs 1:7a puts it, "The fear of the Lord is the beginning of knowledge."

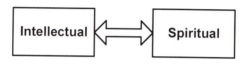

Asking students to reflect on this interconnection will help them understand that compartmentalization of faith and intellect should be avoided.

- *Do I recognize that my intellectual beliefs influence my spiritual beliefs and life activity?* For example, the intellectual belief that life is a zero-sum game where one person must lose if another is to gain will have a substantially negative impact on the spiritual idea of hope. Such a belief also would likely push the spirituality toward pessimism rather than optimism.

- *Do I recognize that my spiritual beliefs influence my intellectual beliefs?* For example, believing that mankind was created by and in the image of God gives us an enormous amount of information about human nature, our own minds and spiritual strivings, our purpose, and our destiny. Spiritual knowledge greatly expands intellectual knowledge, awareness, and understanding.

- *Do I understand the connection between the intellectual and the spiritual?* Belief, feelings, and all intellectual activity take place in the mind. The mind seeks unity. Being double minded is a sign of a conflict or a problem. Spiritual ideas and intellectual concepts are both thoughts, thus making the two inextricably interconnected.

- *Do I understand that Biblical knowledge is a type of knowledge, and that it is an essential part of my total knowledge base?* Some Biblical knowledge (information about angels, for example) is of a different order or category than, say, scientific knowledge, but much Biblical knowledge is directly relevant and in the same arena as "worldly" knowledge. The Bible gives us an exact piece of knowledge to account for the perceived design of plants and animals, for example.

- *Do I understand that all knowledge needs to be interconnected and coherent?* If some of our ideas contradict other of our ideas, we cannot be said to have knowledge. Instead we have only confusion or at the very most, "candidates for knowledge."

3.4.3 FACT AND VALUE

People's values influence both how they interpret facts and what they identify as a fact in the first place. The supposed separation of fact and value in science is just not realistic. (See Appendix 4 for an extended discussion.) Our values have a great impact on what to research, what we find, and what it means. And, of course, facts influence our values because we respond to arguments and evidence and shape our sense of what is right or wrong in part based on what we experience and observe.

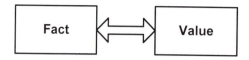

We should remain committed to a Biblical moral foundation, only nuanced by how we interpret and apply it based on particular facts. In practice, the separation of fact and value means the separation of fact and selected (rejected) values, such as moral constraints, social implications, and the like. Science is deeply involved in values. Depending on the values held and promoted, this involvement can be good, bad, necessary, or unnecessary. For example, it is a (good) value preference that results should be empirical rather than whimsical; it is a (good) value preference that we should make rational rather than irrational decisions; it is a (not necessary, perhaps even bad) value preference for some people that all evidence for a given phenomenon should point toward materialism.

- *Do I understand how someone's values (my own and those of other knowledge creators and analysts) influence what will be judged to be a fact or allowed as evidence for a fact?* Perhaps the most obvious kinds of examples can be found in connection with naturalist/materialist commitments versus theistic commitments. Those who are committed to finding a natural explanation for every phenomenon will not see any supernatural events (or persons) as even possibly factual. A miracle cannot be factual in their value system.

- *Do I understand how the things that I and others believe to be facts can influence our moral and spiritual values?* For example, those who believe that the mind is merely a product of the electrochemical activity of the brain are more likely to believe that free will is an illusion and that our actions and beliefs (including moral and spiritual actions and beliefs) are determined by brain chemistry.

While there may not be a formal course on decompartmentalism, students can learn this habit of thinking by beginning with the early steps outlined in Chapter 4 below. Another effective way to help students with this task is to have them practice the unification of spiritual activity with life activity and with intellectual activity, as described in the exercise here.

Exercise

Have students read Brother Lawrence's short book, *The Practice of the Presence of God.* There are many editions and it is available free online for reading or printing.[67] This little book, by a 17th century French Carmelite, encourages the Christian to keep God present and in constant communication at all times, talking to him as one would to a nearby companion. With a sense that God is always present, students should be better able to see the connections among all their learning, experience, and work. Have them practice God's presence in all their activities for a week or so and then write a short paper describing their experience.

3.5 New Disciplinary Knowledge and Interpretation

It is rather obvious that integration cannot take place without knowing what the ideas are that need to be integrated. However, too many students fail to understand the claims, the argument, the supporting evidence, or the context of the claims. They want to approve or reject before they understand, and seldom do they want to look for any good when they suspect the quality of the data.

---

[67] For online reading or printing, go to http://www.ccel.org/1/lawrence/practice/ or to http://www.practicegodspresence.com/brotherlawrence/index.html.

Remember that in a large percentage of cases where faith appears to be in conflict with academic learning, the conflict is over interpretations framed by a non-Christian worldview and not over actual facts or data.

3.5.1 A Decompartmentalized Faith

For historical reasons, ranging from the pietism of the nineteenth and early twentieth centuries to the contemporary cultural pressures exerted by scientism and secularism, there has been a tendency to fragment reality, dividing the spiritual from the material, and to encourage the view that religion is a private matter, largely unrelated to the secular issues of the day. For many students, the effect of this pressure has been to compartmentalize their Christian faith, and to view their religion and spiritual experience as a separate realm of existence, disconnected from the rest of life. George Barna notes that "because the Christian faith is not associated in people's minds with a comprehensively different way of life than they would lead if they were not Christian, the impact of that faith is largely limited to those dimensions of thought and behavior that are obviously religious in nature."[68] Until Christian students can learn to connect their faith to their academic and life concerns, they will be unable to integrate faith and learning successfully.

For this reason, the process of decompartmentalization —or better, noncompartmentalization—is essential to prepare for the process of faith-learning integration and to practice it when learning new disciplinary knowledge. Students who continue to hold their faith separate from the rest of life (behaving, learning, and thinking) will not only learn little about integration but will be in danger of having the expanding area of learning take over their men-

---

[68] "Survey Shows Faith Impacts Some Behaviors But Not Others." Barna Research Online. October 22, 2002. Retrieved from http://www.barna.org.

tal—and spiritual—life, even further marginalizing their faith.

3.5.2 GENERAL UNIFICATION QUESTIONS

These questions seek to give students insight into the Big Picture:

- *How do I understand the claim that "All truth is God's truth"?* Most students have probably heard this statement before, but they may not have given it much thought beyond the realm of religion. It may be helpful to ask them to clarify this question, or to ask questions such as, "Is the fact that water is made up of one oxygen and two hydrogen atoms part of God's truth?" So-called secular (that is, non-Biblical) knowledge is part of God's truth, too.

- *How does the fact that I live in a world created by God affect the way I perceive it and understand it?* Every bug, every tree, every person, every chemical process, and every rock came from the mind of God. What does that mean? If we are created in God's image (of which part is the ability to know and to reason) and if he created the world, what does that mean for our capacity both to know the world and to learn about God, its creator?

- *How can I apply Christian knowledge as a touchstone of evaluation to test other knowledge claims?* This is one of the key integrative questions, which may be difficult at the initial stages of integrative thinking to answer well. And yet this question brings up the idea that all knowledge must harmonize and be coherent, and that the standard for harmonization is Christian knowledge.

Another way to view the rejection of a compartmentalized faith and the embracing of a Biblically based integration is to say that Christians must pursue a "Grand Unification Theory" (to borrow a term from physics) that explains the interrelatedness of everything in the moral, spiritual, and physical world.

3.6 Critical Thinking

Students, on their part, must avoid sloppy thinking, cognitive biases, fallacies of argument, and so on. And as they approach the new knowledge claims that are to be integrated, they must be able to detect slanting, selected data, unsupported claims, worldview biases, distorted facts, and so on and so on — but also, worthy, fair, reasonable, and true claims.

The culture war is not only a spiritual and moral war. It is an information war. Sixty-two percent of Christian teens agree with the statement that "The Bible is totally accurate in all of its teachings," and yet fifty-three percent agree with the statement that "When Jesus Christ lived on earth He committed sins, like other people,"[69] a belief that clearly conflicts with Biblical teaching (as in Hebrews 4:15, 2 Corinthians 5:21, and 1 John 3:5). That a large number of teens can believe these incompatible claims shows the lack of critical thinking ability, at least in terms of intellectual coherence.

At the same time, however, most students have been exposed to the concept of critical thinking, the habit of viewing arguments and claims with caution, if not outright skepticism. Most high school students can pick apart the claims of an advertisement and point out the fallacies and emotional appeals. They are becoming better information consumers than their parents or their grandpar-

---

[69] "Teenagers' Beliefs Moving Farther From Biblical Perspectives." Barna Research Online. October 23, 2000. <http://www.barna.org>.

ents, just in time for an age where so much information is suspect, deceptive, or simply false. However weak students' critical thinking skills may be in relation to faith concepts, educators can build on what students do know and on their cautious attitude about knowledge claims, to present the idea and practice of faith and learning integration as a critical thinking activity.

Critical thinking skills become the fourth foundation stone needed to support the process of faith-learning integration because effective integration requires the ability to analyze and test knowledge claims, determine logical consistency, identify fallacies, evaluate arguments and evidence, and seek reasonable explanations. Good thinking is required to bring together and connect current knowledge of every kind with new knowledge.

The first step in making this connection is to examine the nature of critical thinking itself. Critical thinking, in the process of analysis of information, includes the evaluation of arguments and fact claims not only as to their factual nature, their completeness, and their fairness, but also the way they are clothed—in other words, the semantics of their presentation. Implied in analysis is the evaluation of arguments and fact claims for coherence, consistency, reasonableness, adequacy, and the like. Judgments or conclusions are based on this evaluation. But evaluation involves standards, axioms, or values. And standards, axioms, and values are either a part of or derive from one's worldview. Thus, our conceptual model from Section 3.3.1:

can be simplified by collapsing "worldview" and "standards" (which includes values and axioms, etc.) into one called "values" and "evaluation, analysis" and "judgment" into one called "critical thinking," thusly:

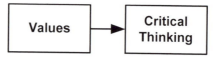

The point is that critical thinking is in its very essence bound to and dependent on values and is not simply an algorithmic application of the rules of logic. The source of the values underlying judgment becomes a matter of keen interest for the Christian. Depending on one's values, very different propositions may be held to be or not to be rational, true, or coherent. Whether a fact is considered good evidence for an argument depends on one's values regarding what constitutes good evidence. (Recall the discussion above about the influence of values on the identification of decision-making criteria.)

The second step in making the connection is to look at the nature of integration. And here I begin not with the integration of faith and learning, but the general integration of knowledge with knowledge. As we saw at the beginning of the book, the integration of knowledge is a normal, even necessary process of learning, a task common to all learners. Every new knowledge claim is automatically examined to determine how it fits in with currently held knowledge. That is, new information is subjected to some tests before being accepted. It is tested first for consistency with what is already known in order to ensure that there is no logical or factual contradiction between the new and the received. Secondly, the information is checked for overall coherence with a unified view of reality. How does it square with knowledge in the same area, in other areas, with one's larger beliefs about the world, with one's basic presuppositions and values?

For every learner and scholar, then, secular or Christian, knowledge integration depends on first, what is already known or believed to be true (a sort of personal set of beliefs) and second, what is likely or possible to be also true. This latter dependency involves not only disciplinary methodologies and predictive theorization, but metaphysical commitments, worldviews, and even politics and ideology.

 A good training exercise for critical thinking is to assign a specific, relatively small topic with two or more divergent camps. Have the students research each side, not necessarily to decide who is right, but to discover how confident each side can be in the strength of their evidence and the certainty of their conclusions. I found it effective to use the Shroud of Turin as a topic because (1) it relates to Christianity and so has some interest, even to Protestant students, and (2) there are books "absolutely proving beyond doubt" that the Shroud is the burial garment of Christ, and there are other books "absolutely proving beyond doubt" that the Shroud is no such item. And there is even a book that claims "both sides are wrong."

Exercise

A major principle of supply and demand is that almost anything in high demand will be counterfeited. This principle applies to information also. When ideologues need ammunition for their side in the information war, the quality of that information is often not examined. Many studies are flawed, many claims are distorted or even untrue, interpretations or opinions are presented as undeniable facts, and as in many other areas of life, exaggeration permeates the environment.

Good critical thinking skills are a necessary part of integration, then, to help students avoid unquestioning acceptance of disputable claims. In what may seem to be a paradox of epistemology, a love of truth is often shown best by a healthy skepticism toward knowledge claims.

Unhealthy skepticism, where nothing is believed, prevents us from attaining any truth. But healthy skepticism, that questions claims and demands support for them, helps us filter out the false and distorted and gives us the opportunity to identify the genuine.

Questions that will help students approach knowledge claims with more caution include these:

- *How do I know that claim is true?* Many students have the view that education is about memorizing knowledge. They take knowledge as found. In other words, they accept assertions about the world without wondering about the evidence for those assertions. While it is true that we accept most knowledge claims on the basis of authority, the difficulty is that many knowledge claims are either not true at all or are distorted in some way. Encouraging students to challenge the claims they encounter is a healthy way to keep them from being victimized by propaganda or ideology. There is an increasing tendency simply to assert conclusions rather than provide evidence for them. Students must learn to ask, "What is the evidence for that conclusion?" Remind students, also, that there is a third choice other than "believe this claim," and "don't believe this claim": that choice is "remember this claim without judging it either true or false."

- *What alternative ideas oppose that idea?* Most ideas have qualifications, counterclaims, or even direct opposition from alternative ideas. A common method of silently biasing an argument is to present only one solution or possibility and to ignore or even deny or at least disparage all other alternatives (which, in fact, may better fit the data or solve the problem). When students hear that "there is no opposition to this" or that "those who oppose this are fanatics or immorally motivated," they should be suspicious and look for the other side(s). "The first to plead his case seems right, until another comes and examines him" (Proverbs 18:17).

- *What has been omitted or ignored?* Selection is one of the chief methods for slanting an argument. What is omitted (counter arguments, opposing data, conflicting interpretations, unexplainable evidence) that might have a dramatic effect on a given knowledge claim or theory if allowed to be presented? The great difficulty with omission is that the alternative information is invisible. What is invisible is often assumed not to exist.

- *Is there an agenda or ideology behind this conclusion?* Conclusions or evidence given in support of controversial positions or highly political beliefs may need to have extra scrutiny given them because the temptation to distort or even fabricate evidence is strong. Proponents of strongly held beliefs sometimes admit poor evidence with little scrutiny because it agrees with their position.

- *How does the structure of a question limit the possible answers?* Questions that provide false dilemmas ("Was the king a hero or a criminal?") or that otherwise limit the realm from which answers can be drawn ("What financial remedies are there for crime?") may seek to restrain the arena of possibility unfairly.

- *What is the worldview behind the claim or implied by it?* Are the assumptions of naturalism or materialism being made (so that there can be no supernatural aspects to any truth)? Does the claim imply a relativism of truth or values?

- *How does the claim or conclusion fit in with Christian truth?* Can the claim be harmonized with Biblical knowledge?

> The goal of the integration of faith and learning is to connect the two—Biblical truth and academic knowledge—into a unified, coherent whole. This task can be performed successfully only if, on the one hand, the relevant Biblical truth is known and understood accurately and if, on the other hand, the academic knowledge is true and accurate.

3.6.1 Skills for Critical Thinking

Barry Beyer suggests a list of ten critical thinking skills in his book, *Practical Strategies for the Teaching of Thinking.*[70] This list is a useful starting point.

- *Distinguishing between verifiable facts and value claims.* Many, if not most, presentations of information mix together testable facts and value-laden interpretations or philosophical claims (often in the guise of facts). Additionally, while some people like to claim that some areas of learning "separate fact and value," such a thing is not possible. Decisions about what to research, what results mean, whether an observation represents a fact or an interpretation or both or neither—these are all value-laden decisions. The blurring of fact and value is common, and it may be especially so among those who assume that they have eliminated values from the equation.

- *Distinguishing relevant from irrelevant information, claims, or reasons.* A popular error here is the presentation of an anecdote in the place of real data. Generalizing from a vivid, persuasive, "just so" exam-

---

[70] Barry K. Beyer, *Practical Strategies for the Teaching of Thinking.* Boston: Allyn and Bacon, 1987, p. 27. The italicized items are Beyer's; the comments after them are my own.

ple is fairly common. Also common is the presentation of true but irrelevant facts as if they offered proof for an inference.

- *Determining the factual accuracy of a statement.* A fact claim may be accurate, partial, distorted, inaccurate, or filtered. Students must learn to distinguish between a provable fact and a fact claim or inferential conclusion presented as a fact.

- *Determining the credibility of a source.* Sources, even highly authoritative sources, are not infallible because even the most respected can be wrong or subject to bias or worldview conditioning. And the conclusions of some sources may be in doubt because of conflict of interest. The determination of credibility (and how much credibility) is a skill based on experience and judgment.

- *Identifying ambiguous claims or arguments.* A common source of ambiguity is the failure to distinguish between two related concepts, almost inviting confusion. An example would be discussing the correlation of two factors in a way that implies that one causes the other (but not arguing one way or the other), or not distinguishing between the mere presence of a chemical and a harmful level of that chemical in the context of an argument about food safety. (For example, some ordinary foods contain arsenic, but not in significant amounts.)

- *Identifying unstated assumptions.* Assumptions range from the very large and philosophical (about the presence or absence of God in the universe, for example) to the small. As an example of the latter, the claim, "Our vitamins have three times the amount of thiamine as the leading brand," conveys the implication that "our vitamins" are better, based on the unstated assumption that "three times the amount of thiamine" is better than a lesser amount.

- *Detecting bias.* The information world has gone deeply political in the last few decades. With the influence of postmodernist attitudes especially, overt bias has even gained something like respect. However, to the rationally minded, bias, especially hidden or disguised bias, is problematic and can lead to deception. A particularly subtle and therefore popular method of bias is the use of selection—instead of a rounded picture of things, picking out only the positive or negative aspects or just the details that support the arguer's position. Students should learn to detect such biases of presentation as
  - o slanted presentation
  - o selected evidence
  - o straw man (unfair presentation of opposing ideas)
  - o hyperbole (exaggeration)
  - o biased definitions or biased terms of discourse ("pro-choice" versus "anti-choice")
- *Identifying informal logical fallacies.* There are many fallacies of reasoning; these are the most important to know:[71]
  - o hasty generalization
  - o dicto simpliciter (sweeping generalization)
  - o ad hominem (personal attack)
  - o ad populum (appeal to popularity)
  - o begging the question (circular reasoning)
  - o irrelevance
  - o faulty analogy
  - o ad verecundiam (appeal to prestige)

---

[71] A good textbook on critical thinking should cover most or all of these fallacies and errors.

- o contrary to fact error
- o contradictory premises
- o self-refutation (self-referential absurdity)
- o false dilemma
- o appeal to ignorance
- o tu quoque (you do it yourself)
- o appeal to pity
- o appeal to force
- o compound questions
- o emotive language
- o weasel words
- o composition
- o division
- o vicious abstraction
- o equivocation
- o accent
- *Identifying formal errors of logic,* including
  - o invalid syllogism
  - o affirming the consequent
  - o denying the antecedent
  - o affirming a disjunct
- *Recognizing and understanding cognitive biases,* especially
  - o availability
  - o recency
  - o anchoring
  - o confirmation
  - o contrast
  - o framing
  - o familiarity
- *Recognizing logical inconsistencies in a line of reasoning.* Question-begging arguments (also called circular reasoning) are fairly common, where what was originally in need of proof is later used as evidence for a supporting point or even for itself. For exam-

ple, the argument, "All those who are truly expert in the field believe that X is the case," is circular because it implies that those who do not believe that X is the case are not truly expert in the field. Similarly, self-refuting statements, sometimes called self-referential absurdities, fail to meet their own requirements. For example, "There is no such thing as truth," "Language cannot convey meaning," "All generalizations are false," are logically inconsistent statements.

- *Determining the strength of an argument or claim.* It is important for students to understand that arguments exist along a continuum of strength. Some arguments are stronger than others. Weak arguments can be added together to make strong cases (this is how criminal investigations often proceed). Not all evidence is equal.

One way to teach critical thinking in a course that cannot afford a lot of extra time in class to discuss it is to have students create a critical thinking mini-textbook. To do this, assign each student one or two of the fallacies, cognitive biases, or other errors listed above. Have them research a definition and several examples. Combine their results into an online reference guide. Give a quiz on the guide one or two times during the term, to make sure they are reading it.

Exercise

3.6.2 CRITICAL THINKING IN FAITH-LEARNING INTEGRATION

It is crucial for Christians to develop critical thinking skills, the skills of analysis and evaluation, a cautious attitude toward knowledge claims, and an awareness of the use of information as a cultural weapon. The lists above serve as a starting place, but critical thinking as a faith-learning integrative tool must go beyond it to include a deeper understanding of how the arena of knowledge works. In addition to the traditional critical thinking cur-

riculum, including such topics as semantics, logical fallacies, fact and interpretation, selection and slanting, and so
on, students need to study somewhat subtler concepts:

- The role of worldviews in determining what constitutes a fact or counts as evidence and the different
  conclusions about facts and evidence found in natu-
  ralism/materialism, postmodernism, and Christianity.
- Bringing under analysis and critique the very
  worldviews that produce many contemporary
  knowledge claims. What is the best view of reality
  (the most holistic ontology), the best road to truth
  (the most rational epistemology), and the best
  source of value judgments (the most objective axiology).
- The nature of knowledge claims and the role of political, sociological, and methodological factors in
  constructing claims.
- The use of misinformation, disinformation, selection, and suppression of evidence in an environment of information warfare.
- The presentation of controversial positions as moral
  imperatives, where favored positions are cast in
  positively emotive, moral terms such as "justice,"
  "freedom," "fairness," "choice," "compassion," and
  "rights" while disfavored positions are cast in nega-
  tively emotive, moral terms such as "blaming the
  victim," "oppression," "racism," "sexism," "hate
  speech," "intolerance," and "mean-spirited."
- The role of information provenance on credibility
  and the problems of conflict of interest in sources.
- The use of agenda scholarship to advance ideology.
- The identification of underlying assumptions in inferential arguments.

ne control of what is allowed to be discussed or gued, with what terms, and under what condions. This might be called discourse control. In)stmodern terms, we do not seek to discover truth, we seek to advance our narrative over our opponent's narrative. Whose narrative gets discussed can make quite a difference in how problems, solutions, facts, actions, and so on are viewed and evaluated.

If, as is sometimes said, the primary goal of education is learning how to think, then we can connect this process to faith and learning integration to develop not only critical thinkers, but critical thinkers committed to Biblical authority and the Christian worldview as unifying principles for all knowledge. The Scriptural admonition to "examine everything carefully" (1 Thessalonians 5:21) should apply to everything. The critical thinking foundation stone prepares students for integration (and takes them along the way) by providing them with tools and thinking habits for examining and connecting both the special revelation (the Biblical framework of reality) and the general revelation (the natural world). Faith-learning integration as a critical thinking activity produces several desirable characteristics:

- A rational view of reality—all reality—not a truncated and therefore ultimately irrational view as in naturalism or a view of reality seen as inaccessible or non-existent as in postmodernism
- An intellectually coherent system of belief, without missing or self-contradictory elements
- A commitment to truth as the highest goal, not subservient to politics, ideology, or power
- An all-encompassing, circumspect, and holistic view of life

Exercise

A good way to sharpen students' critical thinking abilities and combine their thinking with faith issues is to have them explore some of the urban legends that include religious components. Urban legends represent just the kind of misinformation that is so casually passed around and believed without thought or analysis. For example, there is the well-known claim that Procter and Gamble donates money to the Church of Satan. A good research source for this type of urban legend is urbanlegends.about.com, where the "Religion" link takes the reader to many varied stories and claims. Describe one of these legends to students and have them research it to discover whether there is any truth behind it. Discuss the results in class. (Note: www.snopes.com also has a "Religion" section.)

As thoughtful Christians, we want to make sense of all we experience, see, feel, learn, read, and strive for, using our God-given intellects to examine, evaluate, and approve, alter, or reject the claims we encounter.

3.6.3 ENCOURAGING LEARNING BY SHAPING ATTITUDES

Ideally, students should come to love learning everything—but not believe everything they learn. To achieve this ideal state, students must give up their naïve view of knowledge—that they just memorize the books and lectures and drink it all in—and they must avoid the rejection of knowledge altogether just because some of it is wrong or biased. One way to address this problem is to borrow an idea from Aristotle.

In his *Nicomachean Ethics*, Aristotle proposes a model wherein each virtue is a mean between extremes, each extreme representing a vice. For example, the virtue of generosity is a mean between the excess of extravagance and the deficiency of stinginess. This model might be useful to describe how we can approach knowledge claims.

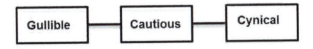

On the one hand, we don't want to believe everything we hear or read. That would make us hopelessly gullible, open to every advertising claim, urban legend, political rhetoric, and hoax. On the other hand, we don't want to reject all knowledge claims and not believe anything. That would make us cynics, viewing everything we hear as an attempted manipulation. In between these two attitudes is the cautious approach to knowledge claims, where we keep our critical thinking processors humming along, our baloney detectors operating, and our analysis engines running at full speed.

Here are some more words that can be used to help students grasp the concept of meeting new knowledge with a positive, cautious attitude.

Extreme Acceptance	Ideal Mean	Extreme Rejection
credulous	thoughtful	dismissing
uncritical	aware	disregarding
naïve	careful	scornful

It would seem plausible that the gullible student would benefit most from understanding this model, and that might be so. However, it seems that too many students who have become cynical about information or knowledge claims have also become all the more gullible when it comes to "junk knowledge" such as urban legends and conspiracy theories. Possibly because, by rejecting so much knowledge without analyzing it for quality, they never develop the information processing skills (also known as critical thinking skills) that would help them avoid falling for such information fakery. It cannot be overemphasized how important it is to develop a sober, circumspect, careful, cautious, fair, optimistically skeptical attitude toward knowledge claims.

In his 1500-page book about the assassination of President Kennedy, Vincent Bugliosi lists 44 groups or organizations named by conspiracy theorists as having been involved in the assassination. And he also lists 214 individuals alleged to have been co-conspirators, together with 82 individuals named as assassins by various conspiracy theorists.[72] Ask students to select a conspiracy theory and bring evidence supporting and rebutting it. There are many to choose from:

Exercise

- TWA 800
- Twin Towers / 9-11
- Protocols of the Elders of Zion
- Pan Am 103
- Assassination of Martin Luther King, Jr.

What if you can't evaluate a claim?

Students probably do not have extensive databases of true, integrated knowledge, either of Scripture or of general learning, and they might lack the thinking tools to evaluate claims (that's why they are in your classes). Therefore, they should be taught that one of the keys to integration is to learn what is being claimed without either committing to its truth or rejecting it as false:

You can remember something without necessarily believing it.

Students should be reminded that it's always okay simply to file away what they are learning; they do not have to put an "I believe this" or an "I don't believe this" tag on the information.

Students who do not learn how to integrate their faith with their academic learning early on in their undergraduate careers may never learn to do so effectively, with the result that they may face faith-daunting challenges later in

---

[72] *Reclaiming History: The Assassination of President John F. Kennedy,* New York: W. W. Norton, 2007, pp. 1489-1498.

their academic careers (undergraduate or graduate). The emphasis on integration at Christian colleges and universities must be continuous, deep, and thorough. The foundations can be built alongside faith-learning integrative tasks, but the earlier the foundations are laid and the more robust they are built, the more successful the process of integration can become.

3.6.4 EXAMINING THE SOURCES OF VALUES AND BELIEFS

A vital part of learning to think critically, as well as developing a quality worldview, is to understand the role of personal values in the arenas of analysis, inference, and even facts. (See Appendix 4 for an extensive discussion of the interrelationship between facts and values.) How and where and why students get their personal values certainly influences the quality of their thinking, and their capacity to engage in effective integration. Therefore, students need to perform a robust self-analysis as part of their critical thinking training.

Successful self-analysis results in the ability to examine and evaluate one's personal process of belief formation. The culture is tremendously powerful, so much so in fact that it is sometimes more influential in belief formation than Bible reading, church attendance, and Christian educational practice. It's significant that one of the most fundamental pieces of ancient Greek philosophy is "Know yourself." And Paul enjoins believers to examine themselves in regard to their faith (2 Cor. 13:5, 1 Cor. 11:28). The problem is that Christians often do not.

Another area of critical thinking needed to prepare students for successful integration, then, is the development of a capacity for self-analysis. Students must develop the habit of asking questions about their beliefs, values, and attitudes. They must begin to look inward, to engage in metacognition, thinking about their own thinking and what lies under it. The goal is to identify and diminish the influence of values that conflict with Biblical values, the insidious influence of harmful values absorbed from the surrounding cultural mix, and to increase the role of Biblical values. And in what may seem to be a counterintuitive way, genuine self-analysis will help combat and remedy the rampant narcissism that infects so many people today. Relevant self-analysis questions include the following:

Identity and Source of Values and Beliefs. Too many values and beliefs come from popular culture. Students need to ask whether their values reflect Biblical teaching or such substitutes as pleasure, expediency, cultural norms, "coolness," selfishness, peer pressure, "whatever feels comfortable," relativism, and so forth.

- *What are my values?* A deliberate listing of values is an excellent exercise. Many people have values they do not think about. One way to help students expose their values is to offer them choices between values, in conflict situations. Would you study for the test or go out for pizza? If ten people are starving in a lifeboat, would you agree to cannibalism to save nine? Spiritual values as well as moral and personal values should be explored.

- *What values are reflected by my behavior and choices?* To a large extent, we are what we do, rather than what we say we are. It is surprising how many shoplifters vehemently declare that they are not thieves, but that they have this problem about taking things from the store that they haven't paid for. Another way to think about this is to say that many times we think we possess certain values that by our behavior we show that we really do not possess. The shock of recognition at this discovery should cause us to examine ourselves. Who are we really? Who do we want to become?

- *Where did I get my values?* This question may prove impossible to answer in many instances or at least for certain values, because in addition to Christian sources (the Bible, Sunday School, sermons) we tend to adopt values from many other sources: media, experiences, advertisements, anecdotes, peer pressure, authoritative pronouncements. Nevertheless, asking students to examine a value (tolerance, anti-drugs, permissible styles of dress, attitudes toward work) to discover its source is a good exercise. For example, where does the common antipathy toward turning in a wrongdoer come from? The negative attitude toward "ratting" on another person is a value from the criminal underclass.

- *Are those values good?* A student was once asked to fill out a card listing her life's major goals. She wrote two: "Have fun and serve the Lord." We should examine our values for quality.

- *Where did I get that belief?* This may be a good question to probe into students' beliefs about astrology, urban legends, and some of the more common ideas floating in the culture (cultural relativism, what behaviors are morally permissible, even the purpose of education).

Quality of Values and Beliefs. Elsewhere I have defined quality as "a measure of excellence," referring to "how well something measures up to its ideal state" based on "a set of controlling criteria."[73] By using appropriate criteria, we can evaluate the quality of our values and beliefs. Sometimes we discover that too many are harmful, confused, incoherent, or self-contradictory.

---

[73] Robert A. Harris, *Creative Problem Solving: A Step-by-Step Approach.* Los Angeles: Pyrczak Publishing, 2002, p. 93.

- *Does that belief make sense?* While some things in Biblical teaching are above reason, none are contrary to reason. We should strive to make the world make sense as a whole, and all of our beliefs should be consistent with a reasonable view of reality.
- *Is that belief really true?* The postmodern answer is, "What a quaint question." But we are called to be a people of truth, who should want our beliefs to conform to the way things actually are. Christian epistemology includes the correspondence theory of truth.
- *Is that belief Biblical?* An idea may not necessarily be explicitly mentioned in the Bible to be considered Biblical. If the belief can be derived from or harmonizes with Scriptural principles or doctrines, then it generally may be considered Biblical.
- *What is the evidence for that belief?* Evidence, under the Christian worldview, includes facts, inferences, arguments, Scriptural passages, reasons, and personal experience. Evidence might not constitute a proof, but there should be some reasonable support for a belief.
- *Are my values and beliefs coherent with each other?* Again, some people hold beliefs that are logically inconsistent with each other.
- *What is my standard for evaluating my values and beliefs?* Students should be encouraged to identify how they evaluate the values they hold as well as how closely they measure up in behavior to those values. Evaluating values on the basis of popularity, fad, political correctness, peer influence or whether "it feels right" or "I'm comfortable with it" creates a shifting sand. Not evaluating values or beliefs at all can result in holding suboptimal or even harmful ones. Beliefs left unexamined can lose strength (be-

cause they are not refreshed and reconfirmed) and can either be lost or turn into superstitions.

Consequences of Values and Beliefs. Our values and beliefs influence the way we think, plan, act, and respond to others and to events. What we believe affects our choices and attitudes as well as our aspirations.

- *What are the implications of that belief?* Ideas have consequences, as the saying is. Many people hold beliefs without thinking about their logical implications.

- *Are my beliefs livable?* This question allows students to think about whether they hold beliefs that are impossible to live up to or beliefs that conflict with each other.

- *Do I live consistently in accord with my values?* Are we like the Pharisees, who say one thing and do another, or do we strive to match our actions to what we say we believe they should be?

- *Is my faith commitment evident in my actions and choices?* Do we claim to adhere to the ten commandments, but then feel free to download copyrighted music illegally or make copies of copyrighted software and give it to our friends?

The Basis for Decision Making. A worldview is not merely a collection of propositions given intellectual assent. It forms the basis for decision making. Decisions are based on criteria, which are themselves based on values, which are part of one's worldview. In fact, you can discover with a good degree of accuracy most people's real worldviews by examining the decisions they make and observing how they live.

Generally a decision process examines the choices or alternatives available and applies a set of criteria to each alternative to see how well each alternative measures up to each criterion. Not only are the criteria themselves based on or influenced by values, but the importance (or weight) given to each criterion is a product of personal values also.

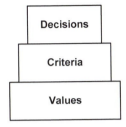

The following questions will help students explore the relationship between their values and the decisions they make:

- *What is my method for choosing or adopting values?* Values are best chosen deliberately, either by making an intellectual commitment to them or by developing habits that reflect good values. Unfortunately, many of us fall into values by adopting behavioral habits without thinking too much (or at all) about the values those behaviors reflect.
- *What is my basis for decision making?* When faced with a decision of any kind, whether moral, economic, or simply where to eat, what is the process I use to decide? What general principles do I use?
- *How do I determine the criteria for my decision making?* Criteria are based on values: What values do I use? Criteria are positive factors that must be met. For example, low cost might be a criterion for a vacation.
- *How do I decide how important each criterion is in the decision process?* Someone might include the criterion of "good gasoline mileage" in an automobile purchasing decision, but if the criterion has very lit-

tle importance (and is thus overpowered by other criteria, such as "powerful and sporty"), then it will have little influence on the decision.

- *How do I determine which choices or alternatives to include and which to exclude?* Most people, when faced with a decision about how to get some cash, do not include "rob a bank" as one of the alternatives. When you decide on a set of alternatives from which to choose, what is your system for including and excluding them? Note once again, that your system of values comes into play at every turn in the decision-making process.

- *How do I predict the possible consequences of my decision?* All decisions result in a variety of consequences. Often we think about only the desired consequences and do not focus much on undesired consequences. And there is always the possibility of unforeseen consequences. Do I engage in some analysis (depending on the seriousness of the decision) to think about consequences, good and bad?

Exercise

Develop an exercise in moral decision making that will lend itself to the application of clear Scriptural principles. (An example might be someone selling a house knowing that the roof leaks. Should the buyers be told?) Have students develop criteria for the decision and the values underlying the criteria. Have them develop alternatives and the values underlying the inclusion or exclusion of an allowed alternative. Then have them make the decision.

Life has gotten so busy, and there are so many choices for our attention and time that few people, especially students, seem to take time to engage in introspection or self-analysis. And yet, without some engagement with the self, people are likely to develop habits and values that they might not otherwise want if they had thought things over earlier. The culture is so powerful and is so constantly blaring its values everywhere that without some intentionality and self-examination, those often poor values are likely to seep in.

There is no special course for developing self-analysis. It should be a process encouraged in every course. Using the Socratic method of asking questions like those listed above will help students to engage in self-examination both inside and outside of class. Note that it is important to prepare students for the Socratic method. Too many teachers ask questions with predetermined right answers and ask a follow-up question only when the student gives the wrong answer to the first question. The effect is that a second question is seen as something akin to punishment, causing the students to fear follow-up questions. They bring this fear of multiple questions with them to college. It is crucial, however, to ask the "second question," such as "Why do you think that?" or "Where did you get that idea?" or "What is your evidence for that assertion?"

The postmodern environment has taught students that all ideas are acceptable and that no support for any idea is needed: "That just happens to be my personal belief and how dare you question my sincerity by asking for evidence." The results of the attitude are that first, no real thinking is needed before indulging an opinion about something and second, rational argument and persuasion about important issues are made difficult if not impossible. Faculty should help students remedy these attitudes and empower them to become strong, rational, circumspect thinkers.

Chapter Summary

This chapter provided information for students and for faculty as they prepare their students for doing integrative work. It presented some of the important preparatory knowledge, skills, and attitudes needed for doing integration effectively. A thorough familiarity with the Bible—what it says, and what it means—is an obvious starting point, because Biblical teaching is at the heart of what is to be integrated.

There is a proverb, "The more you know, the better you can see." This thought sums up the desirability or the need for an ever-growing stock of general knowledge. We learn by analogy and comparison (contrast, too), so having something we can compare new knowledge to helps us understand and remember it.

The chapter concluded with a discussion of critical thinking skills. Learning how to think clearly and to analyze ideas is a fundamentally essential skill, both for developing and strengthening Christian faith and for finding success in life and work.

Questions for Thought and Discussion

1. Explain the role of each of the four components needed for successful integration. Why is each required and what are the consequences if one is weak or missing? Give examples of each component.

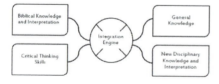

2. What is the relationship between facts and values? Why is it important to understand this?

3. Explain the concepts of compartmentalism and decompartmentalism of faith. What are the effects on someone who compartmentalizes?
4. What is the connection between intellectual and spiritual formation? How can the intellect support spiritual growth and strength?

Activities
1. Partner with one or two other faculty members from different departments and design a set of general education requirements that support the need for students to have the necessary background for faith-learning integration, as described in this chapter. Identify specific course names and an outline of content for each.
2. Look over the list of logical fallacies, cognitive biases, and so forth in Section 3.6.1. How many of them are you familiar with? Can you give definitions and examples of each one? Make a list of the ones that you might teach to your students because of their relevance in your discipline.
3. Write out your personal hermeneutic process. What steps do you take when you want further clarity on the meaning of a Biblical passage or teaching?

Notes

4

4. INTEGRATIVE FRAMES: THE WAY FORWARD

Philosophers of science have repeatedly demonstrated that more than one theoretical construction can always be placed upon a given collection of data.
— Thomas Kuhn[74]

Overview
This chapter answers the following questions:
- What are the various views about or philosophical approaches to faith-learning integration?
- What are the practical benefits and drawbacks of each approach?
- What are some specific examples of integrative work that use the different approaches?
- What are the degrees or depths of integrative work available to the Christian scholar?
- What are some specific practices and behaviors that faculty can engage in to connect faith with their teaching?

---

[74] *The Structure of Scientific Revolutions*, 2nd Ed. Chicago: Univ. of Chicago Press, 1970, p. 76.

4.1 Alternative Views of Integration

When approaching the task of integrating the truths of the Christian faith with their academic disciplines, faculty and students can choose from among several different philosophical understandings about the relationship between the two sources of knowledge. The hope is that, as practitioners develop their skills and grow more confident in their worldview, they will adopt one of the higher views or a combination of higher views. Here is a brief description of each.[75]

4.1.1 The Two Realms View

The two realms view avoids any tension between faith and learning, but neither is it a genuine type of integration because in this view, the teachings of Christian faith and the content of academic learning exist in separate realms of truth or knowledge. Christianity, it is said, treats the aspect of reality known as religion, while academic subject matter exists in the aspect of reality known variously as science, empiricism, or fact. These two realms or "magisteria" exist independently and therefore there is no conflict between the truth claims of either.

There are, however, several problems with this view.

- Two realms implies that there are actually not just two aspects of reality, but two realities that somehow exist in parallel and do not interact, overlap, or connect. Such a stance prevents the development of a unified worldview, that interdynamic holism that provides the coherence to our understanding of reality that is a major goal of education and life.

---

[75] For this chapter, I have relied on some ideas and occasional phrasing from the relevant sections of my earlier book, *The Integration of Faith and Learning: A Worldview Approach,* Eugene, OR: Cascade Books, 2004.

- As a practical matter, two realms is unworkable because the two areas do come into contact and into conflict. When, for example, the science of eugenics became popular in many countries, proponents like Margaret Sanger worried about "human weeds" and how to improve the gene pool through compulsory sterilization, forced abortion and so on. Today, science is mapping the human genome, where parents (and eventually the state?) might once again decide to eliminate the genetically imperfect.[76] Certainly this is an area where Christian values do indeed intersect with science. Maintaining the two realms view would silence the moral voice of the faith. This example should make it clear that science deals with a lot more than just mixing chemicals to make plastic or ant spray. It is involved with moral choices also, choices where the Christian "realm" has an important stake.

- Setting the truth claims of Christianity off to one side while the truth claims of the academic disciplines are front and center, not merely marginalizes Christian truth but dismisses it as irrelevant to the arena of learning.

- Such a position smacks of relativism. It is similar to that of little kids who say, "That may be true for you but it isn't true for me." Or, "Oh, that's your religious 'truth,' but we're talking about 'true truth,' in other words, science."

- The clear implication becomes that the worldview, methodology, assumptions, and conclusions of the disciplines represent and embody true knowledge, while Christian truth claims are merely "religious

---

[76] Ross Douthat, "Eugenics, Past and Future," *New York Times*, June 9, 2012. Retrieved from http://www.nytimes.com/ 2012/06/10/ opinion/sunday/ douthat-eugenics-past-and-future.html?_r=0.

beliefs," nice for people who like that sort of thing, but best kept away from the academy and from people serious about real knowledge.

- Two realms privileges one set of metaphysical commitments while marginalizing another. Science is quite encumbered by certain philosophical assumptions (such as that the natural world is all that exists). In fact, as professor Edward Davis notes, "For many in the modern world, science itself wears the mantle of religion. . . ."[77] And true religion does not permit competition or heresy, so any such threats are marginalized.

Hypothetical Examples

Biological evolution from the Two Realms view:

Typical secular scientist: Humans evolved through the unguided, purposeless process of accidental, random mutations operated on by natural selection.

Possible Christian Two-Realm view: God created our spirit.[78]

Psychology from the Two Realms view:

Typical secular psychologist: The mind is merely a product of the electrochemical activity of the brain.

Possible Christian Two Realms view: In the spiritual realm, we say that people have souls.

4.1.2 The False Distinction View

The False Distinction view of integration asserts that no special integrative work is needed to join Christian knowledge with academic content because "all

---

[77] "Some Comments on the Course, 'Introduction to Christianity and Science,'" retrieved from <www.messiah.edu/hpages/facstaff/davis/course.html>.

[78] The examples of Christian viewpoints under each view of integration are only possibilities for illustration and clarification and do not necessarily represent the viewpoint of all followers of that model.

truth is God's truth," and "all knowledge is one." Whatever the source of knowledge, it is under the sovereignty of God and will be automatically integrated as the faculty member or student learns.

The false distinction view appears to be the two-realms view in sheep's clothing. For if there is no need to examine academic content for worldview bias, say, that would seem to imply that all academic content is to be accepted as is. And then it must follow that Christian knowledge has no role to play.

And there are some issues with this view:

- The differing worldviews of Christianity and, say, naturalism, Marxism, or postmodernism necessarily put claims about knowledge into conflict. Naturalism, for example, rules out knowledge from revelation.

- The conflict over knowledge claims is more often one of interpretation or understanding of the data than it is over the data themselves. We must acknowledge that no automatic integration can take place when competing epistemologies look at the same data so differently.

- The belief that integration is automatic is "overthrown by the experience of every hour" (to steal a phrase from my favorite 18th Century author, Samuel Johnson). We know that there is conflict between many conclusions drawn from disciplinary frames of interpretation and that of our faith.

Hypothetical Examples
Biological evolution from the False Distinction view

Typical secular scientist: Humans evolved through the unguided, purposeless process of accidental, random mutations operated on by natural selection.

Possible Christian False Distinction view: God guided the evolutionary process.

Psychology from the False Distinction view:

Typical secular psychologist: The mind is merely a product of the electrochemical activity of the brain.

Possible Christian False Distinction view: God is in charge of our mind-brain.

4.1.3 THE COMPATIBILIST VIEW

▷≫ Compatibilists are harmonizers, looking for points of agreement between discipline and faith. The commonality might be at the theoretical level (agreement on what constitutes evidence, the goal of objectivity, the use of reason and logic, the belief that truth is worth seeking, and so forth). And the commonality can be one of shared conclusions or interpretations. The work of the compatibilist then includes the following:

- **Identify, connect, and elaborate the points of commonality**—shared values, ideas, conclusions, and knowledge. Compatibilists can use the same scientific method, the same data sets, and do the same kinds of experiments as their secular counterparts. There is a high degree of harmony and similarity between secular and Christian in the practice of mathematics, chemistry, nursing, physical education, engineering, and so on, and these subject areas can be connected to faith by elaborating on the ideas of an orderly, rational universe, created and sustained by an intelligent Creator who set up what we call the "laws of nature."
- **Supplement with Christian knowledge** the partial view of knowledge from limited worldviews such as naturalism. After studying the described complexity of a biological system in the textbook, add

the that the appearance of design is real—the system was designed by a Designer.

- **Add academic knowledge to Biblical knowledge** to extend our understanding of the world and of its Creator. Provide an example from nature that amplifies a Biblical text. A study of ant behavior would certainly flesh out Proverbs 6:6-8: "Go to the ant, O sluggard. Observe her ways and be wise, Which, having no chief, officer or ruler, prepares her food in the summer and gathers her provision in the harvest."

- **Employ Christian subject matter** or worldview knowledge within the paradigms supported by the discipline. Bring in Christian poets and novelists in literature classes, Christian philosophers in philosophy classes, or Christian characters and events involving Christians in history classes.

- **Include Christian biographies.** Many of the important figures in mathematics and science and in other disciplines were devoted Christians, and these facts should be emphasized in classes where these figures are mentioned.[79] A Google search on "scientists who were Christian," "Christian historians," "Christian philosophers," and so on can turn up some useful information.

- Engage in research that involves Christian themes or practices.

A good example of this last bullet is a two-year study by the National Center on Addiction and Substance Abuse at Columbia University, where researchers "examined the link between God, religion, and spirituality and substance

---

[79] For a list of hundreds of Christians in science, from 313 AD to the present day, see the list on Wikipedia at http://en.wikipedia.org/wiki/ List_of_Christian_thinkers_in_science.

abuse prevention, treatment, and recovery."[80] The researchers found that those people with religious commitments were much more likely to avoid substance abuse either initially or as recovering addicts.[81] Connecting faith to a discipline through a study like this shows the relevance of faith values to disciplinary content, and, in fact, makes faith values a part of disciplinary content.

The compatibilist view is worth adopting as one of the techniques of integration because it has several positive aspects. Indeed, to help students learn integrative practices, it is a good idea to begin with compatibilist work because it creates a positive attitude toward learning and integration. Students could begin integrative work by studying simple facts about the natural world. I, for example, am fascinated by the properties of water. Study its forms — liquid, ice, snow, steam — its use as an almost universal solvent, its perpetual recyclability, and so on.

Far from being soft on disciplinary errors, compatibilists can actually be quiet transformationists (see Section 4.1.5) by working with Christian or faith-related topics, as we saw in the example above. The content of every discipline changes over time, for it is made up of what gets noticed, discussed, and promoted.

For example, Feminist literary studies began with women professors (1) going back into the past to find long-forgotten works with proto-feminist themes, (2) writing and teaching about them, and (3) working out feminist literary theories. When they still needed more power and prestige, instead of attacking the ruling interpretive paradigms (Marxism and deconstructionism, in many cases), they worked in parallel with them. Christians in every dis-

---

[80] November, 2001. Available at http://www.casacolumbia.org/ addiction-research/reports/so-help-me-god-substance-abuse-religion-spirituality.
[81] Ibid.

cipline can do similar work, thus gradually transforming the discipline itself, at least in a way that's more inclusive.

To use the literature example, just as feminists mined the past for proto-feminist novels and nonfiction, so Christian literature professors could delve into the huge literature of earlier eras to find worthy Christian books, both fiction (for the English department) and nonfiction (for philosophy and political science, and even for historical purposes). The secular bias and selection of books, ideas, attitudes, even events from the past gives us a wrong impression about what it was really like. Most of the books sold and read to pieces were religious books. (See Chapter 6 for further discussion of this idea as an integrative practice.)

Benefits of compatibilism include these:

- Compatibilism enables students to see that disciplinary learning can strengthen their faith and love for God and his creation, while their faith improves their understanding of what otherwise is secular subject matter. In other words, compatibilism allows students to see how putting a Christian perspective on academic content can provide a better picture of both discipline and faith.

- Because the more aggressive integration techniques involve criticizing some disciplinary assumptions and conclusions, seeking compatible aspects helps students avoid developing either an anti-intellectualism ("disciplinary knowledge is bad so why study it?") or a self-righteous snobbery ("*we* have the truth and they don't").

- Compatibilism makes an excellent argument for convincing students of the value of doing the work of faith-learning integration, as they see how faith knowledge can help inform and extend disciplinary knowledge.

Exercise

A good way to get students' feet wet in the practice of integration is to have them write or discuss the compatibilities and conflicts between Christian knowledge and values and those expressed in a book about values. For a literature, history, classics, history of Christianity, or philosophy course, or as part of a cornerstone course, assign students to read a book about values such as a Greek or Roman classic. These books are in fact easy to understand by even freshman students, who soon start to brag, "I'm reading Aristotle!" or "I can read Cicero!" Then in class discussion or in papers, have students identify the harmonies (compatibilities) between Christianity and stoicism. For a more rounded analysis, have them identify conflicts also. Here is a brief list to think about:

- Aristotle, *Nicomachean Ethics*
- Cicero, *On Duties* (also called *On Moral Obligation*)
- Seneca, *Letters from a Stoic*
- Marcus Aurelius, *Meditations*

Compatibilism is a good place to start and a good ongoing practice as a general method of integration. However, employing it as the only model limits the faculty member and can send the wrong message to students.

- There is a danger that seeking only harmony between faith and discipline will ignore or downplay the real differences and conflicts between theoretical approaches, worldviews, and interpretations.
- Students might get the idea that learning doesn't require the careful, circumspect analysis that is actually required for discerning the true from the not-so-true.

Hypothetical Examples
Biological evolution from the compatibilist view

Typical secular scientist: Humans evolved through the unguided, purposeless process of accidental, random mutations operated on by natural selection.

Possible Christian Compatibilist: Both secular and Christian scientists agree that the human body is marvelously put together, in beauty and complexity. The operation of individual cells, for instance, is remarkable and dramatic. "I will give thanks to You, for I am fearfully and wonderfully made; wonderful are Your works, and my soul knows it very well" (Psalm 138:14).

Psychology from the Compatibilist view:

Typical secular psychologist: The mind is merely a product of the electrochemical activity of the brain.

Possible Christian Compatibilist view: Positron emission tomography (PET) scans show how the brain lights up when someone prays.

4.1.4 THE INTERPRETIVE COMPATIBILIST VIEW

▶▷ Interpretive compatibilists seek to harmonize Christian knowledge and disciplinary learning by applying alternate or unusual interpretations to Biblical or disciplinary knowledge claims in a way that produces agreement or eliminates conflict. Interpretive compatibilism can be a highly controversial practice among Christians in the cases where it is Christian knowledge that is the object of this adjustment of received interpretations. As we have said, most of the apparent conflict between Christian knowledge and disciplinary knowledge arises from conflicting interpretations (inferences, conclusions) rather than a conflict over facts or data. (Although what constitutes a fact is often open to interpretation also.)

The practice of interpretive compatibilism includes:

- **Interpret Biblical texts in a way that harmonizes them with current disciplinary interpretations.** An interpretive compatibilist, for example, might argue that the Bible is compatible with the current disciplinary view that the Earth is 4.5 billion years old[82] by interpreting Genesis through the "day-age" theory (every creation day was an age of unnamed extent), or by saying that the creation account in Genesis is "poetic" or should not be taken literally. (Young-earth creationists, who tend to be reconstructionists, oppose such interpretations. See Section 4.1.6 below.)

- **Interpret disciplinary theory or claims in a way that harmonizes them with Scripture.** Similarly, an interpretive compatibilist might harmonize Scripture and disciplinary thought by interpreting the theory of quantum tunneling as a method that Jesus used to pass through walls in John 20:26 without violating the laws of physics.

Speaking of the laws of physics, or more broadly, the laws of nature, an important point needs to be made. Professor of philosophy R. F. Holland emphasizes that "when someone says that a miracle is a violation of the laws of nature," he or she might be confusing actual laws, whose violation is a crime, and so-called natural laws, which are descriptions of phenomena, not prescriptions about criminal behavior. Holland says,

> But are the laws of nature in any sense prescriptions? Maybe they are in the sense that they prescribe to us what we are to expect, but since we formulated the laws this is really a matter of our offering prescriptions or recipes to ourselves. And we can certainly fail to act on these prescriptions. But the occurrences which the laws are about are not prescribed to; they are simply

---

[82] See Roger C. Wiens, "Radiometric Dating: A Christian Perspective," available onine at http:// www.asa3.org/ ASA/ resources/ Wiens2002.pdf

*de*scribed. And if anything should happen of which we are inclined to say that it goes counter to a law of nature, what this must mean is that the description we have framed has been, not flouted or violated, but falsified. We have encountered something that the description does not fit and we must therefore withdraw or modify our description. The law was wrong; we framed it wrongly; or rather what we framed has turned out not to have been a law.[83]

The laws of nature have been formulated inductively from the observation of occurrences and patterns. An event that does not conform to the observed patterns is not therefore by definition impossible; it could be a black swan event — a previously unobserved occurrence which requires modification of the "law."

Interpretive compatibilism must be employed with caution for two reasons. First, disciplinary knowledge changes over time, with theories giving way to new concepts. It would be an embarrassment to interpret Scripture in a way that conforms with current disciplinary thinking only to have that thinking abandoned later on. (Good thing earlier scientists didn't try to reconcile the Bible with the theory of phlogiston.)

Second, there can be a tendency to force an interpretation onto Scripture when it really does not fit. For example, it would amount to misinterpretation to say that passages in conflict with current disciplinary theories are "poetry," "metaphorical," or "symbolic," when the context of those passages clearly shows that they were intended to be understood as historical accounts.

---

[83] R. F. Holland, *Against Empiricism: On Education, Epistemology, and Value.* Totowa, New Jersey: Barnes and Noble, 1980, p. 175.

4.1.5 The Transformationist View

Transformationists believe that, while the knowledge claims of the discipline do have much in common or in harmony with Christianity, the methodology of the discipline has produced some errors of outlook and interpretation, and has arbitrarily narrowed or even truncated the scope of knowledge available to it — by omitting or ignoring Christian truth and insight.

In other words, transformationists are revisionists — or better, reformers — who want to improve their discipline. They engage in the following activities:

- **Use the Christian worldview and Christian knowledge as a touchstone** for correcting the errors in the discipline, such as misinterpretations of fact or data, ideology masquerading as knowledge, and inferences that are not supported by the evidence.

- **Separate real knowledge** from claims that are partial, distorted, slanted, deceptive, or even false. Add the real knowledge to the set of beliefs, and remember the false as false.

- **Identify and expose the powerful distortions** produced by ideological bias and Procrustean or formulaic interpretations. The transformationists can proceed to dismantle illogical arguments and point out the misuse of data.

- **Clearly differentiate between claims of knowledge or truth and genuine knowledge or truth.** It's a well-known phenomenon that many people mix truth with opinion, logical ideas, wishful thinking, and interpretations as a method of gaining credibility. "Make your opinion look like a fact," it is said, "and you'll have a greater chance of convincing people." Here, once again, we see the importance of critical thinking and the need for skilled analysis. Much of the work of transformationists involves corrective critiques based on sharp, clear evaluation and wise judgment.

Exercise Have students locate a short article written from an evolutionary perspective but using the language and metaphors of design and intentionality. For example, it is not uncommon for articles discussing evolutionary development to use phrases such as, "as nature intended," "needed larger wings to fly," "a new body plan," and so forth.

In class discussion or in a paper have students rewrite the article form a creationist or intelligent design perspective and then comment on the effect of interpretive lenses.

While compatibilists usually overlook differences between worldviews or assumptions behind disciplinary practices, in a "let's all get along" mindset, transformationists are more frank about identifying and correcting error. They follow Romans 12:2, where Paul says,

> And do not be conformed to this world, but be transformed by the renewing of your mind, that you may prove what the will of God is, that which is good and acceptable and perfect.

Transformationists are not necessarily confrontational, or interested in toe-to-toe combat. They instead might work in areas that the discipline has ignored. They know that the academy helps set the focus of the culture, and if they bring new subject matter and new ideas to bear in their discipline, the culture will eventually pay attention and perhaps even be changed. (That's why, of course, the defenders of the reigning secular paradigms are so virulent when they encounter those who find fault with the framework they have erected.)

An excellent example of a transformationist is historian Jeffrey Burton Russell, who was troubled by the persistent myth that Columbus proved the earth was not flat, supposedly to the surprise of many educated Europeans. Actually, Burton knew, "All educated people throughout Europe knew the earth's spherical shape and its approximate circumference."[84] What had happened was that in the nineteenth century, a handful of anti-Christian writers made up the story of flat earth believers as a way to discredit Christianity:

> If Christians had for centuries insisted that the earth was flat against clear and available evidence, they must be not only enemies of scientific truth, but contemptible and pitiful enemies.[85]

The myth spread rapidly through the nineteenth century, and is even present in some textbooks today. Russell exposed the myth in his book, *Inventing the Flat Earth: Columbus and Modern Historians*, thereby transforming one corner of historical knowledge, and redeeming the reputation of believers who had been wrongly sneered at.

Russell's solid scholarship commanded respect for his well-documented conclusions.

Another example of transformationist work that departed from mainstream theory—or perhaps extended it and applied it in a new way—but that did not overtly attack any reigning paradigms is *Faith of the Fatherless: The Psychology of Atheism* by Paul Vitz. Psychologist Vitz notes that a "significant part of the atheist position" has been to attribute the source of religious belief to psychological causes—to claim that God is a "projection of psychological needs."[86] Without necessarily accepting this claim, Vitz

---

[84] *Inventing the Flat Earth: Columbus and Modern Historians*. Westport, CT: Praeger Publishers, 1991, p. 2.
[85] Ibid., p. 43.
[86] Paul C. Vitz, *Faith of the Fatherless: The Psychology of Atheism*. Dallas: Spence Publishing, 1999, pp. 4, 131.

develops a new hypothesis that atheism is caused in many cases by the psychological effects suffered from experiencing a "defective" father during the atheist's youth.[87] He outlines the influence of neglectful, abusive, and absent fathers on prominent atheists such as Friedrich Nietzsche, David Hume, Bertrand Russell, Jean-Paul Sartre, Albert Camus, Arthur Schopenhauer, Thomas Hobbes, Sigmund Freud, and many others.

Vitz also discusses the upbringing of a number of theists who are known for their defense of Christianity or Judaism, including Blaise Pascal, George Berkeley, Joseph Butler, Thomas Reid, Edmund Burke, Moses Mendelssohn, William Paley, and many others. In each case, he says, these writers had generally kind, loving fathers.

The book is a fascinating and thought-provoking study, one unlikely to come from a secular professor. Indeed, professor Vitz notes that he himself was an atheist during his undergraduate and graduate years as a psychology student, partly because he "wanted to take part, to be comfortable, in the new, glamorous secular world"[88] and partly because he "wanted to be accepted" by his graduate school professors, all of whom rejected religion decisively.[89]

In a word, then, transformationist work can involve finding faith-relevant but neglected topics in a disciplinary area and developing them. Perhaps a way to describe this kind of transformationism is that it offers a new focus in the discipline.

Hypothetical Examples
Biological evolution from the Transformationist view

---

[87] Op. Cit,. p. 15.
[88] Ibid., p. 134.
[89] Ibid., p. 135.

Typical secular scientist: Humans evolved through the unguided, purposeless process of accidental, random mutations operated on by natural selection.

Possible Christian Transformationist: Human beings show evidence of a Designer, and the beauty and complexity of the human body rule out development through accidental processes. Biology needs to open its doors to evidence of a designer and give up its anti-supernaturalism.

Psychology from the Transformationist view:

Typical secular psychologist: The mind is merely a product of the electrochemical activity of the brain.

Possible Christian Transformationist view: The empirical evidence has turned against mind-brain monism and toward dualism. Research needs to continue along these lines, where individuals can use their minds to change obsessions and habits stuck in their brains.

4.1.6 THE RECONSTRUCTIONIST VIEW

Reconstructionists believe that their discipline, or its focus, has gone astray and is so hopelessly corrupt or pervaded by anti-Christian bias that a new start needs to be made.

Perhaps an example from literary studies will clarify this. As mentioned in Chapter 1 (Section 1.1.4), Duke University literature professor Frank Lentricchia said, "I believe that what is now called literary criticism is a form of Xeroxing. Tell me your theory and I'll tell you in advance what you'll say about any work.[90] In literary studies, reconstructionists do not believe that the interpretive schools of Marxism, feminism, or deconstructionism can be revised or improved sufficiently to bring about compatibilities with Christian viewpoints. So, what is required is either a return to "traditional interpretations" (that were

---

[90] "Last Will and Testament of an Ex-Literary Critic," *Lingua Franca,* September-October 1996, page 64.

practiced before the current ideological methods took over) or the new development of a Christian literary theory.

Of the practitioners of the various views of integration, reconstructionists face the most daunting task, the greatest risks, and the guaranteed hostility and rejection by most of their secular peers. But they also have perhaps the greatest promise of moving forward Christian scholarship and knowledge, and even eventually gaining academic respect.

Exercise

If your discipline is one of those that has been encumbered by politicized theories or ideologies, have your students outline "A Christian Theory of ---." Have them explore what they might keep from the theories currently in vogue and what they might create new and why. In their outline, students should include a defense of the new theory, explaining how it would result in new knowledge and a new view of knowledge that others will find illuminating.

Reconstructionists can expect an especially cold shoulder in disciplines where a particular theoretical model has become entrenched. Philosopher of science Imre Lakatos notes that changing, much less dropping, a given interpretive model for a different one, is usually resisted:

> After a period of initial empirical success scientists may decide not to allow the theory to be refuted. Once they have taken this decision, they solve (or dissolve) the apparent anomalies by auxiliary hypotheses or other "conventionalist stratagems."[91]

---

[91] "Falsification and the Methodology of Scientific Research Programmes," in Imre Lakatos and Alan Musgrave, Eds., *Criticism and the Growth of Knowledge*. Cambridge: Cambridge University Press, 1970, pp. 104-105.

And, as Max Planck noted, people who have invested their careers in working under a controlling paradigm are unwilling to hear that it should be replaced:

> A new scientific truth does not triumph by convincing its opponents and making them see the light, but rather because its opponents eventually die, and a new generation grows up that is familiar with it.[92]

However, the good news is that, like transformationists, reconstructionists do not need to attack directly current interpretive frames or methodologies. While demolishing the erroneous towers of an anti-Christian ideology would be a noble task, it is also possible for Christian scholars to work in parallel, applying their own new vision or theory without explicitly criticizing the status quo in detail. Areas such as history, political science, economics, sociology, and others where parallel work is easier to do are areas where reconstructionists might be able to flourish.

An example of a reconstructionist work in the area of literature and literary criticism is John Gardner's *On Moral Fiction*. Gardner thought that modern literary works had lost their traditional moral frame: "Either they pointlessly waste our time, saying and doing nothing, or they celebrate ugliness and futility, scoffing at good."[93] And the critics, Gardner says, have ceased to evaluate works for their moral quality or utility and have taken to analyzing technique.[94] He therefore proposed that literature and criticism return to a concern with moral effect:

---

[92] Quoted in Thomas Kuhn, *The Structure of Scientific Revolutions*. 2nd Ed. Chicago: University of Chicago Press, 1970, p. 151.
[93] John Gardner, *On Moral Fiction*. New York: Basic Books, 1978, p. 16.
[94] Ibid., pp.16-17.

Nothing could be more obvious, it seems to me, than that art should be moral and that the first business of criticism, at least some of the time, should be to judge works of literature (or painting or even music) on grounds of the production's moral worth.[95]

Hypothetical Examples

Biological evolution from the Reconstructionist view

Typical secular scientist: Humans evolved through the unguided, purposeless process of accidental, random mutations operated on by natural selection.

Possible Christian Reconstructionist: Enough of this materialist superstition. The evidence speaks: Darwin and Company got it wrong. Secular scientists are so intent on escaping from God that they are confusing horizontal variation with vertical evolution. We need to start from reality: "For since the creation of the world His invisible attributes, His eternal power and divine nature, have been clearly seen, being understood through what has been made, so that they are without excuse" (Romans 1:20). It's time to reinvent biology along more accurate lines and interpret the natural world using a better paradigm.

Psychology from the Reconstructionist view:

Typical secular psychologist: The mind is merely a product of the electrochemical activity of the brain.

Possible Christian Reconstructionist view: Psychology needs to explore much more deeply the spiritual dynamics of the human being, how sin wreaks havoc on mental health, and the psychic benefits of knowing God.

---

[95] Ibid., p. 18.

4.2 Steps Toward the Integration Process

As we have noted, most new faculty at Christian universities arrive there after being educated at secular graduate schools, where the integration of faith and learning has not only been neglected but was probably vigorously opposed. These new faculty face the challenge of developing workable models to bring faith and learning together, especially if they believe as I do, that integration involves much more than merely connecting faith and learning, much more than presenting secular knowledge in a Christian environment, more even that presenting secular knowledge "from a Christian point of view."

Students are in a similar position. Many have graduated from public high schools where religion continues to be squeezed out at every corner. Even those who have attended Christian high schools may not have learned how to bring faith together with the subject matter content of their studies in such a way that the two become unified and coherent.

Faculty and students who are unfamiliar with the integration process may be more comfortable easing into it through a series of steps that allow them to lay down successively robust foundational levels. This section describes one possible taxonomy. After growing comfortable connecting faith and learning according to the activities described in one level, the student or professor can move to the next level, continuing the activities of the previous level(s) and adding those of the new. Those working at Level 4 are ready for more specific integrative tasks, which are described in Chapter 6.

As with most structured approaches, there is some arbitrariness and overlap here. Take these levels and their content as approximate guidelines, not as an algorithm. Bulleted items are more exemplary than exhaustive.

4.2.1. LEVEL 1: LIFE WITNESS

Who you are is crucial. Others look to your behavior before they ask about your beliefs. At this earliest level of foundation-laying for integration, practice your faith. Integration at this level can be accomplished by showing respect for both intellectual pursuits (learning, reasoning, analyzing, openness to ideas) and the power of faith (the value and truth of Biblical revelation, the absoluteness of truth available in Scripture, and the objective standards of faith).

This first level is the place where the concept of integrating "faith, learning, and living" comes into play. In his book, *A Serious Call to a Devout and Holy Life* (1728), William Law lays it out for us:

> All men, therefore, as men, have one and the same important business, to act up to the excellency of their rational nature, and to make reason and order the law of all their designs and actions. All Christians, as Christians, have one and the same calling, to live according to the excellency of the Christian spirit, and to make the sublime precepts of the Gospel the rule and measure of all their tempers in common life.[96]

Another way to think about this life witness step is to quote the old proverb, "You are what you do." In other words, you can say you are kind or generous or forgiving, but if in practice your actions are those of a grudge-holding, stingy, cruel person, then that's who you are.

A Christ-like life witness is important for the task of faith-learning integration because your ethos or character determines to a large extent your credibility. Another saying is, "People want to know who you are before they want to know what you believe."

---

[96] Rpt., New York: Dutton, 1967, Chapter 10 (p. 109).

Everyone at Level 1

- provides lifestyle witness, reflecting Christian and Biblical values in words, attitudes, and actions
- exhibits personal integrity
- gains understanding of Biblical content and applications to life
- bases decisions on Biblical values
- references Scripture as appropriate in discussions

Christian Professor in a Christian School

- prays with students at the beginning of each class, seeking God's blessing and guidance on the lesson, asking that the Holy Spirit will illuminate the minds of the professor and students, and desiring to use the knowledge gained for kingdom building
- reads and applies portions of Scripture relevant to the subject or to the value of learning
- includes Scripture quotations in syllabi and class presentations and discussions
- shares personal faith and spiritual journey with students, telling "war stories" about personal struggles and learning experiences, including the use of knowledge
- behaves Christianly towards students and other professors, revealing the connection between faith and living
- applies Biblical concepts generally to the curriculum (God as creator, designer of a rational universe, maker of our minds able to learn about the creation)
- asks students to share their faith and discuss their academic and spiritual journeys

Christian Professor in a Secular School

- prays privately before class, asking to be a clear model and an effective teacher

- answers questions about faith when asked
- identifies and takes seriously moral and spiritual themes in the subject matter

Christian Student in a Christian School

- shares faith and spiritual journey with fellow students
- behaves Christianly toward all, loving all as brothers and sisters in Christ
- seeks to honor God in studies, taking learning and studying seriously
- shows deference to and trust in God
- uses prayer for help with studies
- engages in corporate worship and Bible study

Christian Student in a Secular School

- shares faith and spiritual journey with fellow students
- answers questions about faith in a winsome, friendly, non-threatening way
- behaves Christianly toward all, loving all as brothers and sisters
- shows deference to and trust in God
- uses prayer for help with studies

4.2.2 LEVEL 2: THE HARMONY OF KNOWLEDGE

At this level, faith and learning are brought together and begin to be unified, and the decompartmentalization of life takes place to merge faith and learning (and living!). Learning and faith influence each other. The focus is on the holism of knowledge, the compatibility of faith and reason, the unity of truth, and the need for revealed truth to complete empirical truth in order to attain a comprehensive picture of reality. There is not a realm of religious truth separate from scientific truth.

This is the level where compatibilists (discussed in Section 4.1.3) do much of their work. For those just starting out in integrative practice, decompartmentalizing can be a frightening experience, especially because so many parts of our culture (universities, news media, TV, film, print media) work so hard to separate faith and "reality." Breaking out of the culturally imposed boxes can be a real challenge.

At this level, students and faculty both recognize the implications of unified knowledge—that faith can enrich, revise, clarify, even correct some aspects of subject matter knowledge, while that same subject matter can amplify and clarify faith.

Everyone at Level 2

- respects all knowledge as unified, believing that "all truth is God's truth"
- develops a thorough knowledge of Biblical content and principles
- begins to apply Biblical knowledge to subject matter (the fall of mankind and social problems, the power of redemption to change lives, the purposefulness of creation reflected in the structure of nature)

Christian Professor in a Christian School

- seeks common ground between faith and scholarly discipline
- shows compatibility between Christian and secular ideas (for example, Christianity and stoicism, Aristotle and Christian ethics or friendship)
- uses Christian and Biblical examples and illustrations
- compares Biblical teaching to good practice in the discipline's subject matter

- argues that Christianity is relevant to learning, that the Bible has much to say about knowledge (human nature, beauty, history, etc.)
- applies Christian knowledge to clarify and supplement subject matter
- applies subject matter to extend and enrich Christian worldview

Christian Professor in a Secular School

- encourages students to be interpretation seeking
- teaches about the importance of choice of media
- alerts students that values underlie views of the world and knowledge (ontology and epistemology) and that these values affect how we learn and our belief about what can be learned
- helps students see that some knowledge claims are tendentious or biased

Christian Student in a Christian School

- prays about learning, studying, and intellectual service
- works with other students on integrative issues
- views the studying of academic content as a spiritual work involving the life of faith as well as the life of the mind

Christian Student in Secular School

- recognizes that apparent conflicts between faith or Biblical knowledge and what is taught may derive from differences of interpretation
- learns but does not automatically accept information that appears to conflict with Biblical knowledge

4.2.3 Level 3: Biblical Authority

The Bible has much to say about the need for thinking, reasoning, analysis, and understanding. It also reveals many truths highly relevant to learning. And, of course, it contains many statements about reality, desired behavior, human nature, and so forth. Therefore, knowing the Bible well is important (Section 3.3.2). Interpreting it correctly is even more important (Section 3.3.3). And applying it to life and knowledge as the authoritative word is a crucial part of the integrative process.

Often we read about the integration of faith and learning in terms of "adding a Christian perspective" to disciplinary knowledge. And that's true; it does. But real integration needs to go beyond adding a perspective, and apply a Biblical standard, whereby disciplinary content can be evaluated.

Everyone at Level 3
- becomes thoroughly familiar with the Bible, studying it in several translations
- develops substantial Biblical hermeneutical principles, including using word studies to clarify the meaning of passages
- upholds the existence of truth, reason, meaning, and objective standards against postmodernist influences
- upholds Biblical authority in the entire world of knowledge

Christian Professor in a Christian School
- models good Biblical interpretive methods
- identifies and applies Biblical principles and texts to specific disciplinary situations

- asks integrative questions, requiring connection between Biblical revelation and disciplinary knowledge claims

Christian Professor in a Secular School
- applies Biblically derived moral, ethical, and value principles to the subject matter
- identifies the basis of traditional law and morality in Judeo-Christian teaching and reveals the logical and practical problems with moral and legal systems that lack this basis

Christian Student in a Christian School
- thinks about integrative questions and works to harmonize presented knowledge claims with Biblical teaching
- uses Biblical authority as aid in understanding studies (for example, the fall of mankind and sinful human nature as explanation for the failure of socio-economic systems that propose the perfectibility of people through government social engineering)

Christian Student in a Secular School
- recognizes that content is not knowledge
- realizes that moral formation is connected with knowledge and that "ideas have consequences"
- uses Biblical knowledge as a guide for understanding the implications of disciplinary knowledge claims

4.2.4 LEVEL 4: SOVEREIGN WORLDVIEW
Those working at Level 4 not only recognize the role of worldview in the definition and acquisition of knowledge but also uphold the Biblical (or Christian) worldview as

the ultimate touchstone for identifying truth, and for testing all knowledge claims.

Level 4 integrators understand the Big Picture—how worldviews shape expectations, perceptions, thinking, inferring, and so forth. Those possessing a Christian worldview understand that it is futile to argue with, say, someone possessing a naturalistic worldview, who claims that Christianity or one of its teachings is "irrational." It is futile to argue because within that worldview, and how it defines what is rational, the arguer is right. Within the Christian worldview, faith in, say the miracle of turning water into wine, is perfectly rational.

Everyone at Level 4

- discerns worldview assumptions underlying claims and interpretations in the subject area
- recognizes the influence of worldviews on epistemological and ontological commitments
- understands that what is reasonable to believe depends on one's personal, metaphysical pre-commitments
- realizes that the supposed tension between faith and reason is actually a wrong attempt to apply one worldview's beliefs about truth and reason onto another worldview's beliefs
- is willing to oppose knowledge claims that conflict with revealed truth

Christian Professor in a Christian School

- teaches that Christian faith should be the organizing episteme that informs and interprets the subject area and all knowledge.
- provides assumption sets alternative to philosophical materialism and postmodernism

- applies a Biblical worldview to scholarly pursuits and knowledge acquisition, developing perhaps a uniquely Christian school of thought within the discipline
- works to qualify, adjust, break out of, or reform the assumption sets of the discipline and offer new, Biblical-based viewpoints (explicitly or implicitly)

Christian Professor in a Secular School

- shares awareness of alternative interpretive schema
- points out assumptions underlying argument networks
- teaches students about worldviews and the development of knowledge (interpretation influenced by worldview, knowledge filters, etc.)
- encourages students to look beyond not only the conclusions of the discipline, but the assumptions and methodology behind the creation of disciplinary knowledge claims

Christian Student in a Christian School

- understands how different worldviews lead to different conclusions
- uses a Biblical faith framework to free himself or herself from prevailing secular academic ideologies

Christian Student in a Secular School

- understands how different worldviews lead to different conclusions
- uses a Biblical faith framework to free himself or herself from prevailing secular academic ideologies
- recognizes the pervasiveness of ideology, and political correctness over objective truth in many disciplinary claims

Following these steps by adopting the practices described under each one allows faculty and students to grow into the practice of integrating faith and learning gradually, until they become comfortable and more experienced. How long an individual remains at one level depends on that person's desire and ability, and on the particular characteristics of the discipline.

CHAPTER SUMMARY

This chapter discussed half a dozen alternative ways of viewing the relationship between faith and learning, together with the implications for the integrative task for each. Each successive view and step represents a more robust, or should we say, aggressive, approach. Faculty and students can choose an approach (hopefully from the last four: compatibilism, interpretive compatibilism, transformationism, and reconstructionism) that suits their comfort level, their perception of need in the discipline, and the ideas for integration they harbor. The last four approaches can be combined, depending on the task at hand.

The second part of the chapter explained another set of steps into the integrative process, whereby those who are beginning or who are nervous or uncertain can start at a simple level and move up gradually into the higher levels.

In a word, this chapter will help faculty and students ease into the integrative life.

Questions for Thought and Discussion

1. Which of the views of integration described in Section 4.1 appeal(s) to you as an operating principle, either to start (if you have not yet begun to integrate) or as an ongoing method?

2. Looking at your discipline as a whole, what view of integration needs to be used in order to incorporate Biblical truth most effectively?

3. Which of the Steps Toward the Integration Process are you practicing in your teaching now, and which do you plan to adopt soon?

Activities

1. Meet with a colleague or as a department and discuss how and to what extent your disciplinary area has been overtaken by frames, ideologies, methodologies, or viewpoints that are incompatible with Christianity. Determine which views of the integrative process appeal to each faculty member, and how your department can proceed to adopt more robust integrative practices.

2. Schedule focus groups with students (five or six per group) to discover to what extent they are aware of and performing integrative work and at which level described in Section 4.2.

Notes

5

5. STRATEGIC INTEGRATIVE PRACTICES

There is no wholly neutral epistemology that can settle disputes over what areas of human knowledge are neutral and objective. Rather, a Christian epistemology must begin . . . not only with common sense but also with data derived from revelation.

−George Marsden[97]

Overview

This chapter answers the following questions:

- How can Scripture be used to begin the process of faith-learning integration?
- How can students be encouraged to value reading and learning, especially materials that conflict with their faith?
- How can integration be accomplished when disciplinary knowledge claims change regularly?
- What are the possible results when Biblical knowledge meets academic knowledge?
- What are the strategic challenges to faith-learning integration?

---

[97] Op. cit., p. 247.

5.1 THE CHRISTIAN APPROACH

In an essay outlining a Christian approach to political science, James Skillen identifies five characteristics of Christian scholarship that apply to every discipline. We have covered most of these in various places in the book, but they bear mentioning again.

1. Identify and clarify the operating philosophies and assumptions possessed by those in the discipline. Skillen says, "A Christian approach to the discipline should include reflection on the roots and predispositions of different theorists' approaches."[98] Christian scholarship should be circumspect, aware of the intellectual—and ideological—environment in which their discipline exists.

2. Discuss and critique the main and alternate approaches to disciplinary content. Says Skillen: "A Christian approach ought to be more empirical, at least in the sense that it tries to account for all or most of the approaches being used . . . rather than being dogmatic in its own approach while ignoring approaches which it finds incompatible with its own."[99] Christian scholars cover other views as a means of informing students of the various standpoints that inform disciplinary practice. Practitioners of other standpoints are not likely to include the Christian perspective.

3. Christian scholars should always be conscious of their worldview. Skillen says that "a Christian approach ought to be fully self-conscious of its own starting point and basic convictions."[100] Performing integrative work ne-

---

[98] James Skillen, "Can There Be a Christian Approach to Political Science?" in Harold Heie and David L. Wolfe, eds. *The Reality of Christian Learning: Strategies for Faith-Discipline Integration.* 1984. Rpt. Eugene, OR: Wipf & Stock 2004, pp. 21-22.

[99] Ibid., p. 22.

[100] Ibid., p. 22.

cessitates a clear awareness of the Christian worldview because that is the touchstone used to assess disciplinary knowledge claims. Thus, it is ever in play.

4. Christian scholars should feel free and be brave enough not only to develop their own theoretical approaches but also to refuse to work within erroneous paradigms. Skillen says, "It [a Christian interpretation] should not be embarrassed to reject the starting points of the dominant political ideologies and philosophies of the day."[101]

> The key to the entire faith-learning integration enterprise lies here: Faculty and scholars need to stop struggling so vainly to accommodate the aggressively secular approaches that have taken over so many disciplines. Expose the false and advance the true.

5. Christian truth is essential to an accurate understanding of humanity. Many of the disciplines are concerned with the human condition—with people: psychology, sociology, anthropology, history, literature, political science, business, and so on. That being the case, it is ridiculous for scholars to imagine that their discipline "can be understood by some neutral, empirical method which can bracket or ignore Christian 'values.'"[102] All the "human" disciplines can benefit from a study of Christian values and human nature as described in the Bible. But "benefit" is much too weak a word. The disciplines actually require revealed knowledge about humanity if they are to be complete and accurate. Anything less produces a shrunken and distorted caricature of what it means to be human.

---

[101] Ibid., p. 22.
[102] Ibid., p. 28.

5.2. ILLUMINATE COURSE CONTENT WITH SCRIPTURE

A good way to remind yourself and a powerful way to bring students' attention to integrative seriousness is to employ relevant Scriptures throughout your courses. It is likely that a large percentage of your students have arrived at your university with a secular high school education, possibly supplemented by a secular community college education. No doubt Biblical relevance to course content was nonexistent. So simply bringing Biblical texts to bear as commentary or illumination on aspects of course content can revolutionize the worldview of many students who have been shoved into intellectual and spiritual compartmentalism by the many years of secular education.

Showing that the Bible has relevance to academic subject matter is a powerful way to help students begin the process of integrating faith and learning. Demonstrating that **the Bible is not merely relevant but essential** for a complete understanding of all reality will further lead to integrative thinking by students.

Every syllabus should have a thematic Biblical epigraph. For my critical thinking classes I have used Isaiah 1:18a: "'Come now, and let us reason together,' says the LORD." (Someone might argue that this is not a passage about critical thinking and is taken out of context. However, the verse does show that the Lord can appeal to human reason to think over a situation and make a rational decision.) I have also used 1 Thessalonians 5:21: "But examine everything carefully; hold fast to that which is good."

Appendix 1 lists many Scriptures relating to learning, truth, wisdom, and so forth. A little thought and some research will no doubt turn up many other appropriate passages for your use.[103]

In addition to a course thematic verse, Scriptures can be used to link Biblical content (including theology) to course content as you proceed through the semester. Whether you use PowerPoint presentations, handouts, activity worksheets, or lecture, you can include verses that help focus, clarify, elaborate, or summarize the day's theme.

Scriptures can also be used to begin presentations and discussions that involve a critical evaluation of an idea or theory that conflicts with Biblical truth. Conflicts are good places to discuss analysis, Biblical interpretation, and disciplinary worldviews. Some questions to raise include

- Why the discrepancy?
- What is the source of the conflict?
- What is the nature of the conflict? (Interpretation, conclusion, fact claim, philosophical precommitment—that is, worldview or ideology)
- Is there a resolution to the conflict?

5.3 STRESS THE VALUE OF LEARNING

Much has been said in this book about erroneous and harmful worldviews, false knowledge claims, and deceptive practices such as the blurring of fact and interpretation. That said, however, students should be encouraged to read widely, study carefully, and learn deeply, not only because knowing the discipline's content is important and useful, but also because there is valuable information in almost every book and every article.

---

[103] You can download a free Bible search tool with many features and extras, all free, from www.e-sword.net.

5.3.1 The Value of Reading

Our culture is so secular now that we cannot expect to find very many books, scholarly articles (or even TV documentaries) presented strictly from our worldview. Nevertheless, there is often important, true, and useful information in even the most secular of sources, and we should make use of them. Of the books I read, the ratio of non-Christian authors to Christian authors is at least 10 to 1. It is safe to say that much of the information I use in my work to serve God, including content for this book, comes from non-Christian sources. I would not be surprised if the same is true for your own work.

There are benefits to reading all kinds of materials, including those written from a non-Christian or even anti-Christian perspective:

- Worthy knowledge can exist amidst bias, falsehood or simply wrong interpretations.
- Secular books and other sources can often be quite accurate and worthy.
- The book or other source provides at least some true and worthy ideas that can be used in building the Kingdom of God.
- There are often arguments or information that can be used either to support the Christian worldview or to criticize lesser worldviews.
- The authors of many works that attempt to criticize Christianity often supply information and commentary that can be used against their own positions.
- That's where the new ideas are.
- It's important to "know your enemy" and gain an understanding of what the arguments are for and against positions the Christian world supports.
- Even sources that would seem to be completely without factual merit (think about some of those

wild conspiracy theories) can be useful for examples, developing critical thinking, or understanding what the claims are and what evidence is brought to bear to support those claims.

Students should be taught that when they read, they must make mental adjustments for the writer's theoretical frame and biases, and then glean the wheat from the tares:

> Finally, brethren, whatever is true, whatever is honorable, whatever is right, whatever is pure, whatever is lovely, whatever is of good repute, if there is any excellence and if anything worthy of praise, dwell on these things. — Philippians 4:8

Developing and feeding the desire to learn — to read, to write, and to think — is crucial for the growth of future Christian leaders, who, in their formative years at the university, are in danger of keeping those subtly anti-intellectual mindsets that were implanted and encouraged by too many well-meaning believers around them in their early years.

5.3.2 READ AND LEARN REASONABLY

Most new knowledge claims come to us based on authority or faith — which is to say, trust in the source. Very little of what we know is the product of reasoning either inductively or deductively. And only a tiny portion of what we know is based on personal experience. When a new knowledge claim is made, we decide whether or not to accept it (or in which of the three silos or buckets to put it) based on several criteria:

- **The evidence for the claim.** Is there data, some persuasive reasons, Scriptural authority, documents, eyewitness accounts?[104] A major problem in the Internet and social media world is that claims circulate without any basis in fact. And when they become familiar enough, many people believe them simply because they have heard the same claim from several sources. (That's why students need to learn about cognitive biases, such as recency, familiarity, and availability.)

- **The significance of the claim.** If the claim is relatively unimportant, and if it does not require further action or decision making, it requires less additional attention or thought than a claim of larger implications. For example, if we read that "the July average high temperature in Death Valley California is 116°F," we are likely to accept it as true even though it might not be. The consequences of being wrong are so small that it doesn't matter very much if we are.

- **The source of the claim.** If the source has apparent legitimacy and credibility—from a track record of reliability, a known authority, or even internal evidence of trustworthiness (such as the absence of ideology or slanting), our reasoning engine is likely to accept the claim as true, at least tentatively. For example, if we read that the deepest part of the ocean is the Challenger Deep, at 36,200 feet, and the source is the National Oceanic and Atmospheric Administration, we can with some reasonableness assume that the figure is trustworthy.

- **The harmony with prior knowledge.** Does the knowledge claim fit rationally together with other

---

[104] By the way, eyewitness testimony of events that take place suddenly, such as an accident or crime, is among the least reliable form of evidence because the eyewitnesses do not have time to process the events accurately.

things we believe? Is the claim something that can actually be known? A fancy term for this criterion is epistemological coherence. Our total body of knowledge must form a coherent whole without internal contradictions.

- **Worldview compatibility.** Is the knowledge claim compatible with what we believe is possible to be real? The fancy term for this test is ontological coherence. (Note, however, that worldview is actually larger than one's ontological set. Worldview includes epistemological commitments—what is and what can be true—together with views of human nature, values, and so on.)

- **The implications claimed.** Facts do not speak for themselves, but must be interpreted. In many instances, the meaning given to facts is dependent on the bias or ideology of the fact presenter. Increasingly, knowledge claims are weaponized to prove or at least argue for an ideological point or to attack a conflicting knowledge claim. Such information warfare, as it is sometimes called, can require a lengthy assessment of even what appears to be a simple piece of empirical data.

As we discussed in Chapter 1, if the claim has some significance and yet, even after some thought or research work, we cannot make a definite judgment about the truth of it, we can remember the claim without having judged it either true or false. Instead, we file it under "it is said" and leave the determination of veracity in suspense. So there are, in fact, several judgments available to our reason:

- accept it ("This is true")
- reject it ("This is false")
- remember it only ("This is uncertain")

Additionally, our reason might tag the new knowledge claim with a qualifying label, such as:

- probable
- plausible
- improbable
- implausible

For example, the claim that, "If the Loch Ness monster exists, it must be a plesiosaur," might have any one of the four labels attached to it depending on the individual's other beliefs.

Once students are up to speed with critical thinking skills, they will also realize that a given knowledge claim might be evaluated as embodying one or more of the following attributes:

- true, fair, accurate, and complete
- distorted
- partial
- misleading
- slanted
- semantically biased (use of emotive language, selected terms of discourse)
- fallacious
- exaggerated
- understated
- out of context

When you present course content whose truth is questionable, tentative, or highly inferential, supply introductory language that lets students know that they should remember but not necessarily give complete credence to it. Some example phrases include

- According to this theory . . .
- Our current understanding is . . .
- This is believed to be . . .
- Available evidence suggests . . .
- Those who support this theory say . . .

- One interpretation of the data is . . .
- It is claimed by those who support this interpretation [or theory] . . .
- What little evidence for this that there is includes . . .
- The evidence isn't all in yet, but it looks as if . . .
- This inference might have more credibility if it were not a product of such a constrained worldview . . .

5.3.3 CHRISTIANITY IS REASONABLE

Learning about the Christian faith and integrating its principles into one's overall knowledge does not require the student to "stop reasoning and just believe." While the source of Christian knowledge (the Bible) differs from the source of disciplinary or secular knowledge, both kinds of knowledge are subject to rational processing.

In other words, instead of speaking of religious faith claims as suprarational (above reason) or extrarational (outside of reason), and certainly not antirational or irrational (against reason), I believe that they are run through the reasoning engine just like other faith claims. The supposed conflict between faith and reason arose through an attempt to apply a secular definition of reason to a Christian worldview. In the secular arena, where God is imaginary, all things of faith are by definition irrational. But in Christendom, faith is completely reasonable. What it is reasonable to believe depends on what is "properly basic" as Alvin Plantinga likes to say, for that person.

> What you properly take to be rational . . . depends upon what sort of metaphysical and religious stance you adopt. . . . And so the dispute as to whether theistic belief is rational can't be settled just by attending to epistemological considerations; it is at bottom not merely an epistemological dispute, but an ontological or theological dispute.[105]

---

[105] Alvin Plantinga quoted in Ronald Nash, *Faith and Reason: Searching for a Rational Faith*, Grand Rapids, MI: Zondervan, 1988, page 91.

In other words, whether you decide that believing in God is rational or irrational depends not so much on your belief about what is true; it fundamentally depends on what you believe about what *can be* true and on what kinds of things it is reasonable to believe.

Let's consider an example from religious faith. Here is a Christian faith claim: Jesus was born of a virgin. Is it reasonable to believe that? If belief in God and the truth of the Bible are in your belief set, then your reasoning engine will assent to that claim as being rational. On the other hand, if you reject the possibility of the existence of God, then of course any talk about God will appear irrational to you, and your reasoning engine, consulting your set of beliefs, will reject the claim that Jesus was born of a virgin. If your worldview permits you to believe only claims based on empirical demonstration, then you cannot accept the virgin birth. (Note, however, that believing "only claims based on empirical demonstration" is an ultimately unsupportable stance, since every worldview is foundationed on unprovable beliefs, such as the existence of the external world, or even the concept that experiments produce meaningful results.)

But just because this knowledge claim is compatible with the individual's existing belief set, why should it be believed? The answer to this is that some faith claims, such as Christian faith claims based on Biblical authority, are considered privileged truth claims and are accepted on the basis of Scriptural authority.

Contrast this with another alleged Christian faith claim: Christians shouldn't chew gum. No doubt the individual's reasoning engine would find no direct Scriptural authority for this claim, and therefore it would not possess privileged status. Therefore, depending on the individual's other beliefs, this knowledge claim would be either acceptable or unacceptable.

The supposed conflict or tension between faith and reason comes from applying a concept of reason from the worldview of naturalism to the concept of faith in the worldview of Christianity. To the naturalist, faith is unreasonable because it has been relegated to an area of magical thinking, imaginary beliefs, and false hopes. But under the Christian worldview, faith is very reasonable.

5.4 REMEMBER BLACK SWANS AND UNICORNS

One of the great challenges to integration, both secular and Christian, is the fact that disciplinary knowledge changes from time to time when the discovery of new data or the reinterpretation of existing data leads to new conclusions and new theorizing.

For example, from early on and up into the late eighteenth century, it was an established empirical fact throughout Europe that all swans were white. "All swans are white," was a true conclusion. If scholars had thought of the phrase then, it would have been described as "settled science." That knowledge could be integrated into the knowledge set of every scientist and every other educated person.

But then, in 1790, black swans were discovered outside of Europe. This surprising event underscores not only the tentativeness of inductive generalizations but the danger of changing one's worldview to accommodate knowledge claims that might turn out later to be incorrect.

There have been so many ideas, theories, and even fact claims that have been challenged or disproved, that good advice when encountering knowledge claims that appear to conflict with Christian truth but which cannot yet be refuted is to file them in the "remember only" silo or knowledge container in your memory. Learn it accurately, but don't be in a hurry to believe it.

5.4.1 DISCIPLINARY KNOWLEDGE CHANGES

Unfortunately, scholars and scientists do not always calmly and rationally pursue objective truth wherever it may lead. There are many examples of worldview biases resulting in predetermined outcomes or questionable interpretations. For a while, many of these ideas gain credence among the scholarly community; but eventually, someone challenges them and exposes their errors. A few prominent examples include theories put forth by Sigmund Freud, Karl Marx, Margaret Mead, and Alfred Kinsey.

There is also a substantial group of authors cautioning us about the suspect nature of scientific and other disciplinary claims. Statistical analyst John H. Fennick says,

> By now of course, we know that the "latest" study will often contradict those that have gone before. . . . While publication of dubious studies is spurred by the struggle for funding and the lure of catchy headlines, I believe it occurs because most practitioners simply don't understand the statistical tools they use. . . .[106]

Fennick continues by noting, "Pure objectivity is hard to find" because of such inhibitors to objectivity as biases, causes to advance, concern over funding, and the disincentive to publish negative results.[107] He concludes, "Not surprisingly, there is a just and rising distrust of the scientific community."[108]

But worse than one study contradicting another is the thesis of epidemiologist John P. A. Ioannidis, who says,

---

[106] In *Studies Show: A Popular Guide to Understanding Scientific Studies.* New York: Prometheus Books, 1997, p. 9.
[107] Fennick, p. 13.
[108] Fennick, p. 13.

There is increasing concern that in modern research, false findings may be the majority or even the vast majority of published research claims. . . . It can be proven that most claimed research findings are false.[109]

Ioannidis concludes that in "many current scientific fields, claimed research findings may often be simply accurate measures of the prevailing bias."[110] As for checks and balances, even the effectiveness of the peer review process has been called into question.[111]

Exercise An interesting discussion about the nature of knowledge and scientific theories can be drawn from physics. Newtonian physics, quantum mechanics, and Einstein's General Theory of Relativity are all generally accepted as true, yet they all conflict with each other. Ask students to do some brief research on these three physics theories and discuss in class how scientific understanding and explanation are sometimes limited.

A good centering for students is to assign a short research project that looks into the history of an idea and how it changed: understanding a historical event or cause to a historical episode, learning about the way false theories were finally rejected (look up phlogiston or n-rays, for example).

5.4.2 CHANGES IN BIBLICAL INTERPRETATION

On the faith side of integration, we know that God's truth is unchanging and eternal and that his word in Scripture is truth. And we also understand that our interpretation of Scripture is not always completely correct. Because

---

[109] "Why Most Published Research Findings Are False," *PLoS Medicine* 2:8 (August 2005), p. 696. <www.plosmedicine.org>.
[110] Ibid.
[111] Hank Campbell, "The Corruption of Peer Review Is Harming Scientific Credibility," *The Wall Street Journal*, July 14, 2014, p. A15.

the Bible is so reliable and the text has been so carefully preserved, I have no examples equivalent to the discovery of black swans. But I do have a minor example or two of interpretive changes.

When the Hebrew Old Testament was translated into Greek, known as the Septuagint, the translators came across a Hebrew word they didn't know the meaning of. The *Reh-em* seemed to be quite a fearsome beast, since, for example, David praises God for rescuing him "from the horns of the *Reh-em*" in Psalm 22:21. For some reason, the Septuagint translators turned the Hebrew *Reh-em* into the Greek *monokeros*, which the translators of both the Geneva Bible and the King James rendered quite literally as unicorn (*mono* = one; *keros* = horn).[112] Eventually, archaeology and further study have identified the most likely candidate for *Reh-em* as an auroch, a wild and aggressive but now extinct bull standing about six feet high at the shoulders. And with enormous horns — um, two, not one. So, God's word was accurate and true all along, even though for a while it contained unicorns. Further research may bring even more clarity and certainty, but for now a modern translation of Psalm 22:21 gives us: "Save me from the mouth of the lion! You have rescued me from the horns of the wild oxen" (HCSB).

Another change in translation gives Scripture a much clearer meaning and makes more plain sense. In the NASB (and many other older translations similarly), John 3:16 reads, "For God so loved the world, that He gave His only begotten Son, that whoever believes in Him shall not perish, but have eternal life." The problem is with the word *begotten*, because we know that Jesus is the eternal, uncreated Son of God. So, in what sense was he begotten? Well, he wasn't.

---

[112] Is it just me or does it seem odd to you that the translators of the Septuagint could render "the horns [plural] of the unicorn [one horn]?

The traditional etymology of *monogenes* in John 3:16 has been assumed to consist of *mono* (one) and *gennao* (beget), with the sense of generate. But this has seemed to imply that God somehow created the Son. Modern interpreters now believe that *monogenes* is derived from *mono* and *genos* (kind, genus), making an accurate translation of *monogenes* as *unique*. Thus the newer translations render John 3:16 as

For God loved the world in this way: He gave His One and Only Son, so that everyone who believes in Him will not perish but have eternal life. (HCSB)

For this is how God loved the world: He gave his unique Son so that everyone who believes in him might not be lost but have eternal life. (ISV)

For God so loved the world, that he gave his only Son, that whoever believes in him should not perish but have eternal life. (ESV)

God loved the people of this world so much that he gave his only Son, so that everyone who has faith in him will have eternal life and never really die. (CEV)

As these anomalies reveal, our understanding of Christian knowledge doesn't change as often or as radically as our understanding of other knowledge, partly because secular knowledge claims can be compromised by poor experimental design or interpretation or by entanglement with ideology.

5.5 DETERMINE THE INTEGRATIVE OUTCOME

When you apply the Christian worldview and its truths to a disciplinary knowledge claim, theoretical approach, value system, ideology, or interpretation, there are several possible outcomes.[113]

1. Christian knowledge affirms disciplinary knowledge or practice. A discipline committed to the truth, rules of evidence, or reason is affirmed in general or a specific knowledge claim is affirmed. Conclusions that harmonize with Biblical truth are affirmed.

2. Christian knowledge supplements disciplinary knowledge. Christian knowledge of human nature can extend and enrich insights about behavior learned in psychology or sociology, for example. Since science and social science are in general committed to methodological naturalism, the conclusions these disciplines allow their practitioners to draw omit any part of the spiritual, supernatural, or nonphysical realm. Knowing about the human personality from a sin and redemption standpoint can add to our understanding of human behavior.

3. Christian knowledge challenges a disciplinary claim. The disciplinary claim might be rejected as false or might need to be qualified or revised. For example, the postmodernist claim that every text has many equally true interpretations is challenged as false.

4. Disciplinary knowledge affirms Christian knowledge. For example, the study of human anatomy or physiology truly puts the meat on the bone of Psalm 139:14a: "I will give thanks to You, for I am fearfully and wonderfully made."

5. Disciplinary knowledge supplements Christian knowledge. Since many disciplines study finer and finer details of things mentioned in the Bible generally, the disciplinary knowledge can often help us understand and extend the depth of the Biblical idea. For example, that little verse in Genesis 1:16b, "He made the stars also," is awe inspiring. And the fact that God has given each one a

---

[113] Adapted from my book, *The Integration of Faith and Learning.*

name was a source of amazement even a few hundred years ago when people believed there were more than 6,000 stars in the heavens:

> Lift up your eyes on high And see who has created these stars, the One who leads forth their host by number; He calls them all by name.
> —Isaiah 40:26

But to learn that estimates of the number of stars now have reached 100,000,000,000,000,000,000,000,000,000 (a hundred octillion), puts the stagger in the data.[114]

6. Disciplinary knowledge challenges Christian knowledge. While the task can be difficult and sometimes impossible, settling a conflict between a disciplinary claim and Christian truth will almost always involve incompatible interpretations rather than incompatible facts. As we have said before, many fact claims are actually elaborate inferences built on a set of assumptions.

> The conflicts between disciplinary knowledge and Christian knowledge are very rarely disagreements over data or facts. While it is common to claim that the conflict involves incompatible fact claims, at issue most of the time are disagreements over interpretations, viewpoints, worldviews, theories, assumptions, methodologies, practices, or some other philosophical (or even subjective) element. Remember that all truth is God's truth. There can be no ultimate conflict between a genuine disciplinary truth and a genuine Biblical truth.

In such cases, an attempt should be made to resolve the conflict, if possible. The options are:

---

[114] Elizabeth Howell, "How Many Stars Are In The Universe?" Space.com, May 31, 2014. < http://www.space.com/26078-how-many-stars-are-there.html>.

- Show that the source of the conflict lies in incompatible epistemologies or worldviews. For example, those who say that miracles are irrational are applying naturalistic or materialistic worldviews to claims in the Christian worldview.
- Show that the disciplinary claim is wrong.
- Determine whether the understanding of the Biblical truth is correct.
- File away the conflict as currently unresolvable.

5.6 REMEMBER: FACT AND INTERPRETATION ARE DIFFERENT

Or if you want to be perfectly accurate, Remember that a Fact Claim and an Interpretation Are Often the Same. That is, what is presented as a fact is often a conclusion based a collection of unstated assumptions, theory-controlled inferences, and networks of arguments. What is represented as a fact is not the solid, objective description of reality that its adherents believe and want us to believe.

Once again, it is a firm belief of the Christian worldview that no Biblical or theological fact conflicts with any scientific fact or discoverable truth, when that fact or truth is a genuine description of reality. Where there is apparent conflict, the issue is a matter of interpretation or understanding of either the observable data or the Biblical text. All truth is God's truth, and the Bible is true and correct in all the original autograph manuscripts.

The same data can often be interpreted in different ways, depending on the design of the experiment, the theoretical frame applied, even the desired outcome. An experiment may support a given theoretical conclusion only under a given worldview or inference frame.

It's also true that the same data set can be interpreted in more than one way. For example, in the 1970s, the residents of Dallas were buying Coca Cola by a margin of three-to-one over Pepsi. So Pepsi commissioned a taste test among Coke drinkers to see if they might not really like Pepsi better when they didn't know which cola they were drinking. To keep them from knowing, the Coke glasses were labeled Q and the Pepsi glasses were labeled M. The data showed that more than half of the Coke drinkers tested preferred Pepsi over Coke.

But then the Coca Cola company repeated the experiment by putting Coke in both glasses. The tasters preferred the Coke in the glasses labeled M over the Coke in the glasses labeled Q. It seems that some people prefer the letter M over the letter Q.[115]

One way to practice integrative scholarship, then, is to locate data that have been misinterpreted, especially in secularist Procrustean fashion, and provide an alternate interpretation. Biology is a field ripe for this.

An extensive discussion of the relationship between fact and value is presented in Appendix 4. It bears close attention because, as we have said, many of the issues and conflicts between Christianity and disciplinary claims come from "facts" that are something else. That's why in this book, we have used the phrase "knowledge claim" to refer to disciplinary ideas.

5.7 INTEGRATIVE CHALLENGES

Even with all the faculty at your college or university agreeing to practice the integration of faith and learning and to teach their students to do the same, there will re-

---

[115] Schuyler W. Huck and Howard M. Sandler, *Rival Hypotheses: Alternative Interpretations of Data Based Conclusions*. New York: Harper and Row, 1979, pp. 11, 158.

main several factors that will make the process a challenge.

5.7.1 Viewpoint and Worldview Disagreement

Within a department, within the institution, and certainly across multiple Christian colleges and universities, one faculty member is likely to differ with another faculty member over some aspect of reality or disciplinary knowledge. The simplest example is the origins controversy. Among Christian faculty, there are

- Young earth creationists
- Old earth creationists
- Progressive creationists
- Intelligent Design adherents
- Theistic evolutionists
- Methodological naturalists
- Two Realms adherents

Each of these viewpoints has multiple flavors or variants. Some can overlap. And this is not even a complete list.

Similarly, students will find some faculty who view postmodernism with favor because it has worked to break the stranglehold of science as the sole arbiter of truth and has allowed "a thousand flowers to bloom." Where all ideas are allowed, some Christians see a favorable environment for Christian faith and learning. Other Christian faculty see postmodernism as an acid that is eating away our ideas of reason, objectivity, and truth, leaving us with emotion, subjectivity, and relativism. Or to use postmodernist lingo, once the totalizing narratives of the patriarchy have been deconstructed and decentered, what we are left with is a struggle to impose hegemonic narratives through naked power. And that's not good.

It is clear that students can and will be confused about what is "the Christian view" or "the correct view" of a subject. Perhaps the best answer that can be given to this question is that worldviews and faith-learning integration are both ultimately personal. The goal is for faculty and students to strive for a coherent view of reality, informed by Christian truth as it is understood in connection with the academic (or any) knowledge claims.

As Christians, we want our beliefs about the world to be processed through and derived from the most rational, logical, complete, objective worldview possible. We do not want to restrict ourselves to a truth-straining worldview such as naturalism that leaves out what we think is the most important part of reality.

While Christians may have substantially different integrative outcomes for a given subject or discipline, the more complete and rational worldview we share should get us closer to a true understanding of ourselves and the natural world than any more restricted worldview whose goal seems to be keeping God out of the equation. Sharing a Scriptural basis of authority gives us hope that we can move ever closer to an interpretive harmony because we share the same objective and unchanging source of truth.

A final encouragement to persevere in spite of differences is knowing that discussion and disagreement are the hallmarks of the academy. The disciplines (where not constrained by politics or ideology) relish point and counterpoint, and there are many flavors of each theoretical or philosophical stance. You might have heard the saying, "When two professors meet, there are three opinions between them."

5.7.2 INTEGRATIVE CHICKEN AND EGG

In Chapter 3, we discussed the need for preparation before faith-learning integration can be practiced successfully. Specifically, students need a knowledge of the Bible, good interpretative skills, critical thinking and analysis skills, and a hefty knowledge base.

So tell me, what are college freshmen to do? I once surveyed my first year college students about their reading habits. I told them that in the "old days" (meaning, say, the 1950's) students entering college had read about 500 books. (I think I read that somewhere at some point, but don't quote me as an authority.) The students reported their own reading had been K-12 textbooks. Not much else. Maybe a magazine here and there. In one class, a student said of a work of nonfiction I had required as ancillary reading, "This is the first book I've ever read all the way through."

Yes, how are freshmen to integrate their faith with their learning? I've had several students who had been saved within months of their first attendance at college. ("I'm trying to stop swearing," one of them told me.) "Biblical knowledge? Oh, yes, I want to read the Bible."

I ask again, what are freshmen to do? In my critical thinking course (a sophomore-level course), one student asked, "Aren't people critical enough already, without needing a course in it?" After I explained that critical thinking was a course in how to think, another student asked, "What if you already know how to think?"

The answer to this vacuum of knowledge and skill challenge, I believe, lies in the verb, *iterate*. Integration, like education itself, is not a linear process, not a simple accumulation of mind stuffing. As we saw in the first chapter, integration is a natural process. It goes on almost automatically—though it is much better when performed intentionally and skillfully. As with other skills, students will get better as they gain experience and knowledge through practice.

My recommendation is that students begin to learn about and practice integrative skills from the first day through graduation, iterating their worldview, thinking ability, knowledge base (and the three silos we've discussed: accept or believe it, reject or disbelieve it, and remember it without judgment). Eventually, they will learn that faith-learning integration is a lifelong process, because learning is a lifelong process. (And we would hope that growing in faith is, too.)

5.7.3 INTEGRATION AND EVOLUTION

The concern on the minds of many Christian faculty interested in integrating faith and learning involves evolutionary theory. Naturalism/materialism can be opposed for its inadequate explanatory power and its transparent atheist agenda. And, as mentioned earlier in this chapter, the errors that have been exposed about the claims of anti-Christians such as Sigmund Freud, Karl Marx, Margaret Mead, and Alfred Kinsey have made it unnecessary to attempt to reconcile their ideas with Christian faith. No need to try to integrate them, except in the sense of study them, remember them, and shake our heads.

But how can or should evolutionary theory be integrated with Biblical truth? It pervades nearly every area of academia. Evolution is still the reigning and only-permitted paradigm in the natural sciences and has a heavy influence in the social sciences. As mathematician David Berlinksi notes, "It serves as the creation myth of our time, assigning properties to nature previously assigned to God. It thus demands an especially ardent form of advocacy."[116] Nothing makes the secular academy more overtly angry than for anyone to oppose Darwinism.

To be sure, some, perhaps many, Christian faculty (again, having been trained in secular graduate schools) have made their peace with Darwin and accepted evolu-

---

[116] David Berlinski, *The Devil's Delusion: Atheism and Its Scientific Pretentions.* New York: Basic Books, 2009, pp. 190-191.

tion as their origins model. The cultural pressure to choose this path is enormous, and faculty looking to be taken seriously by their secular colleagues think that this is the way. So, how does this impact their integrative work?

There are several approaches. Two realms is, I believe, a viewpoint choice originally suggested by secular scientists to placate Christians while at the same time keeping "religion" out of the way. Two Realms' practitioners are likely to keep the Christian perspective as a commentary on secularly modeled accounts (in biology, psychology, etc.). False Distinction practitioners act similarly. Followers of both of these views, if they attempt any integration at all, are apt to reinterpret Biblical texts in ways that harmonize them with current scientific positions.

Compatibilists, or at least Interpretive Compatibilists, who accede to the Darwinian world are likely also to reinterpret the Bible to harmonize with current evolutionary claims or to avoid areas of conflict and seek areas of agreement.

Here are some ideas for teaching that will allow at least some integration to take place.

- **Remind students that to learn and understand the theory is important,** because it permeates the intellectual landscape. At the same time, however, they do not need to believe that it describes what actually happened in the production of life forms. In other words, they are free to believe in some version of creationism or intelligent design, provided they can mount a rational, robust, evidential, Biblical case. (And if they do decide to buy evolutionary theory, they also should be required to mount a rational, robust, evidential, Biblical case.)
- **Teach the controversy.** Whether a faculty member is committed to or skeptical of evolutionary theory, he or she should teach the arguments and evidence

opposing it as well as what can be said in its favor. It is a sad and shameful fact that those subscribing to evolution go to court to stop schools from even mentioning issues or difficulties with the theory.

- **Teach differential probability.** This is a worldview issue. Under one worldview, a theory might seem highly probable, while under another worldview, the same theory will be deemed weak. That is exactly the case here. Under the worldview of naturalism or the practice of methodological naturalism, evolutionary theory appears to be apparently probable because it is the only plausible explanation for life on earth once a creator God is ruled out of bounds.[117] Then, evolution is the only game in town. However, under the worldview of Christianity, evolution must compete with other theories which include theistic components, and these other theories have greater probability than evolution.

What about faculty who favor an origins-by-Creator, every creature "after its kind" belief, instead of evolution? They will have an easier time integrating that position with the Bible, but they still face the work of explaining to students the pervasive presence of the naturalistic model. And, they will face their secular colleagues' scorn, mockery, belittlement, and discrimination, which is the price

---

[117] Thomas Kuhn notes that a given set of data can be explained by more than one theoretical model (see the epigraph to Chapter 4). One of the major criteria for choosing one theoretical model over another is explanatory power—how well the model explains all the data. Unfortunately for the adherents of naturalism, the neo-Darwinist model is rapidly losing explanatory power as empirical investigation of the natural world continues to reveal greater and greater complexity in living forms. The mutation-selection mechanism proposed as the creative engine of evolution simply cannot produce the results found in nature.

reconstructionists must always pay for departing from the wagon wheel ruts of accepted disciplinary roads.

On the other hand, Christian faculty who strive to harmonize the Bible with evolution face their secular colleagues' scorn, mockery, belittlement, and discrimination also because so many of these secular colleagues believe that "no accommodation for God is made in modern evolutionary theory,"[118] and that "we cannot allow a Divine Foot in the door."[119]

Christian faculty are quite willing to allow a Divine Foot in the door, however, so that they are not required to adopt a naturalistic model of origins. They are free to examine the evidence objectively. And rather than have enough faith to believe that the complex machinery of the cell evolved through many single, accidental, undirected, purposeless changes, that the eye has evolved on numerous occasions, or that there are 10^{500} universes, or that the human sense of touch, able to detect surface bumps as small as 13 nanometers,[120] gradually developed because it offered differential reproductive advantages—rather than have enough faith to believe these things which their secular colleagues must believe in order to keep God out of science, Christian faculty and scholars are free to reject the preposterous claims of evolutionary theory.

All that's required is courage.

---

[118] Cedric Davern, *Genetics: Readings from Scientific American, With Introductions by Cedric I. Davern.* San Francisco: W. H. Freeman, 1981, p. 239.

[119] Quoted in Phillip E. Johnson, *Objections Sustained.* Downers Grove, IL: InterVarsity, 1998, p. 72.

[120] Philip Ross, "How Sensitive Is Human Touch? New Research Suggests Our Fingers Can Detect Nano-Wrinkles On Near-Smooth Surfaces." *International Science Times*, Sept. 17, 2013. Online. <http://www.isciencetimes.com /articles/6073/20130917/sensitive-human-touch-new-research-suggests-fingers.htm>.

CHAPTER SUMMARY

This chapter discussed some of the general strategies for performing integrative work, including using Scripture to begin the process and establish a Biblical foundation. Students are encouraged to develop a love of learning and reading—of all kinds of materials, including those whose worldview and conclusions are hostile to Christianity—because there is often worthy knowledge in any source.

Advice was given for handling integrative difficulties, including the common situation where disciplinary knowledge claims change. The various possible results of the integrative activity were discussed, together with some strategic challenges.

Questions for Thought and Discussion

1. How do you normally handle changes in disciplinary content or focus, and how can you construct your integrative approach so that it will be flexible enough to remain connected well?
2. In the past, which integrative outcomes (Section 5.5) have you used? Which are you planning to use in future courses?
3. What other integrative challenges do you foresee in addition to those discussed in Section 5.7?

Activities

1. Consult Appendix 1 and your own knowledge of Scripture and locate a Biblical text that can serve as an epigraph for a syllabus in one of the courses you teach.
2. Locate at least six Scriptures that link thematically to some aspect of a course you teach. Write a brief (three

sentences) connection between each Scripture and the content it links to.

3. Read Appendix 4 on the fact-value dichotomy and explain how facts and values interconnect in your discipline.

4. Meet with other members of your department and discuss faith-learning integrative approaches. Do you find any areas of agreement? Disagreement? Is it possible to develop a unified approach? If not, can you develop a statement for your students explaining the heterogeneity and how they should understand it?

6

6. TACTICAL INTEGRATIVE PRACTICES

Following the godly path means to accept and boldly carry out the challenge of integrating faith and learning by participating in the shaping and teaching of a biblical worldview. Yet the structure and purpose of this worldview must be not only eternally true but also temporally viable.
— Antonio Chiareli[121]

Overview

This chapter answers the following questions:

- What are some practical techniques faculty can use to teach students about faith-learning integration?
- What questions should be asked and answered regarding disciplinary and course content, including worldview issues?
- What are some items that can be included in course syllabi that will help students understand the integration process?
- What are some discipline-specific ideas that can be incorporated into courses in each area?

---

[121] Antonio A. Chiareli, "Christian Worldview and the Social Sciences," in David S. Dockery and Gregroy Alan Thornbury, eds., *Shaping a Christian Worldview: The Foundations of Christian Higher Education.* Nashville: Broadman and Holman, 2002, p. 246.

6.1 Model Integration for Your Students

One of the most powerful methods of learning is imitation: watch an expert and then do what he does. In addition to teaching about integration, then, explain how you do it. Share your integrative research and publication interests with your students. If you are experienced and comfortable doing integrative work, explain your methods to your students and show them examples. Discuss both the easy techniques and the challenges.

If you are still working out integrative processes, by all means share that with your students and ask them for ideas. Supply them with some of the ideas in this book and work together with them to find some additional methods. (You will find that this practice actually increases student esteem for you. Students consider professors who can admit ignorance to be more honest and genuine than professors who can never admit not knowing something.)

Start small and build:

- Begin with compatibilist techniques (see Section 4.1.3) and work your way up.
- Apply the early levels of integration (see Section 4.2) and model the basics for your students.
- Work with a smaller aspect of the subject such as one day's topic. As you work out integrative scholarship during the term, share your progress with your classes.

6.2 Teach Integrative Techniques

Faculty who wish they had learned how to connect their faith commitment with what they were learning in college and graduate school have the opportunity to "pay it forward" by teaching students how to do it.

6.2.1 BEGIN WITH BIBLICAL THEMES

The secularization of the university has, as a major goal, the explanation of all natural and human phenomena without recourse to a role for God and without reference to Biblical teaching. An obvious thrust of integration, then, should be to reestablish Scriptural teaching about human nature.

What does it mean to be human? A first area for exploring connections and disjunctions between disciplinary learning and Christianity is their views of our humanness. Compare the assumed or declared answers to questions such as

- Where did we come from?
- Why are we here?
- What is the meaning and purpose of life?
- What is wrong with life?
- What is the solution or remedy to what is wrong?
- What is our ultimate destiny (after death)?

It's easy to see how different some worldviews are from the Christian worldview. Naturalism is a striking example:

	Christianity	Naturalism
Where did we come from?	Created by a loving God	Evolved from slime
Why are we here?	To love and serve God	Purposeless accident
What is the meaning of life?	Work toward sanctification	None
What is wrong with life?	Sin	Nothing; suffering is normal
What is the solution?	Salvation in Christ	Death
What is our ultimate destiny?	Heaven or Not	Annihilation

Human Nature. A major area for the exploration of integrative themes is that of human nature and the whole story of mankind. The nexus of rebellion, transgression, and redemption is present over and over in the fictional narratives of literature, film, TV, and music videos, and to an extent in art and music. The human-focused disciplines such as sociology, psychology, and cultural anthropology are also interested in this thematic expression.

An interesting area for integrative exploration in literature and film is the modern twist on the redeemer. Traditionally, the movie hero followed the Biblical model by presenting the hero as a type of Christ, who suffered or gave his life for someone, a town, or even the world, often when those being "saved" opposed him. The hero was in some sense better or more knowledgeable than those he rescued.

In modern films, the hero or protagonist is often worse than those whom he rescues, and engages in anti-social, rebellious actions supposedly necessary in order to succeed. (In keeping with the American obsession with individualism, the hero is often a rebel who must work around the folly, stupidity, and opposition of the established authorities, breaking laws and destroying property in order to save the world.)

In many cases, the hero has a dark past and is given the opportunity to redeem himself while saving the world. This is an example of Hollywood's doctrine of works salvation taken to an extreme.

As you know, some ideologies, such as Marxism, advocate the idea that human nature can be changed by the appropriate governmental interventions, and that if Marxist theory is implemented, eventually there will be no need for government and a utopia on earth will prevail. A live question for research, scholarship, and integrative analysis then is to ask: Which method will bring about life change most effectively: structural or environmental changes (such as moving the criminal into a new apartment complex) or personal belief changes (saving the soul and changing the heart) or both (moving out of the neighborhood to a place of positive influence such as a Christian ranch experience)?

Mind and Brain. The adherents of naturalist/materialist philosophy have long argued that the mind is merely an epiphenomenon of the brain. Who we are, at bottom, is merely a collection of electrochemical processes. There is actually no *you* in you. Put another way, you don't really exist. Consequently, free will is an illusion. Everything is determined by the meat grinder in your skull.

Interestingly enough, however, many researchers have discovered that our minds can actually change our brains. This is not just the fact that what we focus on influences the interconnection among brain cells. What's really fascinating is that the mind can oppose the brain and make the brain change its mind, so to speak.

For example, people with Obsessive-Compulsive Disorder (OCD), whose brains kept telling them that they needed to wash their hands, were instructed to talk back to their brain and tell it that they didn't need to wash their hands.[122]

A possible Biblical reference to the mind versus brain idea is in Romans 7:15-25, where Paul says he does "the very thing I hate" (7:15) even though his mind struggles against it. What he calls the "flesh" (7:25) or "sin" that lives in him (7:20) we might say is his brain, sending sinful urges to his mind.

God's Creation and Sovereignty Over an Orderly and Rational Universe. Every discipline can call attention to the fact that we can use reason and analysis to understand the world because it is not the product of a random collocation of atoms and our minds are not the product of chance errors in the replication of DNA. We are God's

---

[122] See, for example, Jeffrey M. Schwartz, MD and Sharon Begley, *The Mind and the Brain,* New York: HarperCollins, 2002; and Andrew Newberg, MD and Mark Robert Waldman, *How God Changes Your Brain,* New York: Ballantine, 2009.

creatures in God's universe and he has given us minds to be curious and experiment and think.

In chemistry, for example, we can perform an experiment and expect that we can rely on the laws of chemistry to operate consistently. In mathematics, we can be confident that if 2x=4 today and 2x=4 tomorrow, x will be 2 on both days.

The Image of God. The neo-Darwinist / naturalist view of humans is that we are the end product of an accidental, undirected, goalless set of random mutations, and that every preserved mutation had some reproductive benefit. And yet, we have features that are not explainable by reproductive advantage, features that are better understood by the idea that we are created in God's image, with a connection to the divine:

- We have a sense of beauty. We enjoy beautiful sunsets, landscapes, flowers, waterfalls and other natural world sights. We also enjoy creating beautiful designs in sculpture, paintings, architecture, and so on.
- We enjoy things in themselves that we find sublime. Did you ever wonder why humans enjoy music? Or reading books? Or making a treehouse? Why do we have such an appetite for humor?
- We have a sense of wonder and awe. Looking at the stars at night, or gazing into a campfire somehow makes us feel a connection with our maker.

Having been created in the image of God has implications enormously different from those derived from being the end result of a collection of accidents. The value of human life is objectively grounded, we have a purpose in life and a hope in death, our spiritual hunger means something, our desire to live a life of purpose serving others (rather than exploiting them) is part of who we are as God's creatures.

6.2.2 REQUIRE INTEGRATIVE ACTIVITIES

Make faith-learning integration activities part of the course requirements. Integration should be among the expressed goals and instructional requirements. Assignments requiring worldview analysis of source materials, essays connecting Christian knowledge with subject matter knowledge, and readings about integrative practices or supporting integrative approaches will all help students improve their integrative skills.

Context awareness is a crucial skill for students to gain. Help them ask, "Where is this person coming from?" or "What are the underlying philosophical assumptions or precommitments here?" Training students to think about these influences should be done in a positive way. We do not want students to view sources with prejudice or to go on epistemological witch hunts. But they do need to be aware of the perspectives and values being applied by the creators of their source material.

Exercise

When you cover a theory, a person famous in your discipline, a literary work, a historical event, or philosophical assertion, ask students (1) to identify the worldview of the idea or figure and (2) to compare the claims or assumptions or values from the idea to the Christian worldview. Class discussion is a good method here. Students can clarify their own worldview while improving their ability to discover the worldviews underlying the content of their discipline.

Many students like to get their information from the Internet, because searching is fast and easy. However, it has been noted that too often students pay more attention to the look of a Web site rather than to indications of authoritativeness. The "simulation of authority" is easy to create, and students can be deceived by a flashy presentation. Encouraging them to perform some source analysis can help prevent gullibility based on appearance.

When you require a research paper (or any research project), have students include an annotated bibliography that includes (1) the reasons they believe the source is reliable (or if not reliable, why they used it), (2) the apparent worldview of the author.

Exercise

In an era where students have grown accustomed to giving their opinions without the need to offer reasons or evidence to support them, it might be a good idea to develop a response sheet that requires students to think more carefully. The sheet could ask several analytic questions, such as:

- What is the worldview, ideology, or value system underlying this [book, article, film, etc.]?
  - o What is the evidence you found in the work that supports this conclusion?
- What assumptions appear to have been made but left unstated by the author?
  - o What is the evidence that caused you to come to this conclusion?
- How do the worldview and the assumptions made affect the argument, conclusions, or central idea of the work?
  - o Support your claims with reasons and examples.
- How do the factors discovered in the analysis above impact your ability to integrate the knowledge claims made in this work?

Once again, teaching faith-learning integration is teaching critical thinking, which is in itself valuable, so taking the time to have students do a little source analysis is worth it because of this double benefit.

6.2.3 BE CIRCUMSPECT TOWARD DISCIPLINARY CONTENT

Integration involves much more that simply testing disciplinary knowledge. Disciplinary knowledge has an enormous contribution to make in extending and supporting the Christian worldview. If, for example, you have ever learned about the hypercomplexity of a biological cell — all the micromachines, little factories, processes, mitosis — your amazement and awe at the power and creativity of God certainly must have increased substantially.

Disciplinary knowledge and the process of integration should be approached positively, not with an attitude of suspicion or hostility. After all, faculty have chosen to study and teach a subject area because they have found worthy knowledge there, and students have come to college believing that they will grow in every area — knowledge, faith, wisdom — by studying under Christian faculty professing a specific discipline.

So, be careful when presenting the integrative process. "Accentuate the positive," as Mom used to say. Or, to be more academic, William Hasker says that we should ask

> what specific contribution does this discipline make to the Christian vision of reality? How does it enable us to understand God, and his world, and our fellow human beings differently than if the insights of the discipline were not available? What insights, projects, and activities does the discipline make possible?[123]

Thousands of scholars, even though they may have done their work under limited or misguided worldviews (or po-

---

[123] "Faith-Learning Integration: An Overview," Christian Scholars Review 21:3 (March 1992), pp. 231-48.

litical ideologies) still have discovered and communicated much that is worthwhile. Think of it as mining and refining ore: You might need to process a lot of rock to get to the gold, but the gold — ah, the gold!

6.2.4 Teach Students the CHRIST Learning Model

The CHRIST Learning Model is designed to help students develop a positive, rational engagement with all learning. The six components represent skills, attitudes and behaviors that produce a healthy approach to and interaction with learning. Not only is this model good for helping students in their academic integrative work, but it will help protect them from the gullibility that causes many young people to fall for urban legends and conspiracy theories. The six components are:

Circumspection

The word means, literally, "looking around" and that's a great metaphor for this part. Circumspection involves

- putting knowledge claims, interpretations, and so on in a larger context:
  - o what is this idea part of?
  - o what are its implications?
  - o what are the underlying assumptions?
  - o are there unintended consequences (the "and then what?" test)
- asking what can be said in favor of it?
- asking what can be said against it?
- considering the source
  - o is the source authoritative?
  - o is the source credible?

Humility

Learning must be approached with an attitude of humility. The intellectually arrogant are often so biased and self-confident that they miss half of knowledge. They pigeonhole ideas before (or without!) investigating them. But those who dismiss ideas without hearing them aren't as well educated as they think.

The humble learner approaches new ideas with respect, with the attitude of, "That's interesting. Let's talk about it." or "Let's hear what you have to say." Even if an idea is ultimately judged to be wrong or even dangerous, those who hear the idea and its support have learned

- that this idea exists and what it is
- who supports it and why
- what influence it has

Approaching learning with humility and deference doesn't mean that you have to accept or agree with every idea you encounter. It means that you should approach learning about everything with an attitude of curiosity. "What else do people believe?" should be a driving force in your learning attitude.

Reason

Being reasonable and using reason in analysis and argument and maintaining a sincere and objective response to new knowledge is key to good learning. Drawing reasonable conclusions, making fair assessments, using reason in summarizing ideas, and using logical arguments when supporting, or critiquing knowledge claims—all these practices reveal the proper engagement with and the right attitude toward learning.

Integrity

The learner is also a contributor to "the great conversation" among all those who engage in the life of the mind. This part of the CHRIST Learning model embodies an ethical component, requiring the learner to

- be as objective and free of bias and prejudice as possible
- treat claims and evidence fairly
- avoid special pleading
- summarize both favored and disfavored ideas fairly and accurately

Using reason means being logical and rational, and possessing integrity means being fair.

Scripture

As Christians, we are utterly blessed to have the Word of God in the Bible, because it provides us with an objective standard of truth and values by which we can test all the claims that come our way, so that

> As a result, we are no longer to be children, tossed here and there by waves and carried about by every wind of doctrine, by the trickery of men, by craftiness in deceitful scheming.
> — Ephesians 4:14

Scripture is the source of spiritual knowledge and the knowledge of human nature. The Bible offers insights, new pathways, and clarifying vantage points that allow us to explore and think about and process new knowledge.

Truth

To me, truth is the most important philosophical commitment one can make. Some people like to object to this assertion, saying that instead of truth, love or loyalty or kindness, or justice or fairness or equality is the most important commitment. However, my reply is that without truth, you cannot have any of the other virtues because nothing good can be built on a foundation that lacks truth.

Truth, then, is the capstone component of the CHRIST Learning model. A strong commitment to truth, wherever it may lead, is the essence of genuine learning.

The table below shows the model. It is a complete fabric: Every component is necessary in order to have genuine learning. Share this model with your students (feel free to photocopy the page) and talk it over with them.

C	Circumspection	But examine everything carefully; hold fast to that which is good. —1 Thess. 5:21
H	Humility	Do nothing from selfishness or empty conceit, but with humility of mind regard one another as more important than yourselves. —Phil. 2:3
R	Reasonableness	But the wisdom from above is first pure, then peaceable, gentle, reasonable, full of mercy and good fruits, unwavering, without hypocrisy. —James 3:17
I	Integrity	But the seed in the good soil, these are the ones who have heard the word in an honest and good heart, and hold it fast, and bear fruit with perseverance. —Luke 8:15
S	Scripture	Sanctify them in the truth; Your word is truth. —John 17:17
T	Truth	And you will know the truth, and the truth will make you free. —John 8:32

6.3 IDENTIFY DISCIPLINARY ISSUES

While just a few worldviews, principally naturalism, postmodernism, and Marxism, dominate academia, every discipline has its own variants and combinations and ideological commitments that impact the methodology of doing work in that subject area. The following sections provide some ideas for sorting out your discipline's fundamental operational methods and philosophical commitments, so that you can help your students understand the relationship between their foundational beliefs and those of the discipline's practitioners.

6.3.1 Discuss Your Discipline's Worldviews

Articulate the assumptions underlying your discipline's values, attitudes, and practices.

- What are your discipline's epistemological assumptions?
  - What can be true?
  - What is not allowed in the arena of truth?
  - How is knowledge defined?
  - How is reason defined?
  - How does your discipline's view of truth compare to a Biblical view?
- What are your discipline's ontological assumptions?
  - What are the dimensions of reality — is reality circumscribed to include only material things?
  - Is God prohibited from involvement in the world?
  - What is the discipline's view of human nature? Is it changeable by changing political structures or by changing human hearts?
- What are your discipline's axiological commitments?
  - What is considered "good" in the discipline?
  - What values are used to judge facts, behaviors, actions, and circumstances?

- o Are values fixed, or are they relative to circumstance, or applied selectively?
- o How do the discipline's values compare to
  Biblical values?
- o Is a particular value system imposed or understood in the discipline, requiring scholars
  to conform? That is, is there pressure to apply certain theories, to be politically correct,
  to exalt a person, group, school, or ideology?
- What methodology does your discipline use in the
  process of engaging in scholarly activity?
  - o Is more than one approach permitted?
  - o Are any approaches forbidden (in the sense
    of resulting in lack of publication, ostraciza-
    tion, or marginalization)?
  - o Are facts restricted to empirically demon-
    strable things?
  - o What is the logic of reasoning in your disci-
    pline?
  - o Does the discipline's methodology constrain
    the search for truth?

Inform students about the presence of interpretive
worldviews in every discipline. Give them a few examples
of scholars or others whose writings reflect an identifiable
worldview.

> **Exercise** A powerfully clarifying exercise would be to take a
> literary work, historical event, scientific finding, or
> psychological observation and present it from each
> of several worldview (or ideological) perspectives,
> such as Marxist, feminist, postmodern, naturalist, or even
> atheist and compare and contrast that viewpoint or interpre-
> tation with one from the Christian worldview.

Knowing where an author is "coming from" provides a
context of understanding that can make negotiating oth-

erwise difficult material much easier. For example, knowing that a literary critic is writing from a deconstructionist viewpoint makes the writing easier to interpret because the reader (student) realizes that the writer's intention is to "problematize the meaning of the text."

6.3.2 Discuss the Textbook's Worldview

Many, if not most, standard textbooks in every field are framed by a particular worldview which deeply influences how the text views knowledge, evidence, and reason and how it treats ideas from other, competing worldviews. For example, the standard, popular textbooks in many areas of study, not just the sciences and social sciences, reflect the prominent embodiment of naturalism because that in a variety of forms is the worldview of higher education in general.

It's important, then, to help students identify and assess the theories, assumptions and conclusions in the textbooks you use. Once students are taught to recognize this, they will be less likely to accept without analysis the viewpoints expressed or the knowledge claims made (an excellent critical thinking skill), and less likely to compartmentalize their learning.

Since active learning is more effective than simply handing the students the answers, assign teams of students (three or four students) to define several common worldviews. Combine these and distribute them to the class.

Exercise

For the following week, have students read an assigned article or chapter in their textbook and identify the worldview that informs it. Have them explain where there are compatibilities with the Christian/Biblical worldview and where there are tensions or conflicts.

6.3.3 Evaluate Disciplinary Content

This practice is at the heart of the integration of faith and learning. To integrate Christian faith with academic content, it is necessary to evaluate the truth claims, methodologies, and worldviews of the discipline using the touchstone of Christian knowledge. This process includes

- **Identifying compatible ideas**, theories, interpretations, and fact claims and extending, applying, and underscoring them. Whenever academic content harmonizes with Christianity, that fact should be made explicit. Truth, even if embedded in a misguided or false philosophy, should be celebrated.
- **Identifying conflicting ideas**, theories, interpretations, and fact claims and exposing their incompatibility, criticizing their weaknesses or errors. Students should learn that it is permissible to object to the conclusions or interpretations of scholars of any theoretical viewpoint (including their own) if they have good, specific reasons to do so.
- **Emphasizing the importance of the integrative activity** by discussing and demonstrating the respect due to all participants in the "great conversation" of the academy. Even though there may be much disagreement, the content deserves serious consideration and respect.

Training students how to evaluate source material for worldview and theoretical influence provides the great bonus of improving their learning. One of the great complaints heard from other faculty is that students either do not do the reading or do not pay much attention to what they read. (Who knew it would be so difficult to read a textbook while listening to an iPod, watching TV, and texting friends?) When students are assigned a worldview analysis of their books or chapters, they are put under pressure to read, think about, learn, and remember the content.

Christian scholars, because so much of so many disciplines has become radicalized and secularized, are inevitably going to find themselves challenging the very foundations of some content areas, and in any case, have an enormous task ahead of them if they are willing to create alternative Christian theoretical approaches.

6.3.4 RECAPTURE LOST PATHWAYS

You've no doubt heard of David Hume, that "sneering infidel" of eighteenth century England, but have you heard of Christian-friendly Thomas Reid, Hume's main critic of the time?[124] You've certainly heard of eighteenth-century philosopher John Locke, famous for his *An Essay Concerning Human Understanding*, but have you read his book, *The Reasonableness of Christianity* (1695)?

The point is, in literature and philosophy at least, the ideas and writings that are emphasized today represent a selection from the vast writings of the past. The writings chosen and emphasized today are not the same as those of earlier eras. In the early twentieth century, for example, Herman Melville was treated as an "also wrote" lesser author. Only when the great secularization of America took place did English departments begin to assign *Moby Dick*, the novel Melville called "a wicked book"[125] that he described as "broiled" in "hell-fire."[126]

So why not look into the past vast cast of characters (books) and see if there are some good but neglected works and ideas that deserve resurrecting? History, biography, literature, government, economics, political science, sociology, and many other fields might have gems waiting for you to unearth and bring back to the attention of the culture. You could require such works in your classes,

---

[124] See Thomas Reid, *An Inquiry into the Human Mind on the Principles of Common Sense*, 4th ed. (1785). Rpt., Ed. Derek R. Brookes, University Park, PA: Pennsylvania State University Press, 1997.
[125] Letter to Nathaniel Hawthorne, November 17[?], 1851.
[126] Letter to Nathaniel Hawthorne, June 29, 1851.

base scholarly articles on them, or even become an editor of a modern version.

6.3.5 CORRECT THE RECORD

For at least 150 years, secular scholars have had their say about what is important, what attitudes and judgments we should have about the past—and about what really happened and even what is true. Needless to say, there has been plenty of omission, distortion, mythmaking, together with agenda-driven interpretations. Why not focus your scholarship on correcting the errors and omissions and misinterpretations of the past? Just for a simple example, how often do the textbooks discuss the deep Christian faith of early scientists, philosophers, mathematicians, and other scholars? Is that so irrelevant?

6.4 SYLLABUS IDEAS

It is important to include in each course syllabus language that specifically addresses the need for the integration of faith and learning. This language should accomplish the following:

- State clearly that the institution and the professor are firmly committed to Biblical authority and that Scripture provides a touchstone for understanding and interpreting the discipline.
- Inform students that integration is their job as well as the professor's.
- Avoid intellectual arrogance or an overly negative tone about erroneous knowledge claims that are part of course content.
- Emphasize the value of learning the course content even though some or much of it has been compromised by a limited worldview (such as naturalism)

or a worldview that lacks objectivity (such as post-modernism).

6.4.1 Defining the Integration of Faith and Learning

It would be a mistake to assume that students know what the phrase "integration of faith and learning" means. If that practice is going to be central to their education and to each course, it is a good idea to define it for their sake.

Here are some sample definitions:

Sample 1

The integration of faith and learning refers to the interconnecting of Christian truth found in the Bible with the subject matter taught in each discipline. Where there is compatibility between the two, the result is a synthesis that extends and enriches both the faith and disciplinary learning. When there is conflict, the Christian worldview seeks to understand the source and nature of the conflict, and, when needed, serves as a corrective to erroneous knowledge claims and philosophical positions.

Sample 2 (from Chapter 1)

The integration of faith and learning refers to the intellectual activity of evaluating and interconnecting the subject matter of the academic disciplines with Biblical truth by discovering the appropriate relationships between them.

Sample 3

Faith-learning integration involves combining and connecting Christian (Biblical) truth with academic learning. Integration might involve accepting, rejecting, or remembering (without accepting or rejecting) the knowledge claims of the discipline.

6.4.2 LANGUAGE FOR INTRODUCING INTEGRATIVE PRACTICE

Too many students, like too many people in the Church, are frankly anti-intellectual. They vaguely realize that a lot of what passes for truth is propaganda, or at least arrives slanted toward politically correct ideologies. The challenge of the Christian university professor, then, is to encourage students to love learning and knowledge while letting them know that there are indeed ideologies, theories, and so forth that are distinctly hostile to Christian faith. Students need to know that wrong or even bad ideas can be important to know.

This section includes some sample language (that you are free to use or adapt) designed to position course practics in a way that students will find valuable.

Sample 1

This course covers the major theories that scholars use to analyze and understand [history, psychology, sociology, etc.], together with the worldviews that shape those theories. We will bring alongside these theoretical approaches the light of Christian knowledge to see what additional understandings we can discover for both [history, whatever] and Christian truth. During this process of analysis and evaluation, we might discover that some disciplinary knowledge does not comport well with Christian knowledge. When this is the case, we will investigate the situation, asking why the discrepancy, and how it can be addressed.

Sample 2

As we cover the material in this course, we will become aware that the same data can be interpreted very differently through the lenses of different worldviews. For example, our textbook was written from the worldview of naturalism, leading its authors to draw conclusions that conflict with the Christian worldview.

(The restrictions imposed by naturalism prevent Christian-compatible conclusions.) Nevertheless, the facts presented by the book are accurate, though from a Christian standpoint the conclusions are sometimes not. It will be our task to (1) learn all the content, including the problematic conclusions (2) separate the true from the erroneous, and (3) integrate the entire content effectively into our knowledge.

Sample 3

Learning about knowledge claims, even those informed and shaped by theories hostile to Christianity, can extend our understanding of the subject area, inform us as to why secular ideas permeate the culture, and give us the knowledge we need to respond to the arguments.

Sample 4

This course will involve learning many more ideas than we can accept as true, because they come from secular theories with a bias toward [materialism, naturalism, postmodernism, etc.]. We need to learn these ideas so that we can respond to them effectively. After all, they shaped — if not defined — the culture we live in.

Sample 5

This is not a course where your only role is to sit and learn right answers, either from the theoreticians and producers of the standard ideas in the discipline or from your professor and those who have criticisms of those standard ideas. Instead, this is a course where you are expected to develop your critical thinking skills, weigh evidence, evaluate truth claims, understand competing worldviews, and draw reasonable inferences about the findings and interpretations of the data that this discipline seeks to understand. You are not here to memorize; you are here to learn and to think.

6.4.3 MISCELLANEOUS COMMENTS

Including some personal comments about your own commitment to Scriptural authority, careful scholarship, and faith-learning integration will help students understand you — where you are coming from — and encourage them to take the coursework more seriously. Here are just some ideas that might suggest some comments of your own:

Sample 1

A personal note. This university, this course, and I, your professor, are firmly committed to Biblical authority, our objective standard of truth. We are also committed to the centrality of Christ in all our endeavors, for he gives meaning, purpose, and direction to our lives and our studies. We owe it to our savior to be faithful to his word and to work carefully and diligently in his service. As the Apostle Paul says, "Whether, then, you eat or drink or whatever you do, do all to the glory of God" (1 Corinthians 10:31).

Sample 2

Remember that the goal of education is to get better, not just to get through. We have the truth and must prepare our hearts and minds to serve the One who gave us that truth. Work diligently to learn the course material so that you will be better able to serve God with all your mind. As Paul says, "Whatever you do, do your work heartily, as for the Lord rather than for men, knowing that from the Lord you will receive the reward of the inheritance. It is the Lord Christ whom you serve" (Colossians 3:23-24).

Sample 3

The difference between this university and a secular school is not simply that here you are taught by Christian faculty. The difference is that you will be learning course content from a Christian perspective, expanded and clarified by the Christian worldview. We believe in truth and in studying a comprehensive and complete view of reality. Secular institutions marginalize the presence of God in the world—whether in creation, history, or human strivings. We, on the other hand, put God in the center of his world and our studies.

Sample 4

Why, you may ask, is Biblical knowledge so important? The Bible not only provides an objective standard for truth and behavior, but it also completes our picture of reality by informing us of facts (such as the nature of God and his plan for salvation) that we could never know without it.

Sample 5

The Bible, properly translated, interpreted, and understood, is authoritative in all declarations of fact regarding nature, history, and human nature, including the overarching theme of creation, temptation, transgression, and redemption. Scripture tells us about the meaning and purpose of life, the goals we should pursue and the evils we should avoid.

6.5 DISCIPLINE-SPECIFIC INTEGRATIVE PRACTICES

This section provides just a few small hints and ideas for pursuing faith-learning integration in various disciplinary areas, either by connecting current content areas with faith knowledge or by suggesting some ideas for pursuing Christian scholarship.

Remember that every discipline should include relevant Scripture references to show the connection between subject and faith.

Faculty in each discipline will no doubt have better ideas than these, and will be familiar with integrative books in their area. But for the sake of new faculty, I offer here a few ideas. I have also included in Appendix 3 a few useful books that offer discussions of discipline-specific ideas written by experts in their field.

6.5.1 ANTHROPOLOGY

Demonstrate that the fall of mankind, not religion and civilization, causes the suffering in societies. One of the main disconnections between the Christian worldview and anthropology is cultural relativism, the idea that however strange or even seemingly unhealthy the practices of other cultures are, those practices must be somehow beneficial ("adaptive" in anthropological terminology).

Perhaps a fruitful area of research would be to identify cultural practices that are harmful and unproductive. Robert Edgerton has produced a powerful argument that many primitive cultures have adopted toxic practices that are objectively harmful to them. This is not a common view. He says, "By asserting that some traditional beliefs and practices are maladaptive because they endanger people's health, happiness, or survival, I am opposing the established tenets of relativism and adaptivism."[127]

Edgerton's book suggests an area for Christian faculty to do integrative research. An analysis of our own modern societies and their cultural values would determine whether they have become maladaptive through the assumption of false or harmful (anti-Christian?) beliefs and practices. Edgerton notes that one of a culture's roles is to rein in what we would call fallen human nature:

---

[127] Robert Edgerton, *Sick Societies: Challenging the Myth of Primitive Harmony.* New York: Free Press, 1992, p. 24.

Many of the predispositions that are commonly believed to exist in humans have the capacity to threaten
society and resist the efforts of culture to constrain
them. The list is a long and familiar one. Donald T.
Campbell has argued that if a society is to survive, it
must develop means to curb human greed, pride, dis-
honesty, covetousness, cowardice, lust, wrath, glut-
tony, envy, thievery, promiscuity, stubbornness, diso-
bedience, and blasphemy.[128]

Edgerton calls for an end to the use of a cultural relativist frame that views the practices of all cultures other
than those of modern societies as adaptive, saying that
such an exploded belief should be replaced by a form of
evaluative analysis, judging the good and the bad social
interactions as just that—transactional enjoyments. This
idea runs counter to the worldview of most scholars, who
still cling to the myth of the Noble Savage made famous
by Jean-Jacques Rousseau in *The Social Contract* (1762). In
fact, most primitive societies are not happily constituted
and Edgerton provides persuasive evidence.

Edgerton's work suggests an idea for professors in
Christian university cultural anthropology departments:
Why not examine sick societies—maybe even in the current West—in terms of Christian thinking and methodology. Or, locate an area in cultural anthropology that appears to have been distorted by relativism and correct the
record.

6.5.2 ART

My suggestion for the Christian artist or teacher of art
history or artistic technique would be to recapture the lost
values that art used to embody. It used to be that art had
the purpose of evoking thoughtful feeling, as the observer

---

[128] Ibid., page 70.

pondered a scene in a painting or admired the beauty of a sculpture. Now that a pile of railroad ties thrown randomly on the floor of the gallery can be more admired than an Old Master painting, something seems to be missing.

Anyway, my suggestion is to use, Philippians 4:8 as the anchor verse for reconstructing the study and creation of art:

> Finally, brethren, whatever is true, whatever is honorable, whatever is right, whatever is pure, whatever is lovely, whatever is of good repute, if there is any excellence and if anything worthy of praise, dwell on these things.

It is said that we can't know the value or worthiness of something until we know its purpose. If someone asks, "Is this painting good or bad, worthy or unworthy?" the return question must be, "What is its purpose?" If the purpose of a painting is merely to splash some color on a drab wall, then a canvas with a red and a blue rectangle might be considered good and worthy for that purpose. If, on the other hand, the purpose is to provoke thinking, produce a feeling of grandeur or the sublime, to lift one's ideas to the spiritual, then perhaps the colored rectangles are not the best choice.

Students learning to create works of art—paintings, sculptures, poems, short stories, plays, novels, songs and other music—all too often mimic secular models, without understanding the differences in purpose of secular art and Christian art. I've seen student literary works, for example, with violence, profanity, and salaciousness, all without a higher purpose, but only because those are characteristic of secular works. Similarly, I've seen paintings and sculptures by Christian students that look as if they had been created by a two year old—because that's what many secular examples appear to be. My own experience with student poetry has caused me to develop some advice to would-be poets and other artists: Creating art is both a talent and a skill. The best art requires practice and revision. Generally, the more effort you put into a work, the better it can be. Learn by imitating the best models and then surpass them. And read *Discourses on Art* by Joshua Reynolds.

6.5.3 ASTRONOMY

"The heavens are telling of the glory of God; And their expanse is declaring the work of His hands" (Psalm 19:1). A starting place for thinking might be the book: *The Privileged Planet: How Our Place in the Cosmos is Designed for Discovery*, by Guillermo Gonzalez and Jay Richards (Washington, D.C.: Regnery, 2004). And for reconstructionists, take on Einstein and the speed of light with Joao Magueijo, *Faster than the Speed of Light: The Story of a Scientific Speculation* (2003, rpt. New York: Penguin Books, 2004).

6.5.4 BIOLOGY

Show that the beauty and complexity of the biological world reveals a Creator. The biological world is replete with testimonies to the power, creativity, and sense of esthetics of our Creator. God's hand can be seen in flowers, metamorphosis, the migration of butterflies.

The saying, "God is as deep as you want to go," finds evidence in the complexity of living cells. YouTube has many good examples. One is "The Inner Life of a Cell" at https:// www. youtube. com/watch?v=FzcTgrxMzZk

A relevant Scripture is, "For since the creation of the world His invisible attributes, His eternal power and divine nature, have been clearly seen, being understood through what has been made, so that they are without excuse" (Romans 1:20).

Thus, even in biology, where the discipline is contorted by evolutionary theory, there is compatibility in many facts (as opposed to interpretations and theoretical claims).

6.5.5 BUSINESS AND ECONOMICS

1. Connect Biblical values or themes to business practices. A couple of examples are *Jesus CEO: Using Ancient Wisdom for Visionary Leadership* by Laurie Beth Jones, and John MacArthur's *Called to Lead: 26 Leadership Lessons from the Life of the Apostle Paul.*

2. Assign case studies where students compare a set of Biblical values (leadership, stewardship, justice, etc.) with the practices of a corporation. Where does the company meet Biblical values and where does it fall short? What advice would you give to the leadership of the company?

3. Develop a theory of service maximization where business decisions take into account the amount of public benefit in addition to profit maximization. For example, suppose you make a new ballpoint pen. Your market analysis shows that you can sell a million pens at $10 each and after costs, make a profit of $6 million. Or, you can sell the pen for one dollar and sell 10 million pens, making a profit of $6 million.

Under the strict rules of efficiency, the decision would be to sell a million at $10. But under the theory of service maximization, you'd sell the pen for a dollar and make 10 million people happy.

6.5.6 CHEMISTRY

Visualizing chemical reactions by drawing out molecular formulas shows how rational and orderly the chemical universe and the creation itself is. We can see the careful hand of God in even simple reactions, such as the fuel cell using hydrogen and oxygen: $2H_2 + O_2 \Rightarrow 2H_2O$. And chemistry shows us the reliability of the universe and its physical standards: mix an acid and a base 1000 times, and you still get the same reaction.

6.5.7 EDUCATION

Astute professors of education can guess what I am going to say here: train your students how to teach the integration of faith and learning. And to do it themselves, of course. If we are to universalize faith-learning integration throughout Christendom, get rid of compartmentalism, and take our place as serious scholars, we need Christians educated in the worldview, process, and practice of integration.

6.5.8 HISTORY

History is the story of humanity. God is the creator of humanity. It seems reasonable that he has watched over mankind during our foolish behaviors. Some questions that arise in this regard include these:

- God obviously intervened in the history of Israel. Has God intervened in the rest of history? Can you see his hand in certain events? How do you know God acted?
- Can you see God's "grand plan for humanity" through the unfolding of historical events?
- How have the effects of fallen human nature been repeatedly expressed through specific events or people? (Read Niccolo Machiavelli, *The Prince*.)
- How have the effects of redeemed human nature been displayed through certain events or people?
- Why have political systems built on the perfectibility of human nature failed? Explore examples.
- Why do so many events provide examples of failed utopianism and how does that connect to the Biblical understanding of human beings?

Exercise

We believe that our sovereign God works in history. The questions are when and how and how can we know? When negative events occur (a dictator, war, disaster), we often ask, "Was this God's will?" I suggest a model of God's will that both complicates and simplifies the question. I believe that the will of God has three aspects.

- Permissive will. These events God allows to happen but does not appoint, desire, or direct. A Biblical example is the deaths of eighteen people in the collapse of the tower of Siloam (Luke 13:4-5).
- Directive will. These events God directs humans to do, but the humans have a choice. That is, God wants these things to occur, but we can resist. Biblical examples include God's direction to Jonah, who fled from obeying until God put the pressure on him, and the rich young ruler who declined to follow Jesus (Matthew 19:16ff, Mark 10:17ff, Luke 18:18ff). I believe that this aspect of God's will is the subject of the petition in the Lord's prayer, "Your will be done" (Matthew 6:10b).
- Executive will. These events are appointed by God as things he commands to be done. "Let there be light" (Genesis 1:3) is a good example, as is Jesus calming the storm (Mark 4:37ff and Luke 8:23ff).

The question is, can this model be applied profitably to modern historical events? It's not always clear in the Bible which aspect applies: Matthew 6:10a says, "Your kingdom come." That sounds like a petition, but isn't the kingdom coming as a matter of appointment? And what about Acts 21:10-14, where Paul insists on going to Jerusalem?

One definition of history is that it is a sometimes tendentious interpretation of selected events the historian thinks are of consequence and believes to have happened. What this means for the Christian scholar is that there are many mistold stories, many untold stories, many forgotten stories, and many highly skewed interpretations of events that often include anti-Christian themes and conclusions. Edward Gibbon's *Decline and Fall of the Roman Empire* is an obvious example.

So, another tack for the Christian historian is to find the faults and correct them.

- Tell the true story behind some of the anti-Christian propaganda. For example, this has been done by several historians who have presented the true story of Galileo and the Catholic church.[129]

- Tell the untold or undertold stories of Christian heroes, martyrs, missionaries, scientists, and ordinary workers. Histories of various events often leave out the fact that the problem solver or star of the event was a committed Christian.
- Correct some of the revisionist histories that ignore the role of faith, or view Christian influence as negative.
- Add back the faith portion of events. Many accounts tell who did what and when, but they neglect to include the role of faith in the personalities and events.

Still another tack would be to assemble and discuss all the evidence for some Biblical event, city, ruler, and so on. An interesting book that does this is *Did Jesus Exist? The Historical Argument for Jesus of Nazareth.*[130] Professor Bart Ehrman, the author, was surprised to learn that a growing group of people deny that Jesus ever lived, when, in fact, "the view that Jesus existed is held by virtually every expert on the planet."[131] A major drawback of the book is that the author has little sympathy with Christianity. Instead, he says, "I am not a Christian, and I have no interest in promoting a Christian cause or a Christian agenda. I am an agnostic with atheist leanings. . . ."[132] It would be nice to have an up-to-date account of the evidence for Jesus'

---

[129] See Philip J. Sampson, *6 Modern Myths About Christianity & Western Civilization.* Downers Grove, IL: InterVarsity, 2001.

[130] Bart D. Ehrman, *Did Jesus Exist? The Historical Argument for Jesus of Nazareth.* New York: Harper One, 2012.

[131] Ibid., p. 4.

[132] Ibid., p. 5.

historical life presented from a sympathetic yet scholarly viewpoint.

And yet again another tack would be to rebalance history. For example, take eighteenth century England. Ah, yes, the age of enlightenment with all those skeptics, where reason finally got the upper hand on blind religion. Hume and Gibbon in England, Voltaire and Diderot in France. But that view comes from looking backward from a secularist point of view. The eighteenth century was actually quite religious (most of the books sold were religious books) and, in fact, the age was rationally faithful. Reason and Christianity were seen by many thinkers as allies. Look at Joseph Butler's *The Analogy of Religion Natural and Revealed to the Constitution and Course of Nature* (1736), or Isaac Watts' *Logic, or The Right Use of Reason in the Inquiry after Truth* (first published in 1724, with 20 editions following). The great evangelical awakening needs to be reemphasized, also.

An interesting book that reveals the often self-serving errors made by agenda-driven and even by simply unskilled historians is David Hackett Fischer, *Historians' Fallacies: Toward a Logic of Historical Thought.* New York: Harper & Row, 1970. In an effort to construct a plausible narrative from the collection of often seemingly unrelated bits of information available, historians face the ongoing challenge of avoiding biases conscious or unconscious that will produce something false and tendentious.

6.5.9 LAW

Law classes should point out that much of even current law is based on Old Testament laws and New Testament principles. The themes of justice, mercy, and even forgiveness are relevant, as is the concept of the tension between justice and equity.

Studying hermeneutics will help students later in their law careers understand and practice good interpretation of conflicting documents or witnesses.

6.5.10 LITERATURE

Literature, whether novels, poems, short stories, or plays, explores human nature and human motivation, together with the consequences of choice. The themes of temptation, rebellion, transgression, fall, infidelity, and sometimes redemption take us through a vicarious world where we can understand others and ourselves. The understanding can be described from any of several interpretive filters, such as Marxist, feminist, and postmodernist.

Unfortunately, these perspectives have taken over English language and literature studies, not to the benefit of literature. These theories read into the works under scrutiny meanings and implications never dreamed of by the author. Rather than combat these schools of interpretation, whose products have been called a form of Xeroxing (see Section 1.1.4), I would encourage literature professors either to take the so-called traditional approach to literary analysis or develop a Christian literary theory. A Christian theory of literature would interpret plot and character in light of the spiritual realities of the heart and motivations and life itself.

Upper division majors should be acquainted with the critical theories now popular, and the philosophy behind each theory should be explored in light of Biblical truth.

Some books to look at:

Barratt, David, Roger Poley, and Leland Ryken, eds., *The Discerning Reader: Christian Perspectives on Literature and Theory*. Grand Rapids, MI: Baker Books, 1995.

Gardner, John. *On Moral Fiction*. New York: Basic Books, 1978. Although Gardner is not writing from the standpoint of a Christian theory of literature, his treatment of "moral fiction" and "moral criticism" shows a light on how Christian professors of literature might proceed.

6.5.11 MATHEMATICS

The language of mathematics provides a powerful way to demonstrate and participate in God's creative power and intelligence and connect an abstract study to the natural and physical world. The divine proportion, Fibonacci series (in nature such as the chambered nautilus and sunflowers), fractal algebra, even geometrical shapes (dodecahedrons, anyone?) can connect math to beauty to God.

Mathematics itself demonstrates the rational quality of our Creator. Specific formulas allow mathematics to describe the operations of the physical world.

6.5.12 MUSIC

Harmony, the mathematical relationships in notes, the emotional impact of music—all point to a creator who enjoys esthetics. Why do we enjoy music? That in itself is evidence for a loving God.

Perhaps an integrative theory could be developed by examining how music is used and misused in the culture: how music controls the emotions and is sometimes used for spiritual enhancement as in worship songs and sometimes used to emotionally justify sin, as in films which feature just the right music during scenes of adultery. Areas ripe for analysis are music videos, popular songs in general, the music of television commercials—what are the spiritual or moral implications of all these and the techniques they use?

How does the type of music we listen to affect us? Is classical music really better for our brains than hip hop? Is contemporary music designed to keep our brains from functioning properly, so that we can't think straight? (Or is popular music actually better for us in some way?)

6.5.13 Philosophy

Like literary criticism, philosophy seems to have diminished itself by moving from a discussion of the great ideas to a focus on minutiae and attempts to prove that God does not exist. My recommendations for integrating philosophy with Christian faith are as follows.

1. Recall that the roots of the word philosophy (*phil* = love, *soph* = wisdom) quite literally means the love of wisdom. So recommendation number one is to return philosophy to the love of wisdom and stop being so esoteric. Aristotle for everyone.

2. Speaking of Aristotle, the major project of medieval thinkers was to reconcile Christianity with the classical philosophers. Why not look into what they did and see what that suggests for today?

3. Since logic and critical thinking fall under the philosophy department, and since thinking skills are so sorely needed, why not elaborate on critical thinking courses?

4. Recover lost or marginalized Christian and otherwise theistic philosophers and teach them.

5. Teach the best of contemporary philosophers like Alvin Plantinga, J.P. Moreland, Nicholas Wolterstorf, William Lane Craig.

6. Philosophy is the traditional home of apologetics, and, especially with the rise of the "new atheism," every student needs skill in defending the faith.

6.5.14 Physics

Going down, down, down, past the smallest particles, is there ultimately an idea making up the substance of the universe? And does quantum entanglement have spiritual implications?

At the least, the fact that the universe is orderly and subject to physical laws and constants shows a rational system created by a rational God.

Has the speed of light changed? Was it faster earlier in the history of the universe? What would be the implications? Start with Joao Magueijo, *Faster than the Speed of Light.* New York: Penguin, 2003.

6.5.15 POLITICAL SCIENCE

God-given government (Romans 13) stands in tension with the ultimate sovereignty of God (Acts 5:29: But Peter and the apostles answered, "We must obey God rather than men"). The role of government to secure peace, safety, liberty, and justice to its members. The fact that much law in the Western world has been derived from or influenced by Biblical principles.

6.5.16 PSYCHOLOGY

The emerging neuroscientific evidence for dualism, that the mind and the brain are separate entities is certainly an area for study and research.

A provocative area is the diagnosing of atheism as a father-figure issue. A relevant book was mentioned in Section 4.1.5: Paul C. Vitz, *Faith of the Fatherless: The Psychology of Atheism.* Dallas: Spence Publishing, 1999.

6.5.17 RELIGION

Since the book of Genesis starts the grand story at the beginning, with a relationship between Adam and Eve and God and later Noah and God, the clear implication is that monotheism preceded polytheism. A study that delineates the evidence for this would be an excellent way to integrate faith and learning. And it would also be transformative because the standard, secular view is that polytheism preceded monotheism.

There is just such a book, *In the Beginning God: A Fresh Look at the Case for Original Monotheism* by Winifried Corduan (Nashville: B&H Academic, 2013). However, more research and more publication in this area might help remedy the polytheist-first bias of religious studies departments in the secular world.

6.5.18 SCIENCE

Many of the assumptions and principles of the scientific method are compatible with Christian faith because science required a Christian worldview in order to be invented. Many scholars have demonstrated this, pointing out that science could not be invented in a pagan world. The table below shows the differences:

Pagan Worldview	Christian and Scientific Worldview
The gods are arbitrary and capricious	God is a rational, purposeful God
Existence is cyclic, rolling in a circle	Existence is linear, where cause and effect are real
Contradictions can be believed at the same time	Objective truth and the rules of logic apply
The world is ultimately a mystery	Humans were created in the image of God, allowing our thinking and reasoning to understand the creation

Because science has been overtaken by an aggressively secular scientism that rejects even the faint aroma of Christian faith, students need to have a better understanding of the harmony of these two arenas. Reviewing some books and articles would be helpful.[133]

Students should also become quite clear about the difference between science and scientism (the belief that the only truths are those coming from science), and they

---

[133] See, for example, Eric V. Snow, "Christianity: A Cause of Modern Science," www.rae.org/jaki.html; Michael Bumbulis, "Christianity and the Birth of Science," www.ldolphin.org/bumbulis/; Stanley Jaki, "Science: Western or What?" *Intercollegiate Review*, Fall 1990 (26:1), pp. 3-12.

should be aware of the political and ideological battles that are fought over theoretical issues.

6.5.19 SOCIOLOGY

The social and cultural aspects of knowledge—what gets discussed and what does not, what can be argued and what cannot—provide fertile ground for the Christian sociologist to examine how various communities, groups, and subgroups control what is "true" and what is "false."

A very informative book in its own right, and a model of doing good faith-learning integration (though I do not know which authors are Christians, if any) is the book, *The Secular Revolution: Power, Interests, and Conflict in the Secularization of American Public Life* edited by Christian Smith (Berkeley: University of California Press, 2003). The essays in the book demonstrate that "the secularization of American public life" was not the inevitable result of modernism or historical inevitability, but was "the successful outcome of an intentional political struggle by secularizing activists to overthrow a religious establishment's control over socially legitimate knowledge."[134]

---

[134] Christian Smith, "Rethinking the Secularization of American Public Life," in Christian Smith, Ed., *The Secular Revolution*. Berkeley: University of California Press, 2003, p. 1.

Chapter Summary

This chapter presented specific, practical methods for integrating faith and learning. It stressed the incorporation of Scripture in teaching students about integrative issues. Assessing and evaluating your discipline to determine its underlying assumptions, filters, and viewpoints was discussed, together with the need to evaluate the textbooks used.

Some samples of information about faith-learning integration that can be included in course syllabi were presented.

Finally, a few thoughts for research and teaching were offered about what various disciplines might find of interest.

Questions for Thought and Discussion

1. Why is it important to "use a positive approach to disciplinary content" when discussing or practicing faith-learning integration?
2. What are some ways textbooks reveal their worldview?
3. Describe the most dominant theoretical approach(es) used in your discipline. Does ideology play a significant role in your discipline's approach(es)?
4. Discuss whether you think that teaching faith-learning integration as part of the CHRIST model of learning is more or less effective than teaching integration by itself.

Activities

1. Develop a course syllabus containing the ideas you found valuable in this chapter. Include Scripture, explanations to students, integrative assignments, and lecture topics about your discipline's integrative issues. Be sure to integrate the integrative material into your course subject matter.

2. Develop a plan for including Christian scholarship in your discipline. It could involve recapturing lost focus, correcting the record, creating a new, Christian theoretical approach, or criticizing a disciplinary practice that is based on an unbiblical worldview.

3. Join with other faculty and administrators to develop a short paragraph related to the institution's commitment to the integration of faith and learning. This statement should be appropriate for inclusion in various places, such as the university Web site, individual course syllabi, promotional brochures, and so on.

Notes

A1

APPENDIX 1: USING SCRIPTURE TO ENCOURAGE INTEGRATION

Have I not written to you excellent things of counsels and knowledge, to make you know the certainty of the words of truth that you may correctly answer him who sent you?
— Proverbs 22:21

To encourage students to see the importance of Biblical truth in their academic work, quoting relevant Scriptures is a good starting point. Note, of course, that the translation you use might have different words from those in the New American Standard Bible (NASB), which is the source of most of the texts in this section as well as in the book overall. However, the sense should be the same.

Just as an example, Acts 17:2 reads in the NASB, "And according to Paul's custom, he went to them, and for three Sabbaths reasoned with them from the Scriptures. . . ." The word translated *reasoned* is the same word that forms the root of the English word *dialog*, from *dia*, *across* and *logos*, *word* or *speak*, so *to speak back and forth*. Other translations render the word *spoke to* (CEV), *held discussions with* (GNB), *reasoned with* (HCSB), *to reason with* (NLT), *reasoned with* (ESV), *had discussions about* (GW), *discussed* (ERV). Other possible translations are *disputed with* or *argued with*. Our habit of turning nouns into verbs would allow us to translate the word *dialogued with*.

A1.1 SCRIPTURES RELATED TO THE MIND AND THINKING

Students who might have come to college with what amounts to an anti-intellectual mindset need to understand how important God sees thinking. We were created in the image of God and are commanded to serve him with our whole being. Jesus says that the most important commandment is,

> You shall love the Lord your God with all your heart, and with all your soul, and with all your mind, and with all your strength.
> —Mark 12:30

We are called to a life of the mind, where we must approach the world of knowledge claims with a bit of caution and circumspection. Commonly, truth and error are mixed together, wrong information is presented as truth, and knowledge claims are used as philosophical weapons. Paul tells us:

> But examine everything carefully; hold fast to that which is good.
> —1 Thessalonians 5:21

Examining everything carefully means that some truth claims are likely to be more reliable and some less reliable than others. And holding fast to that which is good implies both treasuring and sharing that which is good and rejecting that which is not so good.

> The first to plead his case seems right, until another comes and examines him.
> —Proverbs 18:17

This quotation cautions us about drawing conclusions after hearing only one side of an issue. We must be on guard when those who have powerful influences over what "truths" get delivered in our culture prevent opponents from having their say. The first sign of a weak or deceitful argument is the attempt to hinder anyone from answering it.

Similarly, as Christians, and as good citizens, we owe it to others to hear them out before we jump in with our own ideas. Let them explain:

> Let people finish speaking before you try to answer them. That way you will not embarrass yourself and look foolish.
> — Proverbs 18:13 (ERV)

Just as we want to be cautious about secular knowledge claims, so we also want to be cautious about any interpretation of the Bible that seems incongruous with what we already know of the Scriptures. (Remember that Satan quotes Scripture in Matthew 4:6, in an attempt to manipulate Jesus.) In other words, we need to use our God-given minds:

> Beloved, do not believe every spirit, but test the spirits to see whether they are from God, because many false prophets have gone out into the world.
> — John 4:1

Indeed, with so much misinformation and disinformation being circulated in our information-laden world, we need to use our God-given minds not only to "test the spirits," but to test all knowledge claims:

The naive believes everything, but the sensible man considers his steps.
— Proverbs 14:15

In order to become sensible people, we need to practice critical thinking and learn how to analyze arguments and information:

Do not judge according to appearance, but judge with righteous judgment.
— John 7:24

The truth is often hidden while falsehood is offered as truth. In classical times, Truth was depicted in art as a naked woman, because Truth has nothing to hide and is beautiful in herself. Falsehood was depicted as a heavily costumed woman, because she needs artificial decorations to make her lies attractive, and underneath the false front is ugliness.

Growing in thinking skills is part of spiritual maturity, and it protects us from the strategies of those who would harm our faith:

As a result, we are no longer to be children, tossed here and there by waves and carried about by every wind of doctrine, by the trickery of men, by craftiness in deceitful scheming; but speaking the truth in love, we are to grow up in all aspects into Him who is the head, even Christ.
— Ephesians 4:14-15

Only if we develop our thinking ability can we make an effective witness:

But sanctify Christ as Lord in your hearts, always being ready to make a defense to everyone who asks you

to give an account for the hope that is in you, yet with gentleness and reverence.
— 1 Peter 3:15

A1.2 SCRIPTURES ON THE IMPORTANCE OF TRUTH

In a postmodern era, where truth itself is not just called into question but virtually denied objective status, it is important to reaffirm that truth does exist and can be known, especially in the case of God's truth. If we tell ourselves to pay attention, we can find in a surprising number of places Scriptural references and teachings about truth, its importance, and its connection to God.

The Psalms are filled with the connection between God and truth, and of the necessity of having the objective truth about living.

Lovingkindness provides an emotional and physical blessing, while truth provides the intellectual confidence in God that we need in order to be preserved.

You, O LORD, will not withhold Your compassion from me; Your lovingkindness and Your truth will continually preserve me.
— Psalm 40:11

Truth provides an objective standard that can be relied on for guidance through any time and any season. Truth is a light that will lead us to God's holy hill. Hence, the saying, "the light of truth."

O send out Your light and Your truth, let them lead me; let them bring me to Your holy hill and to Your dwelling places.
— Psalm 43:3

Truth must be a focused goal because so many are interested in error, distortion, or their own fabricated stories. We live in a culture where people speak of "narratives" rather than "true accounts," because many do not believe in truth any longer. We must fight for the cause:

> And in Your majesty ride on victoriously, for the cause
> of truth and meekness and righteousness.
> —Psalm 45:4a

God wants truth, not something that pleases us to believe:

> Behold, You desire truth in the innermost being, and in
> the hidden part You will make me know wisdom.
> —Psalm 51:6

Truth is a preserver (of one's integrity, self-respect, life, sanity, health. . . .):

> He will abide before God forever; appoint lovingkind-
> ness and truth that they may preserve him.
> —Psalm 61:7

Truth has the power to save us from the errors of our ways:

> But as for me, my prayer is to You, O LORD, at an ac-
> ceptable time; O God, in the greatness of Your loving-
> kindness, answer me with Your saving truth.
> —Psalm 69:13

> I will also praise You with a harp, even Your truth, O
> my God; to You I will sing praises with the lyre, O Ho-
> ly One of Israel.
> —Psalm 71:22

Our standard of behavior, our objective rulebook, is preserved in the teachings of the Bible:

> Teach me Your way, O LORD; I will walk in Your truth; unite my heart to fear Your name.
> — Psalm 86:11

Truth is not a temporal, temporary idea. God's truth reaches across the cosmos:

> For Your lovingkindness is great above the heavens, And Your truth reaches to the skies.
> — Psalm 108:4

> The works of His hands are truth and justice; all His precepts are sure.
> — Psalm 111:7

> Not to us, O LORD, not to us, but to Your name give glory because of Your lovingkindness, because of Your truth.
> — Psalm 115:1

Our lives can be reasonable and wise because we have an unchanging, objective standard for our behavior towards others and for the rules of living. God's truth does not change the way cultural values do:

> For His lovingkindness is great toward us, and the truth of the LORD is everlasting. Praise the LORD!
> — Psalm 117:2

> Your righteousness is an everlasting righteousness, and Your law is truth.
> — Psalm 119:142

You are near, O LORD, and all Your commandments are truth.

— Psalm 119:151

The sum of Your word is truth, and every one of Your righteous ordinances is everlasting.

— Psalm 119:160

I will bow down toward Your holy temple and give thanks to Your name for Your lovingkindness and Your truth; for You have magnified Your word according to all Your name.

— Psalm 138:2

The LORD is near to all who call upon Him, to all who call upon Him in truth.

— Psalm 145:18

Of course, the Psalms are not the only place we can read about how much God values the truth:

Do not let kindness and truth leave you; bind them around your neck; write them on the tablet of your heart.

— Proverbs 3:3

For my mouth will utter truth; and wickedness is an abomination to my lips.

— Proverbs 8:7

He who speaks truth tells what is right, but a false witness, deceit.

— Proverbs 12:17

Will they not go astray who devise evil? But kindness and truth will be to those who devise good.

— Proverbs 14:22

Loyalty and truth preserve the king, and he upholds his throne by righteousness.

— Proverbs 20:28

Buy truth, and do not sell it; get wisdom and instruction and understanding.

— Proverbs 23:23

Many other Old Testament books also prominently value the truth as it is delivered by God and spoken among men.

The Preacher sought to find delightful words and to write words of truth correctly.

— Ecclesiastes 12:10

Those who err in mind will know the truth, and those who criticize will accept instruction.

— Isaiah 29:24

The mind of the hasty will discern the truth, and the tongue of the stammerers will hasten to speak clearly.

— Isaiah 32:4

These are the things which you should do: speak the truth to one another; judge with truth and judgment for peace in your gates.

— Zechariah 8:16

In the New Testament, John is particularly fond of reminding us that Jesus and the Truth are One.

And the Word became flesh, and dwelt among us, and we saw His glory, glory as of the only begotten from the Father, full of grace and truth.

— John 1:14

For the Law was given through Moses; grace and truth were realized through Jesus Christ.
—John 1:17

But he who practices the truth comes to the Light, so that his deeds may be manifested as having been wrought in God.
—John 3:21

But an hour is coming, and now is, when the true worshipers will worship the Father in spirit and truth; for such people the Father seeks to be His worshipers.
—John 4:23

God is spirit, and those who worship Him must worship in spirit and truth.
—John 4:24

. . . And you will know the truth, and the truth will make you free.
—John 8:32

But because I speak the truth, you do not believe Me.
—John 8:45

Jesus said to him, "I am the way, and the truth, and the life; no one comes to the Father but through Me."
—John 14:6

When the Helper comes, whom I will send to you from the Father, that is the Spirit of truth who proceeds from the Father, He will testify about Me. . . .
—John 15:26

But when He, the Spirit of truth, comes, He will guide you into all the truth; for He will not speak on His own

initiative, but whatever He hears, He will speak; and
He will disclose to you what is to come.
—John 16:13

Sanctify them in the truth; Your word is truth.
—John 17:17

For their sakes I sanctify Myself, that they themselves
also may be sanctified in truth.
—John 17:19

Paul, too, in his epistles to the churches, keeps reminding the church of the critical importance of possessing the
truth. Christianity is not something just made up. Truth is
at its core.

We are warned that some will know the truth, but will
suppress it because they prefer error:

For the wrath of God is revealed from heaven against
all ungodliness and unrighteousness of men who suppress the truth in unrighteousness.
—Romans 1:18

In order to keep God out of their lives and out of the
world, some people deny God by creating a false view of
reality, supported by myths of their own making:

For they exchanged the truth of God for a lie, and wor-
shiped and served the creature rather than the Creator,
who is blessed forever. Amen.
—Romans 1:25

Therefore let us celebrate the feast, not with old leaven,
nor with the leaven of malice and wickedness, but with
the unleavened bread of sincerity and truth.
—1 Corinthians 5:8

[Love] does not rejoice in unrighteousness, but rejoices with the truth.
—1 Corinthians 13:6

But we have renounced the things hidden because of shame, not walking in craftiness or adulterating the word of God, but by the manifestation of truth commending ourselves to every man's conscience in the sight of God.
—2 Corinthians 4:2

For we can do nothing against the truth, but only for the truth.
—2 Corinthians 13:8

Truth must be the common coin of communication with all people:

Therefore, laying aside falsehood, speak truth each one of you with his neighbor, for we are members of one another.
—Ephesians 4:25

Knowing, telling, and doing the truth is the fruit produced by those leaving darkness and coming into the light:

For the fruit of the Light consists in all goodness and righteousness and truth.
—Ephesians 5:9

Truth, in fact, is our defensive armor in the spiritual and intellectual battles we fight:

Stand firm therefore, having girded your loins with truth. . . .
—Ephesians 6:14a

God wants everyone to know the truth:

> Who desires all men to be saved and to come to the knowledge of the truth.
> —1 Timothy 2:4

We find the truth in the word, just as we find the Truth in the Word:

> Sanctify them in the truth; your word is truth.
> —John 17:17

> Be diligent to present yourself approved to God as a workman who does not need to be ashamed, accurately handling the word of truth.
> —2 Timothy 2:15

> In the beginning was the Word.
> —John 1:1a

> And the Word became flesh . . . full of grace and truth.
> —John 1:14

> Jesus said to him, "I am the way, and the truth, and the life. . . ."
> —John 14:6a

> It is the Spirit who testifies, because the Spirit is the truth.
> —1 John 5:6

Just from this partial selection of Scriptures and comments about truth, it is evident how much importance God gives to the idea. He wants us to have a genuine, accurate view of reality, both physical and spiritual. Knowing the truth about God and knowing the truth about ourselves are both essential if we are to live free, satisfying, and joyous lives.

A1.3 SCRIPTURES RELATED TO REASON

God is a God of reason, and he wants his creatures, created in his image, to use reason also. Reason and faith are allies, not opponents, in spite of what the secular modern world claims.

> You shall not hate your brother in your heart, but you shall reason frankly with your neighbor, lest you incur sin because of him.
> — Leviticus 19:17

> "Come now, let us reason together," says the LORD: "though your sins are like scarlet, they shall be as white as snow; though they are red like crimson, they shall become like wool."
> — Isaiah 1:18

> And Paul went in, as was his custom, and on three Sabbath days he reasoned with them from the Scriptures.
> — Acts 17:2

> So he reasoned in the synagogue with the Jews and the devout persons, and in the marketplace every day with those who happened to be there.
> — Acts 17:17

> And he reasoned in the synagogue every Sabbath, and tried to persuade Jews and Greeks.
> — Acts 18:4

When I was a child, I spoke like a child, I thought like a
child, I reasoned like a child. When I became a man, I
gave up childish ways.
— 1 Corinthians 13:11

But the wisdom from above is first pure, then peaceable, gentle, reasonable, full of mercy and good fruits,
unwavering, without hypocrisy.
— James 3:17

A1.4 THE BIBLE AND KNOWLEDGE AND WISDOM

The philosophers' definition of knowledge is "properly
justified true belief." True belief comes from God, and
with his help we convert that into new knowledge. Biblical
knowledge is our touchstone, against which all knowledge
claims are tested. Wisdom is so frequently associated with
knowledge because wisdom is dependent on knowledge
for it to work.

The fear of the LORD is the beginning of wisdom; a
good understanding have all those who do His commandments; His praise endures forever.
— Psalm 111:10

Wisdom and knowledge are (1) learned and (2) learned
with the help of the Lord. Hence, Christian higher education is one answer to this Psalm:

Teach me good discernment and knowledge, for I believe in Your commandments.
— Psalm 119:66

The fear of the LORD is the beginning of knowledge.
— Proverbs 1:7a

Then you will discern the fear of the LORD and discover the knowledge of God.
— Proverbs 2:5

The mouth of the Lord is the word he has spoken to us in the Bible. So Scripture is a source of knowledge and understanding:

For the LORD gives wisdom; from His mouth come knowledge and understanding.
— Proverbs 2:6

For wisdom will enter your heart and knowledge will be pleasant to your soul.
— Proverbs 2:10

Take my instruction and not silver, and knowledge rather than choicest gold.
— Proverbs 8:10

The fear of the LORD is the beginning of wisdom, and the knowledge of the Holy One is understanding.
— Proverbs 9:10

With his mouth the godless man destroys his neighbor, but through knowledge the righteous will be delivered.
— Proverbs 11:9

Those who refuse to acknowledge God simply cannot gain the fullness of wisdom that knowing the Holy One and his word can provide:

A scoffer seeks wisdom and finds none, but knowledge is easy to one who has understanding.
— Proverbs 14:6

The mind of the prudent acquires knowledge, and the ear of the wise seeks knowledge.
— Proverbs 18:15

Also it is not good for a person to be without knowledge, and he who hurries his footsteps errs.
— Proverbs 19:2

Strike a scoffer and the naive may become shrewd, but reprove one who has understanding and he will gain knowledge.
— Proverbs 19:25

There is gold, and an abundance of jewels; but the lips of knowledge are a more precious thing.
— Proverbs 20:15

Incline your ear and hear the words of the wise, and apply your mind to my knowledge.
— Proverbs 22:17

Apply your heart to discipline and your ears to words of knowledge.
— Proverbs 23:12

It is He who changes the times and the epochs; He removes kings and establishes kings; He gives wisdom to wise men and knowledge to men of understanding.
— Daniel 2:21

My people are destroyed for lack of knowledge.
— Hosea 4:6a

For I delight in loyalty rather than sacrifice, and in the knowledge of God rather than burnt offerings.
— Hosea 6:6

Oh, the depth of the riches both of the wisdom and knowledge of God!
— Romans 11:33a

For God, who said, "Light shall shine out of darkness," is the One who has shone in our hearts to give the Light of the knowledge of the glory of God in the face of Christ.
— 2 Corinthians 4:6

O Timothy, guard what has been entrusted to you, avoiding worldly and empty chatter and the opposing arguments of what is falsely called "knowledge"--
— 1 Timothy 6:20

We feel sorry for our secular colleagues, who have committed themselves to a worldview that limits their exploratory and explanatory power, leaving them

always learning and never able to come to the knowledge of the truth.
— 2 Timothy 3:7

A1.5 WISDOM

Wisdom might be defined as the ability to use knowledge appropriately to make good decisions. Wisdom involves the discernment to know how to apply what portion of knowledge and when.

The mouth of the righteous utters wisdom, and his tongue speaks justice.
— Psalm 37:30

My mouth will speak wisdom, and the meditation of my heart will be understanding.
— Psalm 49:3

Behold, You desire truth in the innermost being, and in the hidden part You will make me know wisdom.
— Psalm 51:6

So teach us to number our days, that we may present to You a heart of wisdom.
— Psalm 90:12

O LORD, how many are Your works! In wisdom You have made them all; the earth is full of Your possessions.
— Psalm 104:24

The fear of the LORD is the beginning of wisdom; A good understanding have all those who do His commandments; His praise endures forever.
— Psalm 111:10

Make your ear attentive to wisdom, incline your heart to understanding.
— Proverbs 2:2

For the LORD gives wisdom; from His mouth come knowledge and understanding.
— Proverbs 2:6

He stores up sound wisdom for the upright; He is a shield to those who walk in integrity,
— Proverbs 2:7

For wisdom will enter your heart and knowledge will be pleasant to your soul;
— Proverbs 2:10

A1.6 UNDERSTANDING

Understanding implies a knowledge of how things work—the big picture. A person of understanding knows not only how to, let's say, mix up a batch of chemicals to get shampoo, but he or she knows why it is done that way.

> Give me understanding, that I may observe Your law and keep it with all my heart.
> — Psalm 119:34

> Teach me good discernment and knowledge, for I believe in Your commandments.
> — Psalm 119:66

> Your testimonies are righteous forever; give me understanding that I may live.
> — Psalm 119:144

> How blessed is the man who finds wisdom and the man who gains understanding.
> — Proverbs 3:13

> My son, let them not vanish from your sight; keep sound wisdom and discretion.
> — Proverbs 3:21

> Acquire wisdom! Acquire understanding! Do not forget nor turn away from the words of my mouth.
> — Proverbs 4:5

Again, wisdom helps us make the right decision, while understanding lets us know why:

> The beginning of wisdom is: Acquire wisdom; and with all your acquiring, get understanding.
> — Proverbs 4:7

> My son, give attention to my wisdom, incline your ear to my understanding.
> — Proverbs 5:1

Say to wisdom, "You are my sister," and call understanding your intimate friend.
— Proverbs 7:4

Does not wisdom call, and understanding lift up her
voice?
— Proverbs 8:1

For wisdom is better than jewels; and all desirable
things cannot compare with her.
— Proverbs 8:11

I, wisdom, dwell with prudence, and I find knowledge
and discretion.
— Proverbs 8:12

The fear of the LORD is the beginning of wisdom, and
the knowledge of the Holy One is understanding.
— Proverbs 9:10

On the lips of the discerning, wisdom is found.
— Proverbs 10:13a

The mouth of the righteous flows with wisdom, but the
perverted tongue will be cut out.
— Proverbs 10:31

A scoffer seeks wisdom and finds none, but knowledge
is easy to one who has understanding.
— Proverbs 14:6

Those who reject God, and his truth, turn away from
wisdom and honesty and embrace falsehood and deceit:

The wisdom of the sensible is to understand his way,
but the foolishness of fools is deceit.
— Proverbs 14:8

Wisdom does not need to dress in layer after layer of words. It can come to us simply and directly:

The words of a man's mouth are deep waters; the fountain of wisdom is a bubbling brook.
— Proverbs 18:4

He who gets wisdom loves his own soul; he who keeps understanding will find good.
— Proverbs 19:8

Buy truth, and do not sell it, get wisdom and instruction and understanding.
— Proverbs 23:23

By wisdom a house is built, and by understanding it is established.
— Proverbs 24:3

Conduct yourselves with wisdom toward outsiders, making the most of the opportunity.
— Colossians 4:5

But if any of you lacks wisdom, let him ask of God, who gives to all generously and without reproach, and it will be given to him.
— James 1:5

Who among you is wise and understanding? Let him show by his good behavior his deeds in the gentleness of wisdom.
— James 3:13

But the wisdom from above is first pure, then peaceable, gentle, reasonable, full of mercy and good fruits, unwavering, without hypocrisy.
— James 3:17

A2

APPENDIX 2: ADVANCING INTEGRATION AT THE UNIVERSITY

The founders of theories and movements learned long ago that the way to advance their ideas is to share them constantly, widely, and confidently. Those who want to advance the practice of faith-learning integration, and the Christian worldview's impact on scholarly work and the academic disciplines, including the forwarding of new theoretical approaches grounded in Biblical truth and Christian knowledge, must follow suit and use the many information channels available to them.

This appendix offers some suggestions for broadcasting the good news of Christian scholarship. Importantly, none of them require massive budgets either to start or to maintain. All can be implemented wherever there is sufficient intentionality. Lasting commitment (and a few dollars) can produce soaring results at any institution, together with international impact.

Most Christian colleges and universities, in their promotional materials, assert that one of the benefits of attending their institution is that students will experience the integration of faith and learning (or sometimes faith, learning, and living). Now that accrediting associations are increasingly emphasizing the need for colleges and universities to demonstrate that they practice what they advertise, these suggestions have the added bonus of evidencing that you are doing what you say you do.

Having said all this, and in consideration of the ideas that follow in this appendix, the foremost issue that needs to be formally addressed and resolved is the buy-in or commitment to a faith-and-learning culture. Administrators, faculty, and staff must all agree that interconnecting the Christian faith with every subject and course is the desired goal.

A2.1 Internal Faculty Development

The first steps toward a lively faith-learning integration culture is to provide new and existing faculty with the knowledge, skills, and resources necessary.

A2.1.1 Train new faculty

As we noted earlier, most new faculty earn their graduate degrees at secular universities, often in environments unsupportive of — if not overtly hostile to — Christian faith. They spend years studying subject matter that ignores their faith and instead promotes secularist content, interpretations, theoretical bases, and worldviews. So when they arrive at a Christian institution to teach, they have no idea about integration. Who can blame them for teaching the same content they were taught, with little connection to faith matters?

The first step in advancing integration, then, is to provide new faculty with inservice training in integrative practices. Training could be formal (online or classroom course) or informal (assignments to be completed under the supervision of a mentor).

Here are some possibilities:

- Assign several books relating to the integration of faith and learning to be read and discussed or reported on.
- Assign an integrative essay in which the faculty member explains the connection between Christian knowledge and the content of his or her discipline,

identifying commonalities and conflicts or tensions. The essay should explain how the faculty member expects to address or resolve these areas of disharmony.

- Have the faculty member create a syllabus for each course to be taught, building in appropriate integrative practices. The course facilitator or mentor can then evaluate and comment on the result.

A2.1.2 PROVIDE FACULTY DEVELOPMENT

At least once a year, convene all faculty for a day or two and cover integrative practices.

- Share best practices
- Share success stories
- Use group discussion to address problem areas
- Read and discuss general articles or books on the topic
- Divide into departments to discuss common practices within each discipline, and then report out to the faculty as a whole
- Invite outside speakers to present fresh approaches or new ideas

A2.1.3 EXPAND LIBRARY RESOURCES

In a high traffic area of the library, develop a special collection or a visible section (with display) on integration, available and promoted to both students and faculty, containing books about faith and learning.

A faith-learning integration budget should be established, perhaps funded through a special grant, so that the section can continue to grow with new books and so that it can be promoted with flyers and posters.

Creative promotions could be used to encourage the use of the resources. For example, a Faith-Learning Integration week could be held each term with flyers, emails, posters, and announcements in chapel services. Faculty could assign book reviews.

See Appendix 3 for a list of resources to begin with.

A2.1.4 START AN INTEGRATION NEWSLETTER

Have the academic dean send out a faith-learning integration newsletter each week or two, highlighting books, articles, Web sites, problems and solutions, ideas, upcoming conferences, and so on. Send these to all faculty and staff. Make it clear that faculty are expected to contribute

- news of relevant new books in their discipline
- short articles with suggestions or "what worked for me" stories
- summaries of conference sessions attended about integration
- book and article reviews and summaries (in an era where too much information is a problem, your colleagues would appreciate summaries of significant works)

All of these practices are not just about training. They are about enculturation into the mindset of a Christian university professor. Expect culture shock and allow some time for what might be gradual change. Of course, prospective new faculty must be apprised of the institution's goals and required integrative practices, so that those who are eager and bold enough to participate can be preferred.

A2.2 EXTERNAL ADVANCEMENT

You can't change the world by talking only to each other. The opportunity to reach others has never been better—easier, cheaper, and more powerful—than it is now for those who want to spread their ideas across the world. No faculty member or university needs to feel isolated now that the world is electronically connected to such an extent. And the "old fashioned" ways of sharing and collaborating still work, too.

A2.2.1 ADD AN INTEGRATION SECTION TO YOUR WEB SITE

As you are certainly aware, the Web is the go-to place of first resort when a question arises about nearly anything. Here's a first opportunity to share the institution's growing integrative experience.

Use a special section of your institutional Web site to mount

- articles and ideas from everyone (faculty, staff, administration)
- outstanding student papers relevant to the subject
- bibliographies
- links to content on other Web sites—a very powerful feature

A2.2.2 ORGANIZE CONFERENCES ON INTEGRATION

Departments could organize colloquia in their own discipline, or the university could organize general conferences with discipline-specific or topic-specific breakout sessions. The conferences could be national, or to make it easier and less expensive to participate, regional or even local, where relatively nearby institutions could participate. Conferences offer faculty the opportunity to focus on integrative ideas, share them, and get credit for scholarly activity. Conference papers can be printed or posted online to make them widely available.

And remember that video conferencing using Skype or Google Hangout can make international speakers and participants possible with very little cost.

A2.2.3 START AN ONLINE JOURNAL

Like-minded faculty need a place to share their work. The journal could be (1) discipline specific, featuring articles integrating faith with particular subject matter, (2) general, featuring articles connecting faith with any discipline, or (3) theoretical, where the nature, practice, and process of connecting faith with academic areas is discussed. Naturally, book reviews, notices of conferences, letters to the editor and even job postings could all be included.

Benefits: Such a platform would give faculty an opportunity to publish articles that are not likely to find a welcome outlet elsewhere. And publishing online is not only inexpensive, but the ideas can be released faster (no months-long waits for printing and mailing). Costs do not limit the size of an issue, so you don't need to delay or reject a good article simply because the issue is full. And if the journal is open for reading—no paid subscription required—then the ideas are available to a much wider audience.

What about prestige, you ask? Would a new journal on integrative practices in, say, history get any respect from colleagues in the discipline at large? My answer is, first, respect is earned. The quality of the articles will determine the degree of respect gained. Some academics will always scorn such a journal simply because it involves Christian faith. Second, there is a difference between respect and influence. If the journal is influential and its ideas have impact, it should be counted successful regardless of what its detractors say about it.

There are more than 25,000 peer-reviewed, scholarly journals, many of them available free online. They cover a huge range of subjects and promote many viewpoints, so there's no reason to be shy about joining the great conversation.

Examples: *The Journal of Biblical Integration in Business, The Journal of Psychology and Theology.*

A2.2.4 START A UNIVERSITY OR COLLEGE PRESS

Another inexpensive but powerful way to advance the integration of faith and learning by the college or university as a whole is to publish scholarly books about integrating faith and disciplinary knowledge (and other topics, too).

CreateSpace. A service such as CreateSpace enables publishing books in both Kindle and print formats, which are then made available via Amazon and other outlets.

Because the service is either electronic (Kindle) or print on demand, there is no expense for a press run and no cost for inventory storage. There are no sign-up or up-front fees. The college or university does the typescript, proofreading and editing, and conversion of the book to a pdf. Cover design has several options, including free.

Moreover, because all sales are handled through Amazon, no staff is needed for processing orders.

The only costs are editorial staff time and the purchase of an International Standard Book Number (ISBN) for each book, available from Bowker.

A2.2.5 START AN INSTITUTE

Whether with endowment funds or as part of the university's general budgeting, a cross-disciplinary Institute for Integration Studies could serve all faculty both inside and outside the university. Institutes can sponsor colloquia, invite speakers, sponsor journals, support visiting scholars, coordinate joint research or theoretical activities, and facilitate many other kinds of scholarly engagements.

A2.2.6 WRITE A TEXTBOOK

Not satisfied with the ideological bias of the textbook you use? Why not write your own? By yourself or with the help of colleagues in your academic area, write a textbook presenting the subject from a Christian worldview. Critique the reigning paradigms, retaining and underscoring what is valuable in them while exposing questionable assumptions, correcting errors, and supplementing partial accounts.

One of the great benefits of writing a textbook that integrates faith and learning—or that focuses on the Christian worldview—is that it must include serious discussions of the worldviews and theories that dominate the discipline, as well as include the Christian theory or perspective. Thus, students get a much fuller treatment of the discipline's ideas, together with their overall context.

A2.2.7 WRITE A SCHOLARLY BOOK

As has been suggested in several places in this book, there is an open world for Christian scholars to contribute to the Great Conversation by writing books that renew, reform, regenerate, and review topics in every faculty member's chosen field. Topics of interest to Christians have been mostly neglected by non-Christian scholars, or else they have been treated unfairly or off-handedly.

A2.3 STUDENT DEVELOPMENT

Faculty work at a college or university only in part to pursue scholarship. Much of their role is to teach students. And the faith-learning enterprise is the same. That's why this book, aimed primarily at helping faculty to integrate their faith and learning, also has so much focus on teaching students to do the same.

Here, then, are a few global ideas for advancing the integrative practices at the student level.

A2.3.1 DEVELOP A SUPPORTIVE CORE CURRICULUM

Chapter 3 covered the foundational skills and knowledge that students need in order to perform integrative tasks successfully. Creating a core curriculum (also called general education requirements) that will support these needs is an important step toward building an effective culture where integration is viewed as a normal part of higher education.

These courses or subjects are essential components of a Christian university education and should be part of the required core:

- **Biblical knowledge.** Old and New Testament surveys are already requirements at many Christian colleges and universities. A thorough, deep familiarity and understanding of Scripture is absolutely necessary for every educated Christian.

- **Hermeneutics.** Biblical interpretation instruction might be connected to Bible survey courses, or a separate course could be taught. Interpretive skills are as important as Biblical knowledge because wrongly interpreted Scripture isn't Biblical knowledge. As the proverb says, "The central work of life is interpretation."

- **Critical thinking.** This course would include the study of the principles of analysis, argumentation, evaluation, inductive and deductive thinking, and decision making, together with a knowledge of logical fallacies, cognitive biases, and the many ways of manipulating ideas (disinformation, selection, slanting), and a bit of semantics and semiotics. (See Section 3.6 for additional details.)

- **Integrative techniques.** Students aren't any more familiar with the task of faith-learning integration than are some new faculty, so they need training, too. Many colleges and universities have a Freshman orientation course covering study skills and expectations. Some of these courses are only one or two units because there is not much content to them. Adding some robust training in integrative techniques would add value, substance, and interest to these courses.

- **Worldview awareness.** It need not be an individual course, but in some context students need to be delivered from the naïve approach to the world of information they too often possess. This naïve approach I describe as the acceptance of "knowledge as found," taking in and crediting whatever the student reads or hears without concern about the quality or reliability of the source, including the framing and filtering beliefs of the source.

A2.3.2 CHAPEL

Institutions that have regular chapel services for students can dedicate several sessions each term to host speakers on general worldview, integration, and apologetics topics. A scholar from outside the community could present his or her work to exemplify the process of faith-learning integration.

A2.3.3 PROMOTIONS

We live in the attention economy, where what gets done is what is attended to and what is attended to is what is advertised, promoted, featured, shared, and marketed. To encourage students to continue to think about and engage in integrative activities, the institution should design culture enhancement campaigns, with posters, flyers, contests (essay contests?), and other means of getting attention and maintaining focus.

If anyone objects to this idea, ask that person why Coca Cola advertises. Is it to reach people who have never heard of Coca Cola? ("Coca Cola? What is that? Some kind of soft drink? Maybe I should try it sometime.") Coca Cola advertises to keep the brand name alive amidst the information noise (also known as data smog) that threatens to drown out everything. Getting and keeping attention, maintaining intentionality, is the key. To coin a cliché, "It pays to advertise."

A3

APPENDIX 3: RESOURCES

This appendix supplies a list of books offering more information about the integration of faith and learning and related topics.

Berlinski, David. *The Devil's Delusion: Atheism and Its Scientific Pretentions.* New York: Basic Books, 2009.

Claerbaut, David. *Faith and Learning on the Edge: A Bold New Look at Religion in Higher Education.* Grand Rapids, MI: Zondervan, 2004.
Includes chapters on many disciplinary areas.

Cosgrove, Mark P. *Foundations of Christian Thought: Faith, Learning, and the Christian Worldview.* Grand Rapids, MI: Kregel Publications, 2006.

Dockery, David S., Ed. *Faith and Learning: A Handbook for Christian Higher Education.* Nashville, TN: B&H Academic, 2012.
Includes foundational chapters as well as chapters on many disciplinary areas.

Dockery, David S. *Renewing Minds: Serving Church and Society Through Christian Higher Education.* Revised ed., Nashville, TN: B&H Books, 2008.

Dockery, David S. and Gregory Alan Thornbury, eds. *Shaping a Christian Worldview: The Foundations of Christian Higher Education*. Nashville: Broadman and Holman, 2002.
This collection of essays contains pieces on many individual disciplinary areas in addition to general overviews of integrative issues. 400 pages plus notes.

Dockery, David. "A Bibliography for the Integration of Faith and Learning" (Fall 2007). https://www.uu.edu/ dockery/ FaithLearnBooklet_Fa07.pdf.
Includes 36 pages of resources.

Eaton, Philip. *Engaging the Culture, Changing the World: The Christian University in a Post-Christian World*. Downers Grove, IL: InterVarsity Academic, 2011.

Gaebelein, Frank. *The Pattern of God's Truth: The Integration of Faith and Learning*. Winona Lake, IN: BMH Books, 1985.

Harris, Robert. *The Integration of Faith and Learning: A Worldview Approach*. Eugene, OR: Cascade Books, 2004.
This is my first book on integration, designed for students, especially those attending secular colleges and universities.

Heie, Harold and David L. Wolfe, eds. *The Reality of Christian Learning: Strategies for Faith-Discipline Integration*. 1984, rpt. Eugene, OR: Wipf & Stock, 2004.

Litfin, Duane. *Conceiving the Christian College*. Grand Rapids, MI: William B. Eerdmans, 2004.

Nash, Ronald H. *Worldviews in Conflict: Choosing Christianity in a World of Ideas.* Grand Rapids, MI: Zondervan, 1992.

Sampson, Philip J. *6 Modern Myths about Christianity & Western Civilization.* Downers Grove, IL: InterVarsity Press, 2001.

Smith, Christian, ed. *The Secular Revolution: Power, Interests, and Conflict in the Secularization of American Public Life.* Berkeley: University of California Press, 2003.
This important and fascinating collection of essays reveals that America didn't just happen to grow secular gradually. The secularization was a deliberate effort on the part of those who influenced public knowledge.

Sterk, Andrea, Ed. *Religion, Scholarship, and Higher Education: Perspectives, Models, and Future Prospects.* Notre Dame, IN: University of Notre Dame Press, 2002.
This collection of essays on higher education and religion covers the spectrum of opinion, from "Teaching History as a Christian" to "Enough Already: Universities Do Not Need More Christianity."

Virkler, Henry A. and Karelynne Gerber-Avayo. *Hermeneutics: Principles and Processes of Biblical Interpretation.* 2nd Ed. Nashville, TN: Baker Academic, 2007.

Notes

A4

APPENDIX 4: THE FACT/VALUE DICHOTOMY

The direction in intellectual history since the Enlightenment has been to grant to science the authority to pronounce what is real, true, objective, and rational, while relegating ethics and religion to the realm of subjective opinion and nonrational experience.

Once this definition of knowledge is conceded, then any position that appears to be backed by science will ultimately triumph in the public square over any position that appears based on ethics or religion.

         — Nancy Pearcey[135]

Traditional beliefs and institutions do not have to be annihilated; it is sufficient to drain them of their ancient meanings and fill them with others — particularly if they are reduced to the realm of the subjective and therefore private, of "values" that cannot be "imposed" on others.

         — James Hitchcock[136]

---

[135] Nancy Pearcey, "A New Foundation for Positive Cultural Change: Science and God in the Public Square." *Human Events*, Sept. 15, 2000. Reprinted on the Web at www.leaderu.com/orgs/arn/pearcey/np_hewedgereview091200.htm.

[136] James Hitchcock, "Supremely Modern Liberals: The Unhappy and Abusive Marriage of Liberalism and Modernism," *Touchstone* 17:4 (May 2004), p. 22.

Appendix Overview

One of the objections made by secular academics to the incorporation of Christian truth into disciplinary learning is that facts should be separated from values. Only facts belong in the domain of science. This appendix provides an extended discussion of the inextricable interrelationship between facts and values, demonstrating that the separation of the two is impossible.

A4.1 CONCEPT CONTROL

One of the most significant struggles in the marketplace of ideas takes place over the control of the terms of discourse. Those who can frame a controversial issue in terms they prefer have a great advantage in shaping public opinion. "Are you pro-choice or anti-choice?" is a typical example of this kind of framing. Concept control might be thought of as rigging the debate: You must talk about this controversial issue using my categories, terms, and definitions. As a result, those who have the power to declare the terms of discourse have the power to determine the outcome of the debate, and further, they have the power to determine what is accepted as true or false.

The fact/value dichotomy is a doctrine that arose out of a supreme attempt at concept control. Beginning in the eighteenth century, some of the Enlightenment thinkers declared that values (such as moral obligations) could not be derived from facts. Howard Kendler says,

> The naturalistic fallacy rejects the possibility of deducing ethical statements from non-ethical statements. This principle, more precisely described as the fact/value dichotomy, denies the possibility of logically deriving what *ought* to be from what *is*.[137]

---

[137] Howard H. Kendler, "Psychology and Ethics: Interactions and Conflicts," *Philosophical Psychology* 15:4 (2002), p. 490.

For example, the fact that people in educated countries tended to live better than people in countries where education was rare did not imply and could not imply that education was good or that education ought to be made a public policy choice. Such a claim was a value choice.

In the twentieth century a group of scientists turned philosophers, known as the logical positivists, took the idea of a fact/value dichotomy even further. Perhaps they were troubled by the continued talk about God and religion and morality in the midst of our "scientific world." Or perhaps they simply wanted to define out of existence ideas that opposed their ideas. At any rate, they developed a philosophy that not only emphasized the dichotomy but that held only the "fact" disjunction to be of any worth. As Ernest R. House notes,

> The logical positivists thought that facts could be ascertained and that only facts were the fit subject of science, along with analytic statements like "1 plus 1 equals 2" that were true by definition. Facts were empirical and could be based on pristine observations, a position called foundationalism.
>
> On the other hand, values were something else. Values might be feelings, emotions, or useless metaphysical entities. Whatever they were, they were not subject to scientific analysis. People simply held certain values or believed in certain values or did not. Values were chosen. Rational discussion had little to do with them.[138]

The positivists declared that only facts, derived from experiment and observation, could be called truth, and they rejected all talk about values (including questions or asser-

---

[138] Ernest R House, "Unfinished Business: Causes and Values." *American Journal of Evaluation* 22:3, p. 313.

tions involving ethics, morals, religion, and philosophy) not only as "preferences without foundation"[139] but as meaningless or "non-cognitive" babble. Values were thus depreciated as mere matters of taste and as not subject to rational or objective discussion. To ask whether it is wrong to lie or steal was equivalent to asking whether one prefers chocolate or vanilla ice cream: the answer was just matter of personal taste, ungrounded in any truth or reality because there was no experiment that could be performed to prove the truth of any answer.

As a philosophical movement, positivism died out after only a few years when other philosophers pointed out that positivism's foundational claim involved it in a self-referential absurdity:

> Obviously, if the only kinds of statements capable of meaning are synthetic statements [statements of observable fact], then the answer is going to be along the lines that a statement is meaningful when it is either directly confirmed by experience, or reducible to such direct confirmation. Such a criterion is itself not directly confirmable, and so the criterion of meaning renders itself meaningless.[140]

Positivism's claim that "only statements of observable facts have meaning" was a claim not subject to observation and thus, by its own definition, the claim had no meaning. Thus was the philosophical basis for positivism refuted. Unfortunately, the fact/value dichotomy did not die out with the philosophy. Indeed, positivistic ideas are still

---

[139] James R. Abbott, "Facts, Values, and Evaluative Explanation: Contributions of Leo Strauss to Contemporary Debates." *The American Sociologist* 32:1 (Spring 2001), p. 71.

[140] Alexei Angelides, "The Last Collapse? An Essay Review of Hilary Putnam's The Collapse of the Fact/Value Dichotomy and Other Essays." *Philosophy of Science* 71:3 (July 2004), p. 404.

quite prevalent among many scientists and these ideas have become pervasive in our culture, in part because they allow an easy and thoughtless rejection of value claims. In his book, *The Collapse of the Fact/Value Dichotomy*, philosopher Hilary Putnam observes:

> There are a variety of reasons why we are tempted to draw a line between "facts" and "values" — and to draw it in such a way that "values" are put outside the realm of rational argument altogether. For one thing, it is much easier to say "that's a value judgment," meaning, "that's just a matter of subjective preference," than to do what Socrates tried to teach us: to examine who we are and what our deepest convictions are and hold those convictions up to the searching test of reflective examination.[141]

Insisting on an absolute dichotomy between fact and value, then, becomes little more than a ploy to avoid involving values in scientific or other activity. However, the dichotomy does not remove values from existence or even from science (as we will see); it merely allows the dichotomist to avoid examining his own values rationally, or on the basis of how well or even whether they work. The dichotomist will not accept any so-called "value judgments" into the discussion when offered by a critic, and the dichotomist need not identify or evaluate his own values. Putnam concludes: "The worst thing about the fact/value dichotomy is that in practice it functions as a discussion-stopper, and not just a discussion-stopper, but a thought stopper."[142]

---

[141] Hilary Putnam, *The Collapse of the Fact/Value Dichotomy and Other Essays*, Cambridge, MA: Harvard University Press, 2002, pp. 43-44.
[142] Ibid., p. 44.

A4.2 ERRORS RESULTING FROM THE FACT/VALUE DICHOTOMY

In spite of the ease with which some people reject "value judgments" and insist on "just the facts," the fact/value dichotomy involves a cornucopia of errors. All of the following statements, derived from dichotomy thinking, are false:

1. Since facts and values are separate, with facts being solid and provable and values being matters of personal taste, values play no role in the realm of facts (that is, in science).
2. Values are not involved in the determination of what is a fact.
3. Values are not involved in scientific descriptions of fact.
4. Values are not intermixed in the statement of scientific theories or facts.
5. Values, being matters of personal taste, cannot be reasoned about.
6. Values are completely subjective and have no objective qualities.

If we explore each of these errors, we can see not only why they are, in fact, errors, but we will gain some better understanding about why the fact/value dichotomy does not represent reality accurately.

A4.3 VALUES ARE DEEPLY INVOLVED IN THE ARENA OF FACTS

The practice of science involves much more than the compilation of self-evident facts. Definitions of "true," "fact," "observation" and the like are derived from philosophical considerations, from the epistemology of science, and these "considerations" involve values. Even at the bare level of observation, Putnam says, "epistemic values guide us in pursuing right descriptions of the world."[143]

---

[143] Ibid., p. 32.

The entire operational structure of science—and of all knowledge production—involves the use of standards, which is another term for values. Quoting Richard T. Allen:

> Furthermore, every intellectual enquiry has to be guided by standards for sorting the true from the false, established facts from uncertain ones, interesting facts and problems from those which will tell us nothing new or significant, promising lines of enquiry from probable dead-ends, well conducted from ill-conducted enquiry. They are what R. G. Collingwood called *criteriological* activities, ones which are not only rightly or wrongly performed, but ones of which the performers as they go along necessarily judge the success or failure of their own performances. Being trained in them includes coming to appreciate and observe the standards employed.[144]

Allen concludes, "This, then, is the first breach of the fact-value dichotomy: that knowing itself involves the personal employment of standards, most implicitly, for judging what we know and whether we have succeeded or failed in knowing it."[145]

Physical chemist turned philosopher Michael Polanyi addresses the value-laden nature of the peer evaluation of scientific activity. Polanyi identifies the "standards of scientific merit accepted by the scientific community" as first, plausibility. Scientific journals engage in "censorship" in order to "eliminate obvious absurdities" and "refuse publication merely because the conclusions of a paper appear to be unsound in light of current scientific knowledge." If

---

[144] Richard T. Allen, "Polanyi's Overcoming of the Dichotomy of Fact and Value." Retrieved September 21, 2004 from www.kfki.hu/chemone/polanyi/9602/polanyi1.html.
[145] Ibid.

the results presented in a paper "conflict sharply with the current scientific opinion about the nature of things" the paper "may be totally disregarded" even if the author is "of high distinction in science."[146] Plausibility is obviously a complex judgment based on several value criteria, including fit, correspondence or harmonization, and reasonableness. Arguments or conclusions that lead away from preconceived or accepted ideas may be labeled pseudoscience, even though they are presented with robust evidence and rational methodology.

Polanyi continues by saying, "The second criterion by which the merit of a contribution is assessed may be described as its scientific value, a value that is composed of the following three coefficients: (a) its accuracy, (b) its systematic importance, (c) the intrinsic interest of its subject-matter."[147] While "accuracy" could be seen as an empirically supported concept, "importance" and "interest" are clearly valuative and possibly intersubjective. (Objective importance may be more often a conclusion of historical hindsight than an accurate judgment contemporary with the finding itself.)

Finally, Polanyi says that the "third criterion of scientific merit" is "originality."[148] This, too, involves personal or community values in its determination.

Hilary Putnam notes that "theory selection always presupposes values" (emphasis his)[149] and that in working with theories, "judgments of 'coherence,' 'plausibility,' 'reasonableness,' 'simplicity,' and of what Dirac famously called

[146] Michael Polanyi, "The Republic of Science: Its Political and Economic Theory." *Minerva* 1 (1962), pp. 54-74. Reprinted on the Web and Retrieved August 13, 2014 from
https://www.missouriwestern.edu/orgs/polanyi/mp-repsc.htm.
[147] Ibid.
[148] Ibid.
[149] Putnam, p. 31.

the beauty of a hypothesis, are all normative judgments . . . of 'what ought to be' in the case of reasoning."[150] Putnam later concludes, "In short, judgments of coherence, simplicity, and so on are presupposed by physical science. Yet coherence, simplicity, and the like are values."[151]

Values also come into play in the choice of theories. The concept of underdetermination is that the choice of a given theory to explain a set of facts is underdetermined by those facts. In other words, the facts do not compel the scientist to choose a given theory, because more than one theory will fit the same set of facts equally well. Regarding the choice of theory, Michael Dickson comments:

> It is sometimes suggested (sometimes overtly stated) that, given a set of physical phenomena, there are infinitely many ways to construct an underlying theory that predicts just those phenomena. I am willing to allow that in the purely logical sense, such constructions are possible. However, it is far more interesting to consider whether there are not criteria for a construction to be "reasonable."[152]

In other words, scientists do not proliferate a hundred theories for each data set and then say, "Any of these will explain what we've got." Instead, they apply value-based criteria that will permit them to determine whether or not a theory is "reasonable."

Values are also intimately involved in the working out of conflicts between theory and fact or theory and theory. Quoting Hilary Putnam again:

---

[150] Ibid., p. 31.
[151] Ibid., p. 142.
[152] Michael Dickson, "The Light at the End of the Tunneling: Observation and Underdetermination." *Philosophy of Science* 66:3 (September 1999), pp. S56-S57.

When a theory conflicts with what has previously
been supposed to be fact, we sometimes give up the
theory and we sometimes give up the supposed fact,
and . . . the decision is . . . a matter of informal judgments of coherence, plausibility, simplicity, and the
like. Nor is it the case that when two theories conflict,
scientists wait until the observational data decide between them. . . .[153]

Facing a conflict of theories in the absence of data that
will allow them to choose the definitively better one, Putnam says, scientists choose anyway, based on their value-
laden criteria:

Yet Einstein's theory [of gravitation] was accepted and
Whitehead's theory was rejected fifty years before anyone thought of an observation that would decide between the two. Indeed, a great number of theories must
be rejected on non-observational grounds, for the rule
"Test every theory that occurs to anyone" is impossible
to follow.[154]

Anyone who works with facts must constantly and
necessarily involve values in the process. Values are involved in the ordering and structuring of facts to give understanding or meaning to data. Without the values (or
standards or criteria) needed to evaluate, sort, and interpret facts, researchers would have only endless piles of
unexplained data. Far from being absent in the realm of
facts, values are necessary for the construction and operation of theory, processes, methodology, interpretation, observation, description, and evaluation. Even "the level of

---

[153] Putnam, p. 142.
[154] Ibid., p. 142.

evidence that is required to prove a hypothesis" is a value choice in science.[155]

The problem is not the presence of values in science. The problem is the persistence of this error: the claim that the arena of facts has nothing to do with the arena of values. Those who insist on this error still involve values in their work, but by denying that they do so, they are not likely to recognize the presence of values, not identify their assumptions, and not examine their values. The result can be that ideologues will "masquerade their views as science."[156] Conclusions will be based on hidden philosophical preferences rather than on the weight of evidence, resulting in thinking backwards—concluding first and finding evidence second. In such cases,

> . . . the judgments offered stem from a maze of assumptions only rarely given the light of day. They tend not to spring from reasoned argument. In other words, we gather facts to support assumed rather than argued value commitments, all concealed by the veil of science.[157]

Only by admitting to the role of values in the identification and processing of facts will scientists and others be able to debate openly their value commitments.

A4.4 VALUES ARE INVOLVED IN IDENTIFYING WHAT IS A FACT

Values inform the process and methodology of fact discovery. At the simplest level, values influence which experiments will be performed and which will not. The facts which might result from an experiment will not exist—that is, not be apparent—if that experiment is not per-

---

[155] Kendler, p. 491.
[156] Robert Antonio, quoted in Abbott, p. 53.
[157] Abbott, p. 72.

formed in the first place. Facts are not found in places where they are not sought.

Some facts are the result of observation, experiment or discovery, or even counting. These facts are taken to be self-evident. Other facts, however, are the result of interpretation. There is a robust question about the connection between observation and interpretation. It is sometimes argued that every observation is an interpretation, since facts are seen through a lens of theory. Events that do not conform with what is believed to be possible are dismissed as anomalous, wrong, or incoherent.

Other facts, instead of being observable events, are the product of argument networks, based on or dependent at some level on the values of those presenting the arguments for the ontological status of a given fact. To say that such conclusions are not technically facts is to admit that science deals with and operates on the basis of many non-factual ideas.

Michael Polanyi makes it clear that in order for a fact claim to be accepted by the scientific community, it must pass through a process of evaluation, an evaluation that involves value-judgments:

> Let it also be quite clear that what we have described as the function of scientific authority go[es] far beyond a mere confirmation of facts asserted by science. For one thing, there are no mere facts in science. A scientific fact is one that has been accepted as such by scientific opinion, both on the grounds of the evidence in favour of it and because it appears sufficiently plausible in view of the current scientific conception of the nature of things.[158]

---

158 Polanyi, op. cit.

For example, the search for fossil evidence for human evolution takes place largely in one region of the African continent rather than in any of ten thousand other places in the world, because current "scientific opinion" considers that area of importance to the theory, while other areas such as China are deemed not important. Polanyi continues:

> Besides, science is not a mere collection of facts, but a system of facts based on their scientific interpretation. It is this system that is endorsed by a scientific interest intrinsic to the system; a distribution of interest established by the delicate value-judgments exercised by scientific opinion in sifting and rewarding current contributions to science. Science is what it is, in virtue of the way in which scientific authority constantly eliminates, or else recognizes at various levels of merit, contributions offered to science. In accepting the authority of science we accept the totality of all these value-judgments."[159]

Polanyi concludes by saying that the scientific enterprise operates through a set of traditional values that practitioners adopt when they become scientists and are socialized into the brotherhood, so to speak. Part of these values include the "standards of scientific merit" that help determine what is or is not a fact:

> And remember that each scientist originally established himself as such by joining at some point a network of mutual appreciation extending far beyond his own horizon. Each such acceptance appears then as a submission to a vast range of value-judgments exercised over all the domains of science, which the newly accepted citizen of science henceforth endorses, al–

---

[159] Ibid.

though he knows hardly anything about their subject-matter. Thus, the standards of scientific merit are seen to be transmitted from generation to generation by the affiliation of individuals at a great variety of widely disparate points, in the same way as artistic, moral, or legal traditions are transmitted. We may conclude, therefore, that the appreciation of scientific merit too is based on tradition which succeeding generations accept and develop as their own scientific opinion.[160]

Pronouncements about scientific fact (especially those reducing to argument networks or agreed-upon interpretations) are quite comparable to the pronouncements about truth from the "artistic, moral, or legal traditions," for "the authority of science is essentially traditional" like theirs.[161] And all tradition can be said to include a set of value-judgments. The arts, ethics, law, and science are all practitioner communities, where historical experience has helped to determine what is valuable and what is not, what is to be preserved and what is not. How should the materials of the art or science be approached, practiced, and interpreted? A set of gradually developed values supplies the answers.

Philosopher Hilary Putnam argues for the role of values in the determination of facts on the basis of epistemology. Values, he says, include far more than ethical or moral values, and include the values that shape how we define what knowledge is (what can or cannot be true, for example). He says, "Indeed, once we stop thinking of 'value' as synonymous with 'ethics,' it is quite clear that it [science] *does* presuppose values—it presupposes *epistemic* values."[162] In other words, a commitment to certain values—

---

[160] Ibid.
[161] Ibid.
[162] Putnam, p. 30.

certain beliefs about knowledge and facts and their origin, identification, and confirmation — must be made before we can address the issue of what is or is not factual. Thus, value-judgments and value commitments must precede scientific or other fact-discovering activity. Putnam says:

> *Knowledge of facts presupposes knowledge of values.* This is the position I defend. It might be broken into two separate claims: (i) that the activity of justifying factual claims presupposes value judgments, and (ii) that we must regard those value judgments as capable of being right (as "objective" in philosophical jargon), if we are not to fall into subjectivism with respect to the factual claims themselves.[163]

We will discuss Putnam's second claim, that value-judgments are capable of objectivity, later on. The point to be emphasized here is that "fact and value interpenetrate" through the influence of value-judgments on both theory and epistemology.[164] Epistemology is "interpenetrated" by axiological (value) considerations and choices, and facts are developed within that epistemological framework.

A word of caution is in order here. The claim is not being made that facts and values are the same thing, that is, that "facts" are really only "values" in the dichotomous sense where values are considered merely subjective personal taste. This is the view of the postmodernists, who resolve the fact/value dichotomy by denying the objectivity of facts and place all knowledge claims into the realm of rhetoric and subjectivity — which is to say, values. To reject the fact/value dichotomy is not to reject a fact/value distinction. To say that what is a fact is influenced by values is not to say that facts are necessarily subjective. As we

---

[163] Putnam, p. 137.
[164] Ibid., p. 137.

will see below, and as Putnam has hinted above, value-judgments can possess objectivity.

Another way to clarify this point and to see the role of values in the determination of facts is to think about the difference between what really exists (the pure and complete set of things with genuine ontological status) and what we think, know, or believe to exist. Knowledge of what really exists is the goal not just of science but of all truth seekers. Belief about what exists is the result of our efforts to know, and those efforts are influenced by our values and theories. We seek constantly to approach truth, always trying to improve our theories of knowing (epistemes) in order to get closer. Our theories of knowing shape what we think we are learning, indeed, what we think we are looking at. Michael Dickson writes, "[Einstein said that] what does or does not exist is not determined by what can be observed, but by what is permitted by our best theoretical attempts to make sense of the world."[165] Improving theory improves our knowledge of what really is. When theory prevented the idea of continental drift from appearing credible, few accepted it. When the theory of plate tectonics was further developed, the idea of continental drift became more plausible. Dickson continues:

> Einstein did not deny a connection between what exists and what can be observed — of course a thing cannot be observed if it does not exist. Rather, his point is that one cannot say what exists on the basis of observation alone. Instead, theory tells us what sorts of thing might exist, and from the existence of those sorts of thing, we can then say what sorts of observation are possible. To put the point succinctly, as Heisenberg did (attributing

---

[165] Dickson, p. S50.

these words to Einstein), "the theory determines what you can observe."[166]

A simple example of the influence of theory on observation would be to take an ordinary, educated person and a trained specialist and show both of them an EKG strip, an X-ray of a lung, or a biopsy slide and then ask, "What do you observe?" Both are "looking at" the same thing, and yet each will see something very different because of what we might call the theory of interpretation each has learned. And if the success of diagnostic evaluation is any indication, the trained specialist has a better theory for getting at "what really exists" or what is a deeper truth about the information being observed than the educated but untrained person.

From this discussion, we can understand that there are truths or facts that exist but which are not yet known to us or which, when known, will clarify some wrong beliefs about facts that we currently hold. These implications put further pressure on the fact/value dichotomy. When the positivists developed their philosophy, one of the underlying principles they adopted was the idea of verificationism. As Putnam puts it, verificationism is the belief that "*it is metaphysically impossible for there to be any truths that are not verifiable by human beings*" [emphasis his]. In other words, the only facts are those that can be tested or observed by humans doing experiments. This idea was little more than a subterfuge to eliminate all discussion of values or the use of value-judgments, and it became a main support for the fact/value dichotomy.

However, this idea was soon rejected both in philosophy and science itself. Verificationism, notes Putnam, is "a species of what today is called 'antirealism' because it makes the limits of what can be true of the world depend-

---

[166] Ibid., p. S50.

ent on the limits of human verification-capacities."[167] And as we have just noted, we recognize that there is reality — there are facts — that we either do not yet know or that we perhaps cannot ever know (or at least can never prove empirically). Science has moved well beyond the arena of verifiability, for "it is deeply imbedded in the theories of present-day science that for a number of reasons . . . as a matter of contingent empirical fact, there are many truths that are beyond the power of our species to ascertain."[168] We are unlikely ever to know the exact number of stars in the universe, for example, or the status of existence before the Big Bang. At this writing, it is not known whether the graviton exists (a theoretical particle responsible for the gravitational force) or precisely how gravity works, yet we know there must be some true explanation behind it because gravity itself is real enough. But whether or not we will ever access that true explanation is still an open question.

Even though verificationism was rejected, and even though that rejection removed one of the major supports for the fact/value dichotomy,[169] the dichotomy remains, with those adhering to it still rejecting the role of values in the determination of facts. Why? The fact-value dichotomy is an ideology that permits the sneaking in of value judgments in the guise of facts, of normative claims in the guise of empirical statements. Pretending that values do not enter into the scientific enterprise allows practitioners to reject any role for or discussion of outside values while applying their own value preferences silently. As a result, objective values are rejected while subjective values are quietly entertained. The social sciences have been particularly susceptible to this phenomenon. R. J. Bernstein says:

---

[167] Putnam, p. 123.
[168] Putnam, p. 124.
[169] Putnam, p. 40.

Much of what has been advanced as theory in the social sciences turns out to be disguised ideology. No matter how ambitious or modest the claims of mainstream social scientists to advance empirical theory, they have insisted that the hypotheses and claims they put forth are value-neutral, objective claims subject only to the criteria of public testing, confirmation, and refutation. Yet, . . . these proposed theories secrete values and reflect controversial ideological claims about what is right, good, and just.[170]

When the fact/value dichotomy is insisted upon, instead of true value-neutrality, practitioners promote "surreptitiously visions of a good" even while they deny "science's capability to speak intelligibly on value."[171]

A4.5 VALUES ARE INVOLVED IN THE DESCRIPTION OF FACTS

As we saw in the section above, the determination of what is or is not to be considered a fact is often influenced by theoretical or other value-laden concerns. We may now state further that even the act of describing or labeling— choosing an appropriate word to describe a fact—is often inextricably connected to value concerns. The answer to "What are you looking at?" requires that the barest of observations be connected to an often valuative term. Putnam says that "from Hume on, empiricists—and not only empiricists but many others as well, in and outside of philosophy—failed to appreciate the ways in which factual description and valuation can and must be *entangled*."[172]

---

[170] Quoted in Mark Mays and Guy J. Manaster, "Research: Facts, Values, Theory, Practice, and Unexamined Assumptions." *The Journal of Individual Psychology* 55:2 (Summer, 1999), p. 249.
[171] Abbott, p. 52.
[172] Putnam, p. 27.

Failure to understand the entanglement of description re-sults in a scientist thinking that a description is value free, when, in fact, Putnam says, "'Valuation' and 'description' are interdependent—a possibility that is constantly over-looked by positivists and their ilk."[173] Students of seman-tics can readily suggest the nature of emotive, shaded, eu-phemistic, or colored terms, pointing out the difference in evaluative tone we get when we describe a dog as a "mutt" or a "pooch." Similar, though more subtle, evalua-tions are present in terms such as "well nourished," "premature mortality," and "self-respect."[174] All of these are clearly entangled terms, mixing valuation and descrip-tion.

Terms even seemingly bald or "objective" also reveal that to describe is to evaluate. The application of a word to a thing implies both the fitness of the word to the thing and the connotation carried by the word. Richard Allen offers a striking example:

> At the lowest level of mere chronicle, we say, "the Bat-tle of Waterloo was fought in 1815." Here, surely we have a wholly "objective," unevaluative statement of mere fact, a pure description. On the contrary, "battle" itself signifies the successful results of intentional ac-tions. Using "battle" rather than "collision" or "massa-cre" ascribes an intention to fight on both sides at the very moment of engagement, intentions successfully carried out to the extent that weapons were actually used.[175]

The point is not that (in this case) history is made up of subjective comments about events. The point is that de-scriptive terms often involve evaluative connotations or

---

[173] Ibid., p. 62.
[174] Terms from Amartya Sen, quoted in Putnam, p. 63.
[175] Allen, op. cit.

meanings, thus entangling facts and values. The evaluation can come not in the form of the investigator's moral attitude toward the thing being described or named, but in the mere decision to call something the name normally used for such a thing. When we describe something based on its function or principles of operation, the description implies that the object functions properly—and this represents an evaluation: "To describe this object as a 'calculator' or 'clock' or 'knife,' is tacitly to evaluate it as a correctly and effectively operating machine, instrument or device of that type."[176] If a scientist describes an electromechanical machine as a "pencil sharpener," implied in the description is the idea that the machine will sharpen pencils, and this is an evaluative conclusion relating to its function. If the machine does not sharpen pencils, we would say it is incorrectly described as a "pencil sharpener." It is instead a "broken pencil sharpener" or a "poorly functioning pencil sharpener" because it does not fulfill its intended function well. The assessment is a judgment (valuative) based on an empirical test. Thus an entanglement of fact and value.

The same entanglement applies to the examination of unknown artifacts. When an archaeologist comes upon a stone carving with some intricate shapes and figures, the question may arise, "Is this a calendar or does it just look like a calendar?" The answer must draw upon an evaluation of the functionality of the carvings.

Even in the biological world, purpose must be considered in the process of description, and the declaration of purpose (though it may be implied and not stated) is value-laden. As Allen puts it, "Again, with reference to living things and their operations or actions, description is necessarily evaluation." It would be unfair, he says, to call a dis-

---

[176] Ibid.

eased heart simply "a heart," because that would be misleading. But the difference between diseased and normal, while based on objective criteria, is nevertheless evaluative.

A4.6 VALUES ARE INTERMIXED IN MANY STATEMENTS OF FACT

We have just seen that descriptions often involve values or value-judgments and that, in fact, many terms, applied as descriptive labels, imply value-judgments as part of the legitimacy of their application. In both scientific and everyday use, many statements of fact include both an empirical component and a valuative component without rendering the statement "non-factual" or "subjective." Examples of phrases with "both normative and factual content"[177] might be "a good result," "a promising finding," "a worthwhile experiment," or even "an anomalous result."

The idea that value-judgments cannot be intermixed (or entangled, to use Putnam's term) with facts may come from recognizing that many value-judgments are subjective matters. However, not all are. If a researcher says, "This blood pressure medicine is better than that one because the pill is blue and I like blue pills better than pink pills," we recognize the subjective nature of the claim of "better." But if the researcher says, "This blood pressure medicine is better than that one because this one controls blood pressure without side effects while that one offers little control and causes an increased risk of stroke," we see that the statement of value, "better" is based on value-laden but factual, even empirical, reasons ("controls," "side effects," "increased risk"). To say that the second statement "is not factual because it is only a value-judgment" is clearly in error.

---

[177] J. P. Smit, "The Supposed 'Inseparability' of Fact and Value," *South African Journal of Philosophy* 22:1 (2003), p. 56.

For another example of entanglement, take the statement, "Concrete is a good material to use for sidewalks." This statement would be declared a fact by anyone with experience with concrete sidewalks, even though it also reflects values such as "durability is better than nondurability" or "a hard surface is good for sidewalks." Therefore, fact claims can include value claims without rendering them solipsistic or terminally subjective.

To reject some factual statements as "only value-judgments" because they include objective criteria of assessment would be to cripple our ability to describe the world as we experience it. We may disagree about exactly what makes a surgeon "excellent," or just how good a particular surgeon is, but to say that the difference between an excellent surgeon and a blundering surgeon is "only a matter of personal taste" flies in the face of reality and the differential pain, suffering, and death rates of the two doctors. (See below for a further discussion.)

Putnam sees the intermixing of fact and value in many factual statements as inevitable and necessary, arguing that "the picture of our language in which nothing can be *both* a fact *and* value-laden is wholly inadequate and that an enormous amount of our descriptive vocabulary is and has to be 'entangled.'"[178] Philosopher J. P. Smit says that "knowledge must in some sense reflect value-judgements."[179] Much of what we call and rely on as knowledge—and not personal taste or opinion—includes evaluative aspects.

A4.7 VALUES CAN BE REASONED ABOUT

Proponents of the fact/value dichotomy attempt to denigrate values as mere personal preferences that are beyond rational discussion. If disagreements about moral,

---

[178] Putnam, pp. 61-62.
[179] J. P. Smit, p. 57.

ethical, and other values are the equivalent of arguing over which flavor of ice cream is better, then such discussion is pointless. Such is the ploy of the dichotomists: declare that values are subjective and irrational and then one need not deal with them seriously. (And then sneak one's own values into the marketplace by hiding them within fact claims.)

But Putnam points out that "value disputes [are often not mere social conflicts, but are] *rational disagreements calling for a decision as to where the better reasons lie*" (emphasis his).[180] We can argue and reason about our values, often pointing to higher values held in common and even to objective facts relevant to the point at issue. If two people disagree about whether Joe is a skilled or an incompetent mechanic, they can point to his work for rational support. Whether his wheel alignments cause the car to pull to one side and make the tires wear out in 100 miles or cause the car to run straight down the highway—this evidence can be reasonably brought forward in the dispute.

Leo Strauss offers the example of using objective criteria to make value judgments about a statesman, noting that if the historian shows, by objectively measuring the action of a statesman against the model of "rational action in the circumstances," that the statesman made one blunder after another, he makes an objective value judgment to the effect that the statesman was singularly inept.[181]

In discussions of ethics, we not only can but commonly do argue about what is humane or even right and wrong, without agreeing that a given position is merely a subjective, personal opinion. We offer reasons and evidence to support our positions. The cultural relativists would like us to believe that we cannot evaluate the practices of other

---

[180] Putnam, p. 121.
[181] Leo Strauss, *Natural Right and History*. Chicago: University of Chicago Press, 1953, p. 54.

cultures, but this idea is a mistake. As anthropologist Robert Edgerton has shown in his book, *Sick Societies*, we regularly apply basic ideas of fairness, justice, and human rights to criticize cruel practices in other cultures, such as burning alive the widows of men who have just died (suttee). Edgerton reports one case where the "wife burned with the corpse of her adult husband was only four years old. . . ."[182] Few people would fail to condemn such a practice, and few would base the condemnation on mere personal taste. We would argue instead that the practice violates universal human values, that it is objectively cruel and morally repugnant.

Indeed, Edgerton's book is an excellent piece of evidence in the argument that values can be reasoned about, for he takes on the idea that all cultural practices are somehow "functional" for a given culture and through the use of argument and many examples of dysfunctional (what he calls maladaptive) practices, makes a powerful case for a new view of clearly harmful practices that rejects the idea of cultural relativism: "If we are to understand the processes of cultural adaptation and maladaptation, relativism must be replaced by a form of evaluative analysis."[183]

Economist Amartya Sen argues that not only reasons and arguments but scientific evidence can be brought to bear profitably in value discussions: "Someone disputing a value judgment put forward by someone else can have a scientific discussion on the validity of the value judgment by examining the scientific truth of the underlying factual premises."[184] Many of our judgments are based on facts or assumed facts, and an investigation into the accuracy of

---

[182] Robert B. Edgerton, *Sick Societies: Challenging the Myth of Primitive Harmony*. New York: Free Press, 1992, p.137.
[183] Ibid., p. 207.
[184] Quoted in Putnam, p. 76.

the supporting facts can sway our value judgments based on them. Value judgments such as proposals to reform the welfare system or change the minimum wage, or make virtually any public policy decision—all these are address-able with relevant facts, reasons, and arguments.

Hillary Putnam concurs:

> The moral is clear: when we are dealing with any im-portant value disagreement, we assume that facts are irrelevant at our peril. No convincing logical reason can be given for the logical irrelevance of fact to value judgments, even if we accept the positivist conception of what a "fact" is.[185]

Putnam's conclusion is that the discussion of values and the conclusions drawn regarding them should not be thought of as inherently different from other discussions. He says that "the principle that what is valid for inquiry in general is valid for value inquiry in particular is a power-ful one."[186] Just as we present arguments and evidence to support a claim that a given statement is a "fact," we can similarly present arguments and evidence to support a claim that a given practice is good or bad.

Even "basic values," those values that lie underneath our worldview, those assumptions about reality that we use to find meaning in the events of life, can be argued about. Even though we view such basics as foundational preferences not subject to discussion, the fact is that people do sometimes change them. Otherwise, we would never see someone change from liberal to conservative or non-Christian to Christian or vice versa. However slow or rare this process is, it does occur. And even though the change may result only partly from cognitive change (thinking

---

185 Putnam, p. 78.
186 Ibid., p. 110.

and argument), reasoning can still play a role in such huge value shifts.

A4.8 SOME VALUES ARE OBJECTIVE

Another error created by the fact/value dichotomy is the view that facts and values are separated into the two categories of objective and subjective. That is, the implication of the separation of facts and values is that all facts are objective and all values are subjective. This claim is false. Some values are objective.

Part of the difficulty here is the positivist view of objective and subjective. The positivists tended to see as objective only those statements that were empirically verifiable through some experiment, and considered all non-empirical statements "subjective," which is to say, "personally whimsical, locked into the consciousness of individual subjects, or without interest or value to others."[187] However, aside from the positivists and those still influenced by them, the term *objective* has always referred to a statement whose truth exists outside our personal experience or preferences.

An external source of values, then, such as those identified from natural law or Biblical revelation, provides an independent and external standard for making objective value judgments or moral claims. This externality, this objective authority, clarifies why it is possible to use reason and argument in connection with moral issues (or with "value-judgments" to use that term). Thus, while some value-judgments may be merely subjective ("Eating chocolate-covered ants is bad"), other value-judgments — those that rely on objective criteria — are indeed objective ("Sacrificing babies to demons is wrong").

---

[187] Regenia Gagnier, "Value Theory," *The Johns Hopkins Guide to Literary Theory and Criticism*. Baltimore: Johns Hopkins University Press, 1994, p. 722.

As we mentioned earlier, values come into play in the description of reality. Thus, Hilary Putnam says that "evaluation and description are interwoven and interdependent."[188] J. P. Smit goes further to add that an evaluative description can have a factual component:

> If value-judgements are descriptive, i.e. there is a matter of fact that determines the truth or falsity of value-judgments, then an assertion of value refers to a fact about a given object. Facts about values are then . . . a perfectly delineable subspecies of facts in general. . . .[189]

To clarify, we might say that there are some facts without values attached, as in "There are two pencils on the desk." There are some values that are not strictly factual, being matters of taste or preference, as in, "I like pens better than pencils." Then there are facts with practical values intermixed, as in our earlier example, "Concrete makes a good material for sidewalks." This is the example that would fit Smit's comment above. The assertion of value ("good material for sidewalks") refers to a fact about the concrete (it is durable, hard, easy to put into place, and so on).

Putnam goes beyond the presence of facts as a means of making value-judgments objective and asserts that the rational quality of such judgments can call upon an external, objective standard. For example, in scientific research, certain processes and methods are used that value the compatibility, correlation, and correspondence of results, and these preferences "presuppose judgments of reasonableness. And judgments of reasonableness simply do not fall into classes to which we are able to assign probabili-

---

[188] Putnam, p. 3.
[189] Smit, p. 52.

ties."[190] When an experimenter finds an outlier or anomalous piece of data and rejects it as an error, such a practice involves a "judgment of reasonableness." And, Putnam adds, "I have argued that judgments of reasonableness can be objective, and I have argued that they have all of the typical properties of value judgments."[191] Thus, the scientific method itself "presupposes that we take seriously claims that are not themselves scientific, including value claims of all kinds" and yet science is considered the *sine qua non* of objective engagement.[192]

More overtly ethical (or even moral) values can be objective also, if they are transcendent of the individual or the local society. The values of justice, fairness, truth, and respect for the dead, for example, are nearly universal.

A4.9 OBJECTIONS TO THE OBJECTIVITY OF VALUE JUDGMENTS

The equation between value judgments and subjectivity has been at first argued and now assumed for so long that advocating the possibility of objective value judgments has produced several objections. These are discussed in the following paragraphs.

Objection 1: Our judgments often differ.

This is an objection either from application (how to apply the given standard in a given case) or from degree (where do you draw the line). The application argument may be addressed by pointing to any judicial procedure. In spite of postmodernism's attack on the institution of law, it was and is still generally recognized that objective laws are applied judiciously—that is, with an attempt at fairness, objectivity, and even-handedness. Judges strive for objective judgments (at least in theory), with the idea of

---

[190] Putnam, p. 144.
[191] Ibid., p. 145.
[192] Ibid., p. 143.

applying the law fairly, especially in the hard cases where the line must be drawn carefully. Similarly, even though our judgments may differ, we ought to strive to apply the same principles as accurately and objectively as possible. The fact that we may fail, and even fail often, is not an argument against the principle itself nor its inherent objective status. As Leo Strauss says, though we may differ in the exact application, "It would be absurd to deny that there is an objective difference between a blundering general and a strategic genius."[193]

And whether or not we can come to instant agreement about the degree of rightness or wrongness of something, we still understand that there is a distinction between right and wrong and between bad and worse. Putnam writes that "the condemnation of unspeakable acts . . . requires a strong distinction between conduct that is merely 'not nice' and conduct that is unconditionally *wrong*—and that is what any 'norm,' any universal deontological statement, aims to give us."[194]

Objection 2: Not every person or every society meets the standard.

This is no objection to the standard itself. We all have values we strive for but cannot live up to. That is a comment about our own frailty rather than about the worth of the standard. The very nature of objective (external to ourselves) standards is that they represent ideals we can strive for, even if we cannot always (or ever) fully attain them. When we define standards down to our level, we make them subjective and often ignoble.

Moreover, we may even question the rightness of a particular legal or ethical standard our own society upholds. This is not an argument against the objectivity of

---

[193] Strauss, p. 63.
[194] Putnam, p. 114.

standards, but an argument in favor of them, for it shows that we can see a higher standard than that of our own society. Leo Strauss:

> But the mere fact that we can raise the question of the worth of the ideal of our society shows that there is something in man that is not altogether in slavery to his society, and therefore that we are able, and hence obliged, to look for a standard with reference to which we can judge of the ideals of our own as well as of any other society.[195]

Seeking a standard by which to judge not only our own actions, not only the actions of our society, but the very values our society upholds is a strong indication of the belief in and objectivity of transcendent values.

Objection 3: Not every culture values the standard.
Universal assent to any proposition is not necessary for that proposition to be true or worthy. There is probably no fact of any kind that is not disputed by someone. (Indeed, that is one way science itself advances.) The very assumptions we make about reality (that other minds really exist, that the external world is real, that cause and effect are genuine phenomena) have all been disputed by philosophers. The fact of dispute about a value is not an argument against it. After all, some cultures clearly have maladaptive characteristics. Standards of social consensus are not necessarily objective, for some societies permit cruel and unjust practices. Once again, see Edgerton's book, *Sick Societies*.

Having mentioned science, we might point out that what is true in science at any given time is subject to both disagreement and change. In his essay, "The Search for

---

[195] Strauss, p. 3.

Truths," historian Jacques Barzun notes that "even in those disciplines where exactness and agreement appear at their highest, there is a startling mobility of views. Every day the truths of geology, cosmology, astrophysics, biology, and their sister sciences are upset."[196] Yet science is still an objective enterprise, seeking what is true.

Objection 4: Not every culture practices the value in the same way.

This variance is to be expected because different cultures may be at different places in the striving toward a true understanding and application of a given value. Some cultures may be on the way up, shedding unjust practices of the past, while others may be on the way down, adopting unjust practices (probably in the name of justice) as they grow more corrupt.

Some idealizations may be implemented in more than one way. For example, nearly every culture shares a respect for the dead. In showing this respect, though, some cultures burn their dead, some bury them, some even eat the ashes of their dead. Yet the underlying value is still there.

A4.10 THE POSTMODERNIST ERROR

Some of those who attempt to destabilize (to use a postmodernist term) the fact/value dichotomy do so from a postmodernist perspective, which unfortunately compounds the problem by arguing in the wrong direction. Instead of arguing that (1) there is a difference between facts and values, though as we have seen there is much entanglement, even some interdependence, and (2) values as well as facts can depend on objective support, the postmodernists believe that (1) there is really no difference be-

---

[196] Jacques Barzun, "The Search for Truths," in *A Jacques Barzun Reader*, New York: HarperCollins, 2002, p. 17.

tween facts and values because (2) both ultimately reflect (or refer to) subjective preferences, rhetorical stances, or ideological commitments. In other words, all "facts" are really only values—values as defined by the positivists as merely subjective expressions of personal taste. Science with its fact claims, postmodernists say, is merely a political and rhetorical game designed to gain, hold, and exert power over others.

Such a stance fails both practically and philosophically. It fails practically because we do view facts and values as different from each other in kind, in spite of the complex relationship they have with each other, and it fails philosophically because it is now a truism that postmodernism, followed to it logical conclusion, ends in nihilism and the absence of all facts and all values (other than personal emotions).[197]

A4.11 CONCLUSION

The flight from values—the rebellion against values in order to gain personal moral freedom—was part of the Enlightenment exaltation of empiricism (and hence the influence on positivism, modernism, naturalism, and philosophical materialism—brothers all). The insistence that facts and values have nothing to do with each other is what Putnam calls "the last dogma of empiricism" that has spawned many unworkable philosophies of science:

Apparently any fantasy—the fantasy of doing science using only deductive logic (Popper), the fantasy of vindicating induction deductively (Reichenbach), the fantasy of reducing science to a simple sampling algorithm (Carnap), the fantasy of selecting theories given a mysteriously available set of "true observation conditionals," or, alternatively, "settling for psychology" (both Quine)—is regarded as preferable to rethinking the whole dogma (the

---

[197] For typical comments, see Strauss, pp. 4-6 and Hitchcock, p. 26.

last dogma of empiricism?) that facts are objective and values are subjective and "never the twain shall meet."[198]

Ironically, the Romantic rebellion against authority, the denial of absolutes and the affirmation of relativism—the Nietzschean plunge into nihilism—also caused the postmodernists to reject the objectivity of values. Therefore, though modernists and postmodernists are often seen as philosophical combatants, they have much in common in their view of values and value-judgments.

However, we have seen that both philosophies are incorrect. We have learned instead these truths:

- Facts and values, instead of being utterly separate, are often entangled and inseparable.
- Values, far from being matters of taste, are integral to the process of knowing. In other words, values are essential to the realm of facts. Michael Polanyi notes that "science itself can be pursued and transmitted to succeeding generations only within an elaborate system of traditional beliefs and values, just as traditional beliefs have proved indispensable throughout the life of society."[199]
- Evaluation is often an essential part of description and therefore values are a necessary part of an accurate description of reality.
- Both facts and values can be discussed and handled rationally.
- Value statements (or value-judgments) can be objective.
- Verificationism and falsificationism have both been either abandoned or modified in the arena of fact in order to allow scientific claims that cannot be verified or falsified. So it is unreasonable to insist that

---

[198] Putnam, p. 145.
[199] Polanyi, op. cit.

verificationism or falsificationism must apply to the arena of values — to the arena of non-empirical but objective facts and values.

- It is incorrect to assign all non-empirical truth claims to the realm of values.

Why are values so despised by the modernists? The voice of science enjoys its position of highest epistemological status based in large part on its claims to disinterested universality, its neutrality and objectivity. It has achieved this status in part by claiming for itself the only source of truth or knowledge — truth as whatever and only that which results from its processes and determinations. (This is the view of scientism, not true science.) All other claims to knowledge from other sources — revelation, natural law, tradition, philosophy — are rejected by positivist-influenced modernists as the idle imaginings of subjective preferences (that is, values).

Therefore, having once demonized values as, in essence, "unintelligible claptrap," now to acknowledge that values play a role in the scientific enterprise and that the fact-value dichotomy is false and impossible to maintain, would be extremely difficult. One cannot embrace as essential that which one has long dismissed as unreal. The problem, of course, is that the claim to be "value neutral" simply denies the use of some values while allowing others to sneak in under the guise of being value free.

The intended discussion stopper (and thought stopper), "That's not a fact; it's just a value-judgment," does not hold up. Value-judgments can be objective and rational. They are subject to rational analysis like empirical facts. They can draw upon empirical and non-empirical facts for their basis. They may often be more important than facts because they give meaning to facts.

Notes

A5

APPENDIX 5: A QUICK GLOSSARY

Sometimes students can be confused or even put off by terms and concepts they do not understand. This brief glossary includes simple definitions of some key terms that students need to feel comfortable with in order to prosecute the work of integration — and even the work of learning — effectively.

Cogent. A cogent argument is one that is both true and valid.

Deontology. The study of moral obligation.

Disinformation. False information being spread by someone who knows that it is false. Disinformation is part of information warfare, where lies, smears, rumors, false reports, forged documents, and so forth are used to influence others and attain an end. Compare misinformation.

Episteme. A theory of knowing. A critical area of disagreement that impacts the integration issue is that the proponents of naturalism argue for an episteme that includes only knowledge discoverable through empirical sources, whereas Christians argue for an episteme that includes revelation as an additional source of knowledge.

The point to highlight here is that, while the naturalists claim that their episteme should control the public engagement of knowing, Christians are completely and absolutely within their epistemic rights to assert the inclusion of Biblical truth as an essential part of knowledge. Both the naturalists and the Christians must assume the shape and content of their epistemology. Neither can be proved because they precede proof.

Epistemology. The study of the nature, basis, and limits of knowledge. What is or can be known? What is knowledge, and what is truth? What are the limits of knowledge? What are the sources of knowledge? How can we know something?

Faith. Faith in its broadest sense is belief in a knowledge claim—even though you have not yet or may never be able to experience it or demonstrate it—because its source is a trusted authority. In the Christian sense, faith is trust in the revelation of God in the Bible, while we "see in a mirror dimly" and do not yet have proof. Faith then is belief based on a trusted authority, in the absence of proof. (And that defines about 90% of our knowledge.)

No thoughtful person engages in blind faith. We all want our faith to be reasonable. Paul's main method of evangelism was to use reason as a pathway to faith. (See Acts 17:2 and a host of similar passages.)

Holism, holistic. In epistemological terms, holism is the idea that all knowledge is interconnected, interrelated, and interacting. In Christian terms, a holistic view of knowledge would reject such concepts as the "two-realms view" of truth, where Biblical truth is separate from scientific truth.

Ideology. A firmly committed set of principles, ideas, and values that provide an individual's basic outlook on the world, culture, and society. An ideology serves as an interpreter of new ideas and events. While an ideology is similar to a worldview, worldviews are, in theory at least, subject to constant growth and adjustment, whereas ideologies often tend to be narrow, fixed, and held stubbornly in spite of evidence of weakness.

Integration. Integration as it relates to cognition is the process of bringing new ideas into one's current belief set and seeking to create a coherent wholeness, an interdynamic holism, which is to say, a unified mindset where all the pieces—ideas or beliefs—work together in harmony and produce fruitful results. Integration of all knowledge is necessary to have a coherent, rational view of reality.

My somewhat unusual definition of integration includes knowledge claims we know or believe to be false, and knowledge claims we simply remember but neither believe nor disbelieve, usually because we don't have sufficient evidence to decide whether or not to credit them. I argue that both false and suspended knowledge are nevertheless integrated into our view of reality because they are part of our understanding of things.

Knowledge. The philosophical definition of knowledge is "properly justified true belief." That means that knowledge is a form of belief—a belief that has support and corresponds to reality.

Knowledge claim. This phrase refers to any statement claimed to be true or factual. A knowledge claim can be any of the following (which are examples only and not a complete list):

- A statement of fact. "There are three pencils on the table."
- An interpretation. "Hamlet's problem is that he wants certainty in an uncertain situation."
- An inductive conclusion or inference. "The last three houses that sold in the last few months each went for more than the previous one. So housing prices are rising."
- A deductive conclusion. "Since house prices are rising, our house should sell for much more than we paid for it."
- An assertion or belief. "The best solution to beach litter is to fine the litterers."

These examples are called knowledge claims instead of simply knowledge because they need to be processed by your reasoning-thinking-integrating mind before you accept any of them as actual knowledge. And, in fact, much of the time you will simply remember them as claims without necessarily committing to believing them.

Most of what we read or hear has to be filed under "knowledge claims someone asserts to be true." We simply do not have the time to investigate, experiment, think through, or otherwise verify each the claim. So we just remember them.

Logic. A subcategory of reason, dealing with the rules and principles for drawing valid and cogent inferences and legitimate demonstrations. Sometimes defined as the formal rules of reasoning (with formal meaning according to a correct form).

Formal logic includes the standard syllogism and hypothetical syllogisms (conditional syllogisms, disjunctive, conjunctive). These involve the rules and fallacies relating to deduction. Informal logic includes the material fallacies of reasoning (ad hominem, hasty generalization, etc.), and the arena of semantics (including fallacies such as slanting, selection, emotive language, connotation, and so on).

Misinformation. False information spread by someone who believes it to be true. Compare disinformation.

Noetic. Relating to one's intellectual commitments and processes.

Ontology. Concerned with the nature of existence, being, or reality. One's personal ontology includes everything you think is real, everything you think actually exists and excludes those things you do not believe are real. If you don't believe in Santa Claus, you deny him ontological status in your worldview.

Reason. A methodology used in thinking, drawing conclusions, and working with ideas. Reason connects knowledge with knowledge and draws conclusions based on evidence or arguments. It might be said in the simplest terms that the key to reason is the concept of *because*. That is, a statement is true because of some evidence, principle, premise, or other supporting factor.

Reason draws upon one's personal epistemology (what is thought to be true or possible to be true) and one's personal ontology (what is thought to be real or have actual existence). Thus, what someone declares to be reasonable or unreasonable depends on that person's ontological and epistemological commitments, which obtain quite apart from evidence or proof.

Truth. A statement or idea that describes reality accurately. The correspondence theory of truth defines truth as a statement that corresponds to what really exists.

Valid. An argument is valid if it conforms to the rules applicable to that form of argument. When someone informally says, "That's logical," or "That's illogical," he or she is usually referring to the validity of the argument.

However, an argument can be valid but not true. Remember that validity refers to conformance with the rules. For example, the following syllogism represents a valid argument:

All toasters can fly into outer space.

This appliance is a toaster.

Therefore, this appliance can fly into outer space.

Valid, yes, true no. The problem lies with the first premise, which is false. And herein lies the weakness of deduction. The premises are crucial.

An argument that is both valid and true is known as a cogent argument.

Worldview. An individual's personal theory of everything: all the beliefs, values, and understandings about the world and reality that help life make sense. A worldview offers a way to understand new events and ideas by placing them in an interpretive context.

Colophon
Body text set in Book Antiqua 12-point type
with 11-point type for block quotations.
Headings set in Arial small caps
12-, 11-, and 10-point type

Printed by CreateSpace

Is it Biblical?
Regarding the word *Biblical*. Normally, adjectives formed
from proper nouns are capitalized, just like the proper
nouns themselves: Christ, Christian; Aristotle, Aristotelian.
Scripture, Scriptural. But for some reason, Biblical is commonly rendered *biblical*. I think this usage is a mistake.
Therefore, in this book, I have used *Biblical* rather than *biblical*.